New Labour

New Labour's apparent pragmatism disguises an ideological commitment to particular forms of social science – institutionalism and communitarianism.

New Labour: A critique traces the impact of these forms of social science on New Labour, paying particular attention to the welfare state and the economy. Institutionalism and communitarianism typically objectify aspects of the social world to sustain claims to expert knowledge. Mark Bevir defends and enacts an alternative, interpretive approach to social science. His approach inspires a critique of New Labour as a contingent reworking of a particular socialist tradition.

Key content includes:

- Social science – a historical and philosophical critique
- Institutionalism and communitarianism – impact on centre left
- Welfare state and economy – New Labour's reforms.

New Labour: A critique explores diverse traditions of British socialism, which could open the way to radical alternatives to New Labour based on participation, pluralism, and dialogue.

Mark Bevir is Associate Professor in the Department of Political Science, University of California, Berkeley.

New Labour
A critique

Mark Bevir

Routledge
Taylor & Francis Group

LONDON AND NEW YORK

First published 2005
by Routledge
2 Park Square, Milton Park, Abingdon, Oxon OX14 4RN

Simultaneously published in the USA and Canada
by Routledge
270 Madison Ave, New York, NY 10016

Routledge is an imprint of the Taylor & Francis Group

Typeset in Sabon by
Florence Production Ltd, Stoodleigh, Devon
Printed and bound in Great Britain by
TJ International Ltd, Padstow, Cornwall

British Library Cataloguing in Publication Data
A catalogue record for this book is available
from the British Library

Library of Congress Cataloging in Publication Data
A catalog record for this book has been requested

ISBN 0–415–35924–4 (hbk)
ISBN 0–415–35925–2 (pbk)

To Guy and J

Contents

Preface		ix
Acknowledgements		xi
List of abbreviations		xii
1	Political science	1
2	Institutionalism	29
3	Communitarianism	54
4	The welfare state	83
5	The economy	106
6	Social democracy	128
Notes		157
Bibliography		178
Index		195

Preface

I have written a tract for our times. I would like to be able to say that I have written about what is to be done, but alas, as the reader will find, I have only the vaguest reply to that most important of questions. What I can say is that I have tried to raise doubts about prevailing trends in social democracy and political science, and that in doing so I have tried to point to neglected alternatives that I believe to be preferable to these trends.

I am a social democrat and a political scientist. Yet I shrink somewhat from these labels due to their association, respectively, with statism and positivism. The last twenty-five years have made both labels increasingly awkward ones to own. State socialism, and so perhaps social democracy, has been undermined by the collapse of communism and by changes in Keynesian welfare states. Positivism, and so perhaps political science, has been undermined by the interpretive turn, that is, those theoretical movements that have emphasised the holistic nature of meanings, beliefs, and language as well as their constitutive relationship to actions. While social democrats and political scientists could stick their heads in the sand and deny the importance of these political and intellectual movements, I think that they would be foolish so to do. Once they raise their heads, they confront the issue of how to reform social democracy and political science. To urge the need for reform is not to call for an emphatic break with the past. Rather, social democrats and political scientists can draw on competing strands in their heritage to define their various proposals. To urge reform is merely to foreground the question, what is to be done?

Social democracy and political science are in need of reform. I am not alone in believing this. On the contrary, the dominant movements in social democracy and political science are today ones of self-conscious renewal – New Labour and new institutionalism. In my opinion, however, these movements are bland, complacent, evasive, and mistaken. All too often their advocates identify them with phrases that are so bland it is difficult to imagine anyone disagreeing with them. At times they appear complacent about the adequacy of these vacuous phrases; they seem ignorant of the importance of giving them specific content. At other times, especially when pushed on such matters, they become evasive; perhaps they give their phrases one content when responding to critics while still engaging in practices that implicitly ascribe different content to them. Finally, when they do give content to their vacuous phrases, whether in explicit statements or implicitly in their practice, they often adopt positions that objectify aspects of human life in a way I believe to be mistaken.

Although I am only too aware that I have fallen short in telling readers what is to be done, I hope I will convince them at least that something should be done. If they are devotees of New Labour or the new institutionalism, I hope to encourage them to shrug off their lingering complacency, formulate arguments rather than evade them, and thereby give specific content to their otherwise bland phrase-mongering. If they are sceptical of these movements, I hope to encourage them to formulate alternative narratives of reform.

Acknowledgements

This tract for our times draws on previously published essays, and although I found I chewed over bits of the essays again, they retain much of their original flavour. For permission to reuse material, I thank the editors and publishers of *British Journal of Politics and International Relations*, *Public Administration*, *Public Administration Review*, and *Review of International Political Economy*. David O'Brien was co-author of the original essay in *Public Administration Review*, and I am grateful to him too for allowing me to reuse material from it. I also thank Robert Adcock, Mike Kenny, Rod Rhodes, and Shannon Stimson for useful comments on parts of what I place before you. Finally, I thank Laura for preparing the index, and, much more importantly, for her constant affection and support.

Abbreviations

BIPO	British Institute of Public Opinion
CCS	Commission for Care Standards
CCT	Compulsory Competitive Tendering
DTI	Department of Trade and Industry
EU	European Union
ISB	Invest to Save Budget
NAIRU	Non-accelerating inflation rate of unemployment
NHS	National Health Service
NICE	National Institute for Clinical Excellence
NPM	new public management
PFI	Private Finance Initiative
PPP	Public–Private Partnership
PSA	Public Service Agreement
PSBP	Public Sector Benchmarking Project
SDF	Social Democratic Federation
SERPS	State Earnings-Related Pension
SEU	Social Exclusion Unit

1 Political science

Introduction

On Thursday 1 May 1997, the British electorate returned a Labour government for the first time in over twenty years. Labour's electoral triumph brought to an end the dismal series of defeats at the hands of the Conservatives in 1979, 1982, 1987, and 1992. Labour's return from the electoral wilderness was, it seemed, the long-awaited reward for years spent transforming the Party – a transformation that had begun in the 1980s with the launch of the Policy Review and had reached its symbolic peak when the Party revised Clause IV in order to remove the commitment to nationalisation from its constitution.[1] On the morning of Friday 2 May, Tony Blair, the new Prime Minister, explicitly declared that his government had been elected as New Labour and it would govern as New Labour. Social democracy had been refashioned as an ideology and we would see the results in public policy. Out went state ownership, a collectivist welfare state, and Keynesianism. In came public–private partnerships, joined-up governance, and supply-side reforms.

New Labour portrays itself as the future of social democracy. It implies that it has absorbed the lessons of defeat, come to terms with changes in society, and forged ideas and policies suited to our new times. It suggests that other social democratic parties should follow its Third Way if they want to survive let alone prosper.[2] This suggestion has met a receptive audience since other social democrats are often convinced of the need to rethink some of their cherished beliefs. Throughout Europe, social democratic parties are promoting privatisation, welfare reform, and flexible labour markets.[3] If we look across the Atlantic, we find innumerable parallels and links between New Labour and the New Democrats. Perhaps 'we are all Third Wayers now', as suggested by Robert Reich, Secretary of Labor under President Clinton.[4] New Labour is undoubtedly a prominent model for the future of social democracy. To debate this future, we might engage with New Labour. What are its ideas and policies? Where do they come from? What are the alternatives?

Three contrasts

New Labour advocates joined-up governance as an alternative to the hierarchic bureaucracy it associates with Old Labour and the marketisation
it associates with the New Right. The *Modernising Government* White
Paper of March 1999 expressed the government's vision of 'high-quality
and efficient' public services.[5] The White Paper equated effective public
services with the attempt to make them 'more innovative and responsive
to users and ensure that they are delivered in an efficient and joined-up
way'. It illustrated New Labour's tendency to associate efficiency, quality,
and responsiveness with networks that are characterised by 'collaborative
working across organisational boundaries', and especially with partnerships between government agencies and the voluntary and private sectors.
New administrative institutions – joined-up governance – are said to
promise a panacea for the ills of the state.

We get a rather different view of joined-up governance if we adopt the
bottom-up perspective of the citizen. Social workers provide an account
of the case of Mrs T in the files of a local authority in Northern England.[6]
Mrs T is eighty years old and arthritic. She lives on her own, uses a
walking frame, and can no longer manage pans or cooking. She coped
well until she fell and fractured her wrist. Then she visited the hospital,
which sent her home after treatment. Now a Home Care Manager visits
to assess Mrs T, whom she finds to be slow and having problems holding the walking frame because of the arthritis and fractured wrist: Mrs T
has difficulty with washing, dressing, using the toilet, bathing, cooking,
and shopping. A friend of Mrs T's will visit her twice a week, collect her
pension, and do small amounts of shopping. Mrs T's three children live
away, but they will take it in turns to visit on Sundays when they will
keep the house and garden in good repair. The Home Care Manager asks
for an urgent visit from Occupational Therapy Services to assess Mrs T
for equipment for daily living. While Mrs T waits for this assessment, a
home help will visit at mealtimes and help her with dressing in the morning,
and the friend will visit at about 7 p.m. to help her undress.

An Occupational Therapy Assistant calls two days later. She finds that
Mrs T needs substantial equipment, all of which arrives later that day
except for a grab rail. The Gas Board will call within 48 hours to replace
dials on the cooker. The council's housing services will install an emer-
gency warden-call system by the end of the week. The Home Care Manager
now rearranges the home help. She provides a morning call from her own
services from Monday to Friday and she arranges for a private agency
on Saturday. The home help will assist with buttons, collect shopping and
pension, do some basic cleaning, and do laundry and ironing. The home
care will help Mrs T have a bath one morning a week, and also lay out
breakfast and tea and fill the kettle for the day. A twilight service will
call sometime between seven and nine in the evening from Monday

to Saturday to help Mrs T undress. The Home Care Manager arranges and buys all these different services. The Women's Royal Voluntary Service will deliver Meals on Wheels to Mrs T from Mondays to Fridays. On Saturdays Mrs T will treat herself to a meal cooked and delivered by a local hotel. The Home Care Manager is busy, so now all the help is in place, she will only make a quick visit to Mrs T every six months to check on the arrangements.

The *Modernising Government* White Paper provides a top-down account of the properties of a set of objectified institutions, or rather the properties New Labour thinks characterise such institutions. It implies that joined-up governance possesses intrinsic properties such that it is bound to be responsive and efficient. In contrast, the social workers' account of Mrs T provides us with a bottom-up account of a social practice. It illustrates the operation of joined-up governance by describing the ways in which people act so as to interpret, make, and subvert institutional norms and rules in a particular case. The contrast between objectified institutions and contingent practices is a theme that runs through the ensuing study of New Labour.

Within political science, positivists characteristically objectify institutions, social categories, or human rationality. That is to say, they treat these things as, first, given or fixed and, second, constitutive of human actions. They define institutions by reference to norms or rules that apparently govern the behaviour of the people who fall under them. Or they take a social category, such as class or religious affiliation, as an adequate stand-in, or even explanation, for beliefs and actions that apparently are common to all people who belong within that category. Or they ascribe certain principles of reason to people irrespective of any particular circumstances, beliefs, or motivations. In all these cases, positivists treat institutions, social categories, or rationality as the givens that constitute actions, rather than as the contingent products or properties of actions. I favour, in contrast, an interpretive approach to political science that takes its objects to be contingent practices. Whereas positivists ascribe a fixed content to conventions or norms, I regard them as emergent properties of a practice and so as open to different interpretations within that practice. Whereas positivists portray institutions as fixed by conventions or norms, I think of practices as constantly being remade, with every aspect of them being open, at least in principle, to transformation. Whereas positivists sometimes portray institutions as path-dependent, as if existing norms fix their later development, I believe that every aspect of a practice could change as a result of a contingent contest over meanings.

The contrast between objectified institutions and contingent practices overlaps with that between scientific expertise and democratic dialogue. Whenever positivists objectify institutions, social categories, or rationality, they divorce the objects they study from the contingent beliefs and desires embedded within them: they portray the Labour Party, the working class, or bureaucrats as objects whose properties and actions they can explain, correlate, or model without having to take cognizance of the possibly diverse and conflicting beliefs, desires, and actions of Party members, workers, or civil servants. In doing so, positivists establish the possibility of their claiming a certain expertise. They can claim to reveal how and why political events and processes occur through the application of their abstract explanations, correlations, or models. Sometimes they even claim that their explanations, correlations, or models can predict what will happen under certain circumstances. Hence they can offer expert advice to elite actors about what these latter might achieve and how they might do so. Objectification enables political scientists to claim to possess knowledge of social facts that appear to be given independently of any study of concrete beliefs and desires. It thereby enables them to offer policy advice that appears to be valid independently of any negotiation with those at whom the policies are targeted.

An interpretive approach to political science undercuts the positivist notion of scientific expertise. A concern with practices implies that explanations, correlations, or models are valid only in so far as they happen to capture the beliefs and desires of the relevant actors. It also implies that any policy advice based on explanations, correlations, or models will be effective only in so far as the targets of the policy happen to adopt the beliefs and desires ascribed to them by political scientists. Interpretivism thus shifts our emphasis from expertise to narratives and dialogue. We explain events and processes by ascribing beliefs and desires to actors so as to construct a narrative that locates what we want to explain in its contingent context. And we judge the potential effects of a policy by entering a dialogue with the targets of that policy – a dialogue in which they reveal their beliefs and desires and in which policy-makers negotiate and reformulate the policy to make it fit with those beliefs and desires.

New Labour draws, I will suggest, on an institutionalism that purports to make possible expertise. The contrast between its Third Way and an open community based on a participatory democracy thus constitutes the final theme that runs through the ensuing study of New Labour. Political scientists are not detached experts who neutrally record and explain political events and processes. Rather, they are social actors who intervene in dialogues in ways that have political consequences. We will find, for example, that institutionalism and communitarianism have influenced New Labour. This influence implies that when we challenge the objectification of institutions and the idea of scientific expertise in political science, our critique spills over to apply to aspects of New Labour's socialism as vision and practice. The Third Way with its institutionalist roots confronts a vision of an open community with roots in an interpretive approach.

The ensuing study of New Labour explores three overlapping contrasts between positivism and interpretivism, between expertise and dialogue, and between the Third Way and the open community. These contrasts are characterised, of course, by fuzzy boundaries, not sharp dichotomies. New Labour provides the site at which I explore the fuzzy boundaries between different political sciences and different social democracies. The resulting book resembles a sandwich. The first and last chapters are the slices of bread: they discuss different political sciences and social democracies. The other chapters are the filling in which the overlaps and differences among these political sciences and social democracies are explored through an interpretation of New Labour.

This chapter explores different political sciences. It concentrates on the contrasts between positivism and interpretivism and between expertise and dialogue. To begin, it provides a historical account of the emergence of various approaches to political science. This historical account provides a critical perspective on several varieties of positivism. It suggests that to understand contemporary political science adequately we have to deploy an interpretive approach at odds with positivism. It also suggests that positivism has acted less as a source of independent expertise than as a way of conceptualising objects so as to make them governable. Thereafter this chapter offers a theoretical version of this critique. It explores the nature of the objectification that characterises the leading varieties of positivist political science – behaviouralism, institutionalism, and rational choice. And it explores different forms of interpretation to show how and why they too sometimes encourage similar types of objectification. Together these historical and theoretical explorations of political science provide an account and a defence of a decentred interpretive approach.

A history of political science

The twentieth century witnessed the separation of the study of politics from its antecedents in philosophy, history, and law. In very broad terms, we might divide nineteenth-century political thought into two strands. Enlightenment thinkers such as Jeremy Bentham believed in rational, scientific inquiry. Typically they tried to base social science on an individualistic and hedonistic psychology. Organicist thinkers such as Samuel Coleridge rejected the atomistic analysis of the self as a string of momentary sensations, but unlike pre-Enlightenment thinkers they generally emphasised the unique personality of the individual. The encounter between Enlightenment and organicist ideas opened up the intellectual space in which nineteenth-century philosophers, historians, and jurists wrote on politics. On the one hand, the organicist critique of the Enlightenment reinforced T. B. Macaulay's rejection of the deductive Benthamite method in favour of an inductive Whig philosophy of history.[7] Nineteenth-century liberals began to appeal to history, tradition, and culture as well as to rational self-interest. Even John Stuart Mill drew inspiration from Coleridge and Auguste Comte when he modified his Benthamite heritage to champion an inductive method and to stress the importance of culture as a factor in determining what political system suited a particular society. Walter Bagehot likewise appealed to national character as a basis for the scientific study of politics; he described the British as a moderate, steady people who lacked imagination, enthusiasm, and the impulse to grand theorising, and he suggested that the nature and strength of the British constitution derived from this national character rather than the mythic communion to which Whigs often appealed. On the other hand, the influence of organicism on idealist philosophy and sociology prompted a reading of history as exhibiting a moral progress that was linked to reason and harmony.[8] Bernard Bosanquet and D. G. Ritchie explored the development of moral personality in its social and historical context by appealing to national character, Darwinian processes, and Hegel. Similarly, although L. T. Hobhouse saw conflict as a fact about the world, he insisted that it typically encouraged people to create forms of order that were more in accord with a harmony that also was latent in the world.

Mill, Bagehot, Ritchie, and Hobhouse all exhibited to varying degrees a concern with agency or character, a suspicion of deductive models and scientism, and an awareness of historical contingency. They approached the study of politics through philosophy, history, and law. Politics appears in their work less as a distinct empirical domain governed by its own regularities than as an arena in which character and reason work themselves out, often in an explicitly evolutionary process. The political became established as an empirical domain separate from philosophy, history, and law only when these ideas of character, reason, and evolution began to collapse during the first half of the twentieth century, at first in the wake of modernism and later gaining considerable momentum from the First World War. Theoretical and social dilemmas led to the decline of moralistic and evolutionary approaches and the rise of new ones inspired by an atomistic and analytical empiricism.

The First World War undermined the nineteenth-century faith in reason and moral progress. Observers found it harder and harder to conceive of politics as a realm that expressed moral character or the evolution of reason. Whereas actions had been conceived as conduct infused with the reason and morals of the individual, they now became behaviour to be analysed either apart from any assumptions about mind or in relation to hidden desires and depths which often overpowered reason and morals. The First World War also lent a fillip to forms of scepticism – themselves often responses to the Victorian crisis of faith – that broke the world down into atomistic units instead of making sense of units by placing them in a grand narrative of progress. The resulting modernism focused on discrete, discontinuous elements to be assembled into categories or models rather than moral stories.[9] In philosophy, G. E. Moore and Bertrand Russell pioneered an atomistic and analytical style opposed to the speculative and moralistic tone of T. H. Green or Herbert Spencer. In economics, W. S. Jevons, Alfred Marshall, and A. G. Pigou began to separate economics from the moral sciences and history, thereby opening up the possibility of a discrete empirical domain that could be studied quantitatively and through analytical constructions based on atomistic individuals.

Modernism undermined approaches to the study of politics as expressive of grand philosophical or historical processes. Political actions and institutions became discrete units to be investigated individually prior to being assembled into larger sets based on their similarities and differences. Modernist empiricism inspired a quantitative approach to human behaviour as advocated by Graham Wallas and developed by the British Institute of Public Opinion (BIPO) following its formation in 1937. The BIPO surveyed large numbers of representative individuals on specific issues. It divided people's views on any given issue from their wider webs of belief, and then constructed public opinion analytically out of these atomised views. The modernist nature of this approach contrasts with the idealists' reliance on a case-study style of social work and with a Mass Observation that used varied sources, such as diaries, documentary, and observation, to produce micro-studies of individuals, families, industries, and towns, all of which were conceived as holistic in nature.

Modernist empiricism also inspired a search for typologies in comparative politics. Although James Bryce invoked a comparative method, he continued to locate institutions firmly within the whole of the state of which they were a part and even to argue that all societies were evolving towards democracy.[10] The modernist break with such positions appears only after the First World War in the work of Herman Finer. While Finer's *Foreign Governments at Work*, published in 1921, contains an analytical index of topics that enables the reader to compare similar institutions in different countries, his major work, *Theory and Practice of Modern Government*, published in 1932, proceeds topic by topic, treating each institution in relation to similar ones in other countries rather than in the contextual whole of the other institutions in its own country.[11] Finer thereby introduced the now-familiar strategy of comparing various legislatures or constitutions to establish typologies, a strategy that embodies the modernist gesture of breaking previous wholes into atomistic units to be located next to similar units understood as separable objects of analysis. Whereas the political had been explored in relation to philosophical and historical narratives, modernist empiricism established an epistemic space in which it could be explained by the discovery of laws or regularities based on quantitative analyses of opinion and behaviour or on the creation of suitable typologies.

When we recognise how politics became a discipline separate from philosophy, history, and law, we challenge a history of political science that tells a story of scientific progress based on increased empirical rigour and theoretical sophistication. Far from political science providing us with an increasingly better knowledge of the world, it constructs the world it describes through the deployment of a modernist empiricism committed to atomistic analysis. Instead of praising Wallas, Finer, and others for 'their search for pathways through the intimidating mass of historical and contemporary data', we might explore how modernist empiricism constructs such data so as to promote some modes of inquiry and foreclose others.[12] We might represent putative advances in empirical rigour and theoretical sophistication as masks for the contestable triumph of a particular account of the objects and methods of political science.

In the first half of the twentieth century, modernist empiricism remained a nascent trend that was barely visible among moralistic and evolutionary approaches derived from the liberalism and idealism of the nineteenth century.[13] In the second half of the century, it confronted behaviouralism as an alternative departure from these moralistic and evolutionary approaches. Behaviouralism embodied a predilection for grand theories that claim to possess universality and so are insensitive to agency, history, and contingency. Behaviouralists typically thought that natural science provided a better model for political science than did philosophy, history, or law. In many ways, behaviouralism represented a parallel movement to modernist empiricism in its break with ideas of character, reason, and evolution. Yet behaviouralists typically wanted political scientists to concentrate resolutely on framing and testing hypotheses in terms of objective data, and on devising positive theories, abstract hypotheses, or models that were independent of such data and yet received support from it. This search for general hypotheses and models left little space for the quirks of the particular case.

The 1950s and 1960s witnessed S. E. Finer – the younger brother of Hermann – and Bill Mackenzie establish modernist empiricism respectively in the Universities of Keele and Manchester. Almost immediately afterwards, in the 1960s and 1970s, Jean Blondel and Richard Rose brought behaviouralism respectively to the Universities of Essex and Strathclyde. A contrast with positivist behaviouralism thus became central to the self-image of modernist empiricists. However, the contrast between modernist empiricism and positivism obscures as much as it reveals. It obscures the way they both arose as part of the modernist break with Enlightenment and organicist theories. And it obscures the way in which modernist empiricism soon absorbed behaviouralist themes. Instead of defining modernist empiricism in contrast to positivism, we might highlight their similarity. Unlike earlier moralistic and evolutionary approaches, both of them establish a value-free discipline with a discrete empirical domain. Neither of them attempts primarily to understand the political world by reconstructing it as a whole with a narrative form. Rather, they deploy an atomistic and analytical modernism in order to divide the political world into discrete units that they then reassemble through comparisons and classifications that lead to the discovery of correlations and regularities. No doubt modernist empiricists are more likely than behaviouralists to move from the particular to the general, to immerse themselves in concrete cases before going on to draw comparisons, and to highlight oddities within individual examples. Nonetheless, modernist empiricists such as S. E. Finer clearly resemble the behaviouralists in their belief in comparison across time and space as a means of uncovering regularities and probabilistic explanations to be tested against neutral evidence.

The contrast between modernist empiricism and behaviouralism hides other approaches to political science that appeared during the twentieth century. Rational-choice theory can be seen as yet another response to the dilemmas thrown up in and around the First World War, a response that arose as a reworking of the Enlightenment tradition. Like utilitarianism and contractarianism, rational-choice theory postulates isolated individuals with clear preferences coming together to form a society with a distinct pattern of order. We can even trace a clear line of descent from Bentham through Jevons's theorising of marginal utility to the economists who brought rational-choice theory to the study of politics in the 1950s. Nonetheless, rational-choice theorists, in accord with the modernist break with earlier forms of thinking, rarely share the Benthamite equation of individual rationality with character and progress. They are often preoccupied instead with things such as the implications of our having imperfect information or the danger that free-riding will lead to an insufficient provision of non-excludable goods.

Another response to the dilemmas thrown up by the First World War was a social humanism that arose primarily as idealists grappled with a loss of faith in reason and the universal.[14] R. G. Collingwood, John Macmurray, and later Bernard Crick and Quentin Skinner, perpetuated idealist themes and concerns even as they increasingly moved away from objective idealism. Although they no longer thought of history as straightforwardly exhibiting progress or a moral purpose, they still promoted a vision of political science as the interpretation of intentional actions performed in the context of community. Far from purging political science of intentionality and values, they saw these things as integral to such a science. Thus, we find a far more profound commitment to agency, hostility to scientism, and sensitivity to history among social humanists than we do among modernist empiricists.

The history of political science exhibits a number of overlapping and competing traditions. Yet we have to be careful how we unpack this appeal to traditions. Modernist empiricists might suggest that each tradition or 'idiom' provides a different orientation to facts that in some sense are given independently of the ways we talk about them. They might suggest that we have a bag of intellectual traditions or 'tools', each of which has its own job.[15] Interpretivists would reply that far from thinking of a given empirical domain, we should conceive of the facts as being constructed differently within each of the traditions. Different political scientists deploy different categories that play an active role in constructing the different worlds they depict.

Different approaches to political science construct the world differently. Thus, whereas positivists treat political science as an autonomous professional space for the study of power, we might explore how it has been influenced by power and the state while also influencing them. On the one hand, the state has helped define the discipline through the provision of incentives – such as research grants with specific criteria attached – the impact of higher education policy – including the expansion of particular disciplines or universities – and the definition of a set of significant problems through its access to the media. On the other, political scientists have helped to create new bodies of knowledge on which the state has been able to draw to develop, extend, and transform its activities. Political scientists have constructed and investigated various objects through techniques of quantification, comparison, and classification.

The moralistic and evolutionary approaches to political science that dominated the late nineteenth century reflected a complacent belief in Britain's place at the forefront of a natural and rational progress. Yet it was at this time that social investigators, including Charles Booth, Henry Mayhew, and Seebhom Rowntree, developed new techniques to investigate the lives of the poor.[16] These techniques were not neutral and scientific in the way modernist empiricists might suggest. Far from neutrally recording the actions of the poor, Victorian researchers constructed the poor as a passive category with measurable attributes; they made the poor objects, rather than agents who inherit, transform, and invent the varied beliefs, strategies, and practices by which they make their own lives. Victorian researchers approached the poor in this way because they were missionaries on behalf of character, reason, and morality. They measured the condition of the poor in order to define and prompt the action the middle classes or the state needed to undertake in order to spread civilisation to them. Soon the middle classes and the state began to intrude on people's lives as never before, whether as charity visitors, welfare officers, or home and workplace inspectors.

The rupture associated with the First World War undermined the moralistic basis of this missionary activity. As fact and value became forced apart, so the idea of behaviour replaced that of character. Although social investigators still treated people as passive objects, they increasingly turned their attention from social conditions and character to private opinions and behaviour: the individual became the site of needs, desires, and attitudes, rather than upright or lax morals. Likewise, although the state still attempted to reform moral character, the emphasis increasingly shifted to the control of behaviour, particularly after the Second World War. The study of public opinion arose as a type of knowledge that encouraged political parties and the state to seek to govern the political activity of citizens. In 1966, official census data began to be published by parliamentary constituency thereby facilitating the formation of correlations between voting behaviour and class, age, gender, or region. The study of public opinion joined social surveys and registers of births, deaths, and marriages, as a means of knowing and so governing people. Before long, the decline of the missionary aspect of social surveys, together with a growing prosperity, saw the concern to transform the character of labourers and others supplanted by an interest in identifying their desires. Attempts to define the minimum consumption necessary for moral character gave way to market research into wants that might be met by commercial products.

As the state sought to govern the opinions and the behaviour of its citizens, so politics increasingly became a continuous social process located at the intersection of state and society. And as the state permeated new areas of civil society and private life, so it sought to govern not only the opinions and behaviour of citizens but also its own policies; it sought to monitor its impact on education, employment, health, and housing. These changes in the state overlapped with the emergence of studies of policy and its implementation. Mackenzie tellingly inaugurated the study of pressure groups in Britain by arguing that party programmes now mattered less than did the continuous process of adjusting policies.[17] Before long, political scientists began to open up the Westminster model of British government – a model that depicts a unitary state characterised by parliamentary sovereignty, party control, accountability through elections, and a neutral bureaucracy – in order to explore the policy networks and communities they associated with the differentiated, sectoral functions of a now fragmented executive.[18] In doing so, they began to objectify state functions and activities, thereby providing the state with the possibility of new techniques with which to master its interaction with society; they analysed, compared, and classified networks in the hope of identifying patterns and regularities and thereby improving the state's management of them.

The constant extension of the state's knowledge and activity led to fears of state-overload, bureaucracy, and inefficiency.[19] These fears provided part of the rationale for public choice theory and the new public management. The state increasingly struggled to objectify, monitor, and control not only its interactions with society but also its internal procedures. It turned to financial management and competition to secure accountability, and it turned to regulation to ensure that competition worked appropriately. When the New Right deregulated and privatised functions of the state, it typically used techniques such as auditing and contract to know and govern the agencies that took the place of the state. Likewise, now that New Labour deploys the state to enable individuals and organisations to take active responsibility for themselves, it defines appropriate forms of responsible action and monitors and responds to outcomes. In both cases, although individuals appear as agents already or potentially responsible for their own position, the state still promotes a particular concept of responsibility by giving them skills and opportunities to find employment, to protect their health, or to provide for their future. When political scientists explore these developments, they describe the emergence of new patterns of governance defined as, say, self-governing inter-organisational structures. In doing so, they typically objectify these structures, ascribing specific characteristics to them, and thereby encouraging the state to steer them by adopting techniques such as negotiation and an indirect style of management based on trust.[20]

Positivism has few resources with which to accommodate the preceding history of political science. Because it postulates an empirical world given prior to theory, it struggles to comprehend how changing theoretical commitments gave rise to politics as a discrete object of study. Because it presumes the empirical world to be given, it struggles to grasp how competing traditions actively construct different facts as opposed to merely providing different accounts of the facts. And because it insists on a rigid dichotomy between fact and value, it struggles to understand the ways in which our views of the individual prompt objectifications of aspects of our lives and so interact with the rise of new forms of state power. The preceding history of political science already gives us grounds, therefore, for doubting the adequacy of positivist approaches to political science.

The philosophy of political science

Positivism was subjected to forceful philosophical criticism as early as the 1950s. Today few philosophers, and perhaps few political scientists, would describe themselves as positivists. However, even as political scientists repudiate positivism, so many of their approaches to politics make sense only given positivist assumptions about the possibility of pure experience and the causal nature of social life. Positivist assumptions bedevil behaviouralism, rational choice, and the institutionalism that is the legacy of modernist empiricism. Of course, there are instances of each of these approaches to political science that more or less avoid the objectifying tendency of positivism. Nonetheless, the more exponents of these approaches to political science disentangle themselves from positivist assumptions, the further they depart from the principles that inform their approaches. Political scientists can avoid the problems that derive from entanglement with positivism only if they allow considerable latitude for interpretation, and, if they do this, they implicitly suggest that we would do better to approach political life, and to conceive of political science, in ways more commonly associated with hermeneutics.

Positivism often refers to a vision of a unified science conceived in terms set by a strong empiricist epistemology committed to pure and atomised facts. For our purposes, however, positivism will refer to two theses that draw support from this vision. The first positivist thesis is that we can explain human behaviour in terms of allegedly objective social facts about people in a way that renders beliefs or meanings largely irrelevant to political science: beliefs are, at most, intervening variables. This thesis suggests that behaviour can be correlated with, and perhaps explained by, social categories such as class, economic interest, or institutional position. The second positivist thesis is that the relation between antecedent and consequent in political explanation is a necessary causal one akin to that which characterises natural science. This thesis suggests that political science concerns psychological or social laws rather than historical narratives or the understanding of systems of meaning. When political scientists repudiate positivism, they usually intend to distance themselves only from the idea of pure experience; they remain sympathetic to these two theses. In contrast, I want to argue that once we accept there are no pure experiences, we no longer can adhere to the two positivist theses that inform so much political science.

The first positivist thesis is that we can explain behaviour in terms of allegedly objective social facts rather than beliefs or meanings. Political scientists typically try to avoid direct appeals to beliefs and desires by reducing them to intervening variables. For example, instead of explaining why people vote for the Labour Party by reference to their beliefs, political scientists might do so by saying they are working class. Political scientists then might deal with the anomaly this creates of working-class people who vote Conservative not by examining beliefs but by reference to something such as religious affiliation, gender, or housing occupancy. No doubt few political scientists would want to claim that social class and the like generate actions without passing through human consciousness. They want to imply only that statistical correlations between social class and a particular action allow us to bypass beliefs and desires. Their suggestion is that belonging to a particular class gives one a set of beliefs and desires such that one will act in a given way. For example, to be working class is perhaps to have an interest in, and so a desire for, the redistributive policies historically associated with the Labour Party.

The impossibility of pure experience undermines this first positivist thesis. It implies that we cannot reduce beliefs and desires to mere intervening variables. When we say that someone X in a position Y has given interests Z, we necessarily bring our particular theories to bear in order to derive their interests from their position and even to identify their position. Someone with a different set of theories might believe that someone in position Y has different interests or even that X is not in position Y. The important point here is that how the people we study see their position and their interests must depend on their theories, which might differ significantly from ours. X might possess theories that lead her to see her position as A, not Y, and her interests as B, not Z. For example, some working-class voters might consider themselves to be middle class with an interest in preventing further redistributive measures, while others might consider themselves to be working class but believe that redistributive measures are contrary to the true interests of the workers. Likewise, political scientists cannot reduce people's beliefs about their social class and interests to something such as their religious affiliation, gender, or housing occupancy since these things too are not simply given to people; they too are things that people construct using their particular theories.

The second positivist thesis is that the concept of necessary causation found in the natural sciences also fits political science. This second thesis appears to attract political scientists for two main reasons. Sometimes it represents an attempt to claim the prestige of the natural sciences for a favoured approach: talk of explaining actions by causal laws can sound impressively rigorous compared to avowedly interpretive approaches. At other times it springs from lax thinking: political scientists rightly recognise there is a universal feature of explanation such that to explain something is to relate it to other things, and this leads them wrongly to assume the relationship between *explanans* and *explanandum* also must be universal, where the prestige of natural science ensures they then identify this universal relationship with the scientific concept of causation. The main attractions of the second positivist thesis derive, therefore, from the prestige of the natural sciences. Surely, however, we should not take the success of natural science to preclude other forms of explanation?

The scientific concept of causation is inappropriate for political science since, as we already have found, we cannot reduce beliefs and desires to intervening variables. We can explain actions and practices properly only if we appeal to beliefs and desires, that is to the reasons that inform them. When we explain actions as products of reasons, we imply that the actors concerned in some sense could have reasoned differently, and, if they had done so, they would not have acted as they did. Because actions and practices depend on the reasoned choices of people, they are the products of decisions, rather than the determined outcomes of laws or given processes; after all, choices would not be choices if causal laws fixed their content. Hence political science instantiates a concept of rationality that precludes our explaining actions and practices in ways that embody the concept of causation that operates within the natural sciences. Political science has to come to terms with the inherent contingency of the objects it studies.

Positivism has been widely criticised for its faith in pure experience. Political scientists generally recognise that we cannot approach objects from a theory-neutral position. They seem far less aware that the impossibility of pure experience undermines the two positivist theses I have just discussed. First, because people do not have pure experiences, they always construct their identities, interests, and beliefs in part through their particular theories, so political scientists cannot explain behaviour by reference to allegedly given interests or objective social facts. Second, because social facts do not fix people's identities, interests, and beliefs, we have to explain actions using folk psychology, so political scientists cannot appeal to causal laws; instead they have to evoke the reasons people have for doing what they do.

Contemporary political science harbours a range of traditions. Of these, social humanism tends to inspire interpretive approaches, whereas modernist empiricism with its institutionalist legacy, behaviouralism, and rational choice all tend to fall foul of the preceding critique of positivism. Mind you, as I suggested earlier, boundaries between our aggregate concepts are often fuzzy. These latter traditions are neither monolithic nor explicitly committed to positivism. Rather, they are entangled with the two positivist theses in ways that raise a number of problems for them. When their exponents grapple with these problems, moreover, they often introduce interpretive themes into their approach.

When behaviouralism arrived on British shores, some modernist empiricists quickly made their peace with it. They brought behavioural techniques, as well as a greater interest in voting and public policy, into an uneasy alliance with the comparative and institutional orientation associated with the Westminster model. Other modernist empiricists began, however, to define their approach to political science as peculiarly British in contrast to American behaviouralism. They aligned modernist empiricism especially closely with an institutional approach to political science. The institutional approach focused mainly on descriptions of constitutions, legal systems, the formal organisations of government, and the comparison of these objects across space and time. In the next chapter, we will see how this institutionalism has been refashioned in response to behaviouralism and rational choice. For now, we need to note only that this refashioning entailed a loosening of the concept of an institution to allow for a less formal, more dynamic view of institutions, one that explicitly incorporated rules and norms alongside laws. No doubt institutionalism could be a purely descriptive approach; but if it were, it would offer little more than the trite observation that there are continuities in political practices. For our purposes, what matters is thus the claim that institutions – whether they are understood in terms of laws, rules, or norms – govern and explain actions. Institutionalism implies that laws, rules, or norms have explanatory power because they constitute or structure practices. James March and Johan Olsen define their new institutionalism by arguing that institutions such as the bureaucratic agency or legislative committee are 'collections of standard operating procedures and structures that define and defend interest' and even constitute 'political actors in their own right'.[21] Peter Hall similarly defines institutions as 'formal rules, compliance procedures, and standard operating practices that structure relationships between individuals in various units of the polity and the economy'.[22]

Considerable ambiguity remains, however, as to how we should conceive of institutions once we grant them explanatory power. On the one hand, institutions often appear to have an unacceptably reified form. They are defined as fixed rules or procedures that limit, and perhaps even determine, the actions of the individuals within them. Political scientists are thus able to ignore their contingency, their inner conflicts, and their construction. On the other hand, institutions sometimes are opened up to include cultural factors or meanings in a way that suggests they do not fix such meanings, nor the actions of the individuals who are within them. If we open up institutions in this way, however, we cannot treat them as if they were given. We have to ask instead how meanings and actions are created, recreated, and changed in ways that produce and modify institutions.

By and large institutionalists like to take institutions for granted. They like to treat them as if the people within them are bound to follow the relevant rules; the rules, rather than contingent agency, produce path dependency. But to reify institutions in this way is to rely on the positivist eschewal of interpretation that I have been challenging. Institutionalism, so conceived, assumes that allegedly objective rules prescribe or cause behaviour so that someone in a position X subject to a rule Y will behave in a manner Z. The problem with this assumption is not just that people can wilfully choose to disobey a rule, but also, as we have seen, that we cannot read-off people's beliefs and desires from social facts about them. People who are in a position X might not grasp that they fall under rule Y, or they might understand the implications of rule Y differently from us, and in either of these cases, they might not act in a manner Z even if they intend to follow the rule. We cannot resolve this problem by examining the intentions that are implicit in the rules or norms themselves, as Neville Johnson would have us do, since we have no reason to assume that the intentions, beliefs, and desires of those who now fall under an institution in any way resemble, let alone are identical to, those of the founders of the institution.[23] Instead, we have to disaggregate institutions; we have to explore the contingent beliefs and desires that lead people to act so as to maintain and modify institutions in the ways they do.

Faced with such considerations, institutionalists might open up the concept of an institution to incorporate meanings. They might conceive of an institution as a product of actions informed by the varied and contingent beliefs and desires of the relevant people. We should welcome such a disaggregation of institutionalism. Even as we do so, however, we might wonder whether or not we should still think of the approach as institutionalist in any significant sense. All the explanatory work would be done not by given rules but by the diverse ways in which people understood and applied conventions. Appeals to institutions would be misleading shorthand for the conclusions of explorations into the beliefs and desires of the people who acted so as to maintain and modify the institutions in the way they did.

Behaviouralists, too, generally remain committed to our two positivist theses. Even when they accept a constructive role for theory, deny the possibility of conclusively establishing a particular causal relationship, and accept some form of 'epistemological relativism', they still continue to insist both that explanations are acceptable only if they are falsifiable and that we should isolate variables so as to test such explanations against empirical observations.[24] This falsificationism entangles them with the two positivist theses. First, behaviouralists focus on behaviour without exploring beliefs on the grounds that doing so provides them with brute facts against which to test their theories: beliefs and meanings are explored through their alleged behavioural indicators since these alone are suitable empirical facts. Second, behaviouralists usually seek to test their theories against huge data banks, often using highly sophisticated statistical techniques: they aim to discover quasi-scientific, law-like relations, typically expressed as statistical regularities.

Our critique of positivism implies that the correlations behaviouralists offer us cannot constitute straightforward explanations. Suppose, for example, that we find there is a powerful correlation between being working class and voting Labour. For many behaviouralists, this correlation would suggest that we could explain why people vote Labour by saying they are working class, perhaps even that their being working class causes them to vote Labour. Yet our critique of positivism implies that explanations of actions and practices must appeal to beliefs and desires. Here behaviouralists treat beliefs as intervening variables, so they might unpack their explanation by saying that working-class people vote Labour in the expectation that the Party will promote redistributive measures that will make them better off.[25] Yet we have found that political scientists cannot attribute beliefs and desires to people solely on the grounds of allegedly objective social facts about them. Working-class voters might consider themselves to be well-off and even to stand to benefit from a Conservative government, and yet they still might vote Labour because they believe it will promote social justice and they desire to live in a fair society. The important points here are that if behaviouralists want their correlations to do explanatory work, they have to unpack them in terms of beliefs and desires, and because we cannot ascribe beliefs to people on the basis of allegedly objective social facts, we can unpack correlations in terms of beliefs and desires only through an act of interpretation.

Behaviouralists sometimes try to avoid the problems just discussed by explicitly appealing to beliefs and desires. When they do so, they usually conceive of beliefs and desires as objective attitudes to be discovered and transformed into brute data by means of techniques such as questionnaires and statistics. For many behaviouralists, political culture is a given fact composed of attitudes that are capable of being measured. Yet this behaviouralist approach to political culture does not allow sufficiently for the holistic and constitutive nature of beliefs and desires in relation to actions and practices. For a start, because people do not hold beliefs as a necessary consequence of an objective social fact about them but for reasons of their own, we can make sense of their beliefs only by locating them in the context of the other beliefs that provide their reasons for holding them. Suppose, for example, that behaviouralists establish a correlation between a positive attitude to social justice and voting Labour. They still cannot properly explain people's voting Labour by reference to this attitude; after all, someone who has a positive attitude to social justice still might vote Conservative if they believe still more strongly in conservative values, or if they believe Labour will not implement its manifesto. To grasp why someone with a positive attitude to social justice votes Labour, we have to unpack the other relevant beliefs and desires that relate that attitude to that vote. To explain an action, we cannot merely correlate it with a single isolated attitude; we have to interpret it in relation to a whole set of beliefs and desires.

The holistic quality of beliefs and desires implies not only that practices are constituted by intersubjective meanings but also that we can understand a practice only by grasping the whole web of beliefs on which it is predicated. Consider, for example, the practice of voting.[26] Behaviouralists might describe the act of voting as one in which we indicate a preference from among competing policies or candidates by raising a hand or putting a piece of paper in a box. But appeals to behaviour alone cannot tell us why raising one's hand should amount to voting, or why there would be uproar if someone forced someone else to raise their hand against their will, or why only certain people should be regarded as eligible to vote. We can explain these sorts of things only if we appeal to the intersubjective beliefs that underpin the practice of concern to us. We need to know, for example, that voting is associated with making a free choice and so with a particular concept of the self; we need to know what counts as an infringement of free choice and who is regarded as capable of making such a choice. Practices and beliefs are constitutive of one another. Practices could not exist if people did not have appropriate beliefs. Beliefs would not make sense in the absence of the practices to which they refer.

The behaviouralist concept of an attitude presupposes a particular relationship between beliefs and actions. It presupposes, first, that beliefs can be related individually to actions, and, second, that beliefs can be differentiated from actions. In contrast, I have argued that beliefs form holistic webs and that beliefs are constitutive of actions and practices. Political science is, therefore, an inherently interpretive discipline, for to explain political phenomena, we have to come to terms with the meanings embedded within it, and to do this, we have to interpret beliefs and desires in their relationship to one another.

Let us turn finally to the rational-choice approach to political science. Rational-choice theory presupposes that actors choose an action because they believe it to be the most efficient way of realising a given end. It constructs models of political practices from the assumption that actions are the product of strategic, utility-maximising individuals. Because rational-choice theory conceives of actions as rational strategies for realising the preferences of the actor, it seems to reduce the motives of political actors to self-interest. But, as most rational-choice theorists would recognise, we have no valid grounds for so privileging self-interest.[27] Even when actions happen to have beneficial consequences for the actors, we cannot conclude from this fact alone that the actors did what they did in order to bring about those beneficial consequences. The problems with an exclusive reliance on self-interest have led rational-choice theorists to expand their notion of preference. They have devoted a great deal of effort to showing how altruistic actions might represent complex expressions of self-interest, and they have also moved towards a 'thin' analysis of preferences that does not examine the motives for actions but rather requires them only to be logically consistent.[28] Yet the reduction of all motives to an expanded concept of preference is either true but vacuous or else false. If we extend our concept of preference to cover any motive for action, we enable ourselves to reduce motives to preferences, but we do so at the expense of removing all content from our concept of a preference. Moreover, if we equated people's preferences with the choices revealed by their actions, any explanation of the choices by reference to the preferences would appear to be viciously tautological. The danger of thus slipping into empty tautologies surely requires rational-choice theorists to fill out their account of a preference. Once they do so, however, they seem destined to return to a concept akin to that of self-interest with its well-known problems, problems that include not only the difficulty of allowing for altruism but also the mismatches with all those psychological studies that suggest people do not structure problems or process information in the ways required by expected utility theory.[29]

The attempts of rational-choice theorists to exclude considerations of meaning or belief appear to have run into dead-ends. Concepts such as preference and expected utility cannot be equated with the allegedly given self-interest of the individual actor if only because the way in which an agent sees his self-interest depends upon his wider web of beliefs. But if rational-choice theorists expand the notion of preference so as to detach it from a given self-interest, they end up offering us tautologies. It should not surprise us, therefore, that rational-choice theorists have begun to appeal explicitly to notions such as 'social norms, cultural values, ideology, and group identification'.[30] Rational-choice theorists usually attempt to incorporate beliefs by appealing to norms as a source of preferences. Sometimes the norms they invoke are effectively reducible to self-interest: they ascribe to norms a causal effect not in recognition of their intrinsic motivating power, but in relation to the non-normative costs and benefits of breaking them or complying with them, where these non-normative costs can be both social, as in ostracism, and psychological, as in guilt and embarrassment.[31] At other times they invoke norms that are not reducible to self-interest but merely compatible with it.[32] Norms appear here alongside self-interest as a source of allegedly given preferences: they are added to an actor's fixed preferences so that they enter rational-choice models in the same way as do expected utilities. Norms are treated as atomistic entities so that they can play a role analogous to that of additional variables in behavioural studies. When rational-choice theorists introduce beliefs, they, too, thus ignore their holistic and constitutive nature in relation to actions and practices.

Institutionalism, behaviouralism, and rational choice typically remain committed to the positivist theses that we can explain actions and practices in terms of allegedly objective social facts and that such explanations embody the same concept of causation as do the natural sciences. Yet these two theses fall together with the myth of pure facts given independently of our concepts or theories. Indeed, the positivist programme is so theoretically weak that it is all but extinct in the philosophy of social science. Philosophy has long since moved on from the triumph of those interpretivists who argued for the distinctive nature of human life as meaningful and infused by language, to the study of issues that arise in the context of this triumph of interpretivism.[33] All too often political scientists continue to invest in positivist stock even though it is philosophically bankrupt.

Varieties of interpretation

Institutionalism, behaviouralism, and rational choice remain entangled with a bankrupt positivism. Their entanglement with positivism explains why much political science focuses on objectified social facts at the expense of contingent practices and on scientific expertise at the expense of dialogue. Social humanism generally inspires, in contrast, interpretive approaches to political science that reject the two positivist theses. Once again, though, we should be wary of mistaking fuzzy boundaries for clear-cut dichotomies. Even interpretivists can be seduced by the allure of scientific expertise, and especially by the big pictures created by the objectification of traditions and practices.

Interpretive approaches analyse actions and practices in relation to meanings or culture, rather than laws and norms, correlations between social categories, or deductive models. Of course, the distinction between interpretive approaches and others is not an all or nothing affair; sensible interpretivists allow that legal studies, correlations, and models can play a useful role in our understanding of practices, while sensible institutionalists, behaviouralists, and rational-choice theorists allow that their typologies, correlations, and models can do explanatory work only in so far as they can be unpacked in terms of the actual beliefs and desires of actors. However, we can distinguish a family of interpretive approaches to political science that stand out in that they focus on beliefs or meanings. This overlapping family includes decentred theory, social constructivism, ethnography, post-structuralism, and practical philosophy, and it overlaps with subsets of other approaches such as the constructivist variety of institutionalism.

Interpretivists share sympathy for bottom-up forms of social inquiry as well as a focus on meanings or beliefs. A bottom-up stance has strong links to a rebuttal of positivism. A rejection of pure experience implies that people in the same situation can hold very different beliefs if only because their experiences of that situation can be laden with very different prior theories. No abstract concept, such as a class or an institution, properly can explain people's beliefs, interests, or actions; it can represent only an abstract stand-in for the multiple and complex beliefs and actions of the individuals we classify under it. Interpretivists often conclude, for these sorts of reasons, that social practices require bottom-up studies of the actions and beliefs out of which they emerge. No doubt constructivist institutionalists are more willing than post-structuralists to bypass bottom-up studies so as to focus on the ways in which institutions operate in a given setting.[34] Yet even when constructivists postulate institutional unity, they usually conceive of it as an emergent property based on individual actions in the context of intersubjective norms, which, at least in principle, could be contested. Interpretivists favour bottom-up studies of the ways in which social practices are created, sustained, and transformed through the interplay and contest of the beliefs and meanings embedded in human activity.

Another theme shared by interpretivists is an emphasis on the contingency of social life. This theme too has strong links to a rebuttal of positivism. Once we accept that people in any given situation can interpret that situation and their interests in all sorts of ways, we are pressed to accept that people's actions are radically open. No practice can fix the ways in which its participants will act, let alone how they will innovate within it in response to novel circumstances. Hence our practices are radically contingent; they lack any fixed essence or logical path of development. This emphasis on the contingency of social life explains why interpretivists denaturalise alternative theories. Interpretivists believe that political scientists efface the contingency of social life when they attempt to ground their theories in apparently given facts about the nature of human life, the path-dependence of institutions, or the inexorability of technological or social developments; they believe that political scientists thereby present as natural or inevitable what is in fact contingent. Hence interpretivists try to expose the contingency of those facets of social life that other social scientists represent as natural or inexorable.

Advocates of an interpretive approach to political science usually share a concern with meanings, bottom-up studies, and contingency. However, these shared positions are very broad ones that leave a number of questions unanswered. Of particular importance are questions about the composition and recentring of practices. Interpretivists sometimes respond to these questions in ways that can lure them into objectifying aspects of human life. One problem here is that interpretivists at best disagree, and at worst are confused, about the nature of the meanings that inform actions and practices. Sometimes they imply that meanings exist as quasi-structures that possess a kind of immanent logic or that respond to random fluctuations of power.[35] At other times they understand meanings in terms of the intentionality or beliefs of individuals; they unpack concepts such as ideology, discourse or language as referring only to intersubjective meanings.[36] These two analyses of meaning correspond to different analyses of the relationship of content to context, with the more ethnographic and hermeneutic forms of interpretivism typically inspiring a concern with the intentionality of agents, and the more structuralist forms generating an apparent ambition to avoid all appeals to human agency.

Interpretivists disagree as to whether people are situated agents or passive constructs of social discourses. At times they appear to want to straddle these surely incompatible positions, writing, for example, of one 'constituting oneself' and also being 'constituted as' a subject.[37] At other times, they pay lip-service to the capacity for situated agency while writing empirical studies that concentrate almost exclusively on the ways in which traditions and practices create forms of subjectivity; their empirical studies almost totally neglect the ways in which situated agents create traditions and practices.[38] No doubt post-structuralists in particular concentrate on the construction of subjects because they want to repudiate autonomy. However, we should distinguish clearly here between autonomy and situated agency. Autonomous individuals would be able, at least in principle, to have experiences, to reason, to adopt beliefs, and to act outside of all contexts. In contrast, while situated agents can reason and act in novel ways, they are able to do so only against the background of contexts that influence them. A repudiation of positivism encourages a rejection of autonomy: if all experiences and all reasoning embody theories, people can adopt beliefs only against the background of a prior set of theories, which at least initially must be made available to them by a social discourse or tradition. Yet this rejection of autonomy does not entail a rejection of situated agency: we can accept that people always set out against the background of a social discourse or tradition and still conceive of them as situated agents who can act and reason in novel ways so as to modify this background.

Situated agency manifests itself in the diverse activity we might find taking place against the background of any particular social context. Even if a linguistic context forms the background to people's statements, and a social context forms the background to their actions, the content of their statements and actions does not come directly from these contexts; it comes, rather, from the ways in which they replicate, use, or respond to these contexts in accord with their intentions. Of course, post-structuralists in particular neglect situated agency partly because they want to deny that such intentions are autonomous: they want to insist on the theory-laden nature of all the reasoning and experiences on the basis of which people form intentions. As we have seen, however, we can deny autonomy without renouncing situated agency. People formulate their intentions in a creative process undertaken against the background of a discourse or tradition.

Contemporary interpretivists often replay debates about situated agency in discussions of the relationship of the individual to language. A repudiation of autonomy gets expressed in the claim that the individual is constituted by language. However, this claim remains ambiguous over situated agency. A minimal version of the claim that language constitutes the individual would understand language simply as a metaphor for belief: claim-1 is the unexceptional one that people's thoughts and actions embody their beliefs. A slightly more forceful version of the claim would understand language to indicate that people's beliefs are formed in a social context of existing traditions and discourses: claim-2 is that people's thoughts and actions embody their beliefs, where these beliefs arise against the background of a social tradition. Although claim-2 entails a rejection of autonomy, it is compatible with an account of the individual as a situated agent capable of creative innovations based on local reasoning. We can distinguish, therefore, between two varieties of claim-2. Claim-2a is that people's thoughts and actions embody their beliefs, where beliefs arise against the background of a tradition, but where people are situated agents who can modify the beliefs they inherit through their own local reasoning. Claim-2b is that people's thoughts and actions embody beliefs, where these beliefs arise against the background of traditions that determine the beliefs they might go on to adopt. Although a rejection of positivism encourages interpretivists to adopt claim-2a, they need not be seduced into an entanglement with the much less plausible claim-2b. Quite the contrary, interpretivists should be wary of words, such as 'language', 'discourse', and even 'ideology', which evoke quasi-structures as constitutive of inter-subjectivity rather than emergent properties of it.

The bottom-up orientation of interpretivists encourages a decentred focus on the multiplicity of conflicting actions and micro-practices that come together to create a contingent pattern of rule. However, the confusion among interpretivists on the nature of meanings reappears in the ways in which they suggest political scientists might recentre such bottom-up studies. On the one hand, because the more structuralist forms of interpretivism sometimes appear to reduce meaning and agency to a semiotic code, they can encourage the use of concepts such as ideology, discourse, and power/knowledge as ways of recentring accounts of practices. On the other hand, the broad interpretivist emphases on contingency and particularity often inspire an overt challenge to the validity and naturalness of all terms of recentring, including presumably those of ideology, discourse, and power/knowledge.

Interpretivists oscillate between condemning all totalising concepts and invoking their own. At times they appear to want to straddle these incompatible positions, writing, for example, of the need to replace approaches to political science that appeal to social forces with a focus on 'singular practices' only then to go on to assimilate these practices to an apparently monolithic concept of 'individualising power'.[39] At other times they pay lip-service to the importance of contingency and particularity while writing empirical studies that explain the existence and content of actions and practices in terms of quasi-structures that operate as totalising concepts. For example, many post-structuralists depict discourses or regimes of power as contingent particularities only then to portray performances as manifestations of just these discourses and power-relations rather than as themselves contingent and particular. Today interpretivists are muddled about whether they legitimately can recentre their bottom-up studies, let alone over what concepts they should use so to do.

In a sense, interpretivists, like everyone else, should use the abstract concepts they believe best describe the world. If they find that networks are multiplying, they might invoke a 'network society'; if they find that people are increasingly dealing with risk through personalised health plans, pension provisions, and the like, they might invoke an 'individualising power'; and if they find that a group of people express similar ideas about freedom, the market, the importance of the consumer, and the need to roll back the state, they might invoke a 'discourse of the New Right'. All such aggregate concepts describe broad patterns in the world, so the worth we attach to them will depend on whether or not we believe the relevant patterns exist. Interpretivists have no particular problem in accepting such aggregate concepts as descriptions of the world, although arguably they will be more concerned than others to point to exceptions that do not fit under such generalising terms. Nonetheless, the abstract concepts we deploy in this way are purely descriptive: they do not do any explanatory work. Descriptions of forms of life, power, and speech do not necessarily tell us anything about why those forms of life, power, and speech have arisen or why particular practices, actions, or utterances have the content they do.

The question of recentring becomes awkward for interpretivists with respect to explanatory concepts, not descriptive ones. The more we emphasise the contingency and particularity of beliefs, actions, and practices, the harder it becomes to explain them by reference to a broader logic or social process. All too often, when interpretivists deploy ideology, discourse, or power to do explanatory work, these concepts exhibit the failings of a neglect of situated agency. For example, when ideology or discourse purports not only to describe but also to explain a pattern of belief or speech, it is often conceived as being a quasi-structure composed of units whose relations to one another define the content of the discourse. Meaning thus gets reduced to the allegedly inherent relations between abstract semantic units – woman is structurally defined in binary opposition to man – as opposed to the diverse and contingent beliefs that situated agents come to hold against a social background. The deployment of ideology, discourse, or power as an explanatory concept confronts a number of problems as a consequence of this neglect of situated agency. For a start, the use of ideology as an explanatory concept confronts the problem of accounting for change. If individuals arrive at beliefs and even construct themselves in accord with a fixed and disembodied ideology, they appear to lack the capacity to modify that ideology, so such modifications seem to be inexplicable. In addition, the location of meaning in ideologies or discourses is unclear. Meaning appears to be tied to relationships between semantic units, relationships that are given independently of individuals, their beliefs, and their agency. Yet this disembodied view of meaning would contradict the interpretivist concern with contingency and particularity. A disembodied view of meaning implies that while the rise of an ideology might be contingent, its content is not contingent but rather given by the fixed relationships between the semantic units. Likewise, a disembodied view of meaning implies that although ideologies might be singular, the diverse and particular beliefs people might hold about anything can be assimilated to a single pattern imposed on them by the necessity of the relationships between semantic units.

Interpretivists struggle to recentre their accounts of practices in ways that have explanatory power. They might do so by drawing on the contrast between situated agency and autonomy. When we reject autonomy, we accept that individuals necessarily experience the world in ways that reflect the influence upon them of tradition, ideology, or discourse. Hence our explanatory concepts should indicate how social influences permeate beliefs and actions even on those occasions when the speaker or actor does not recognise such influence. To accept situated agency is, however, to imply that people possess the capacity to adopt beliefs and actions, even novel ones, for reasons of their own, where these beliefs and actions then can transform the social background. Interpretivists might be well advised, therefore, to think of the social context in terms of traditions rather than ideologies or discourses; after all, the concept of a tradition evokes a social structure in which individuals are born and which then acts as the background to their beliefs and actions even while they might modify, develop, and even reject much of their inheritance.

As an explanatory concept, tradition has the advantage over ideology and discourse that it allows properly for situated agency and so provides a means of analysing change. Change arises because of people's ability to adopt beliefs and perform actions for reasons of their own. To think about change in this way is not to suggest that traditions contain an imminent logic that fixes their development. It is to say, rather, that the ways in which people change their beliefs or actions depend on their contingent reasoning. Hence our explanatory concepts should indicate how change arises from a type of reasoning that is neither random nor fixed by logic or given experiences. Interpretivists might be well advised, therefore, to analyse change in terms of the ways in which situated agents respond to dilemmas creatively from within their existing beliefs. A dilemma arises for individuals whenever they adopt a new belief that stands in opposition to their existing ones and so forces a reconsideration of the latter. When people accept a new belief, they pose to their existing beliefs the question of how to accommodate it. They respond to the dilemma, whether explicitly or not, by changing their beliefs so as to accommodate the newcomer.

The concepts of tradition and dilemma provide interpretivists with the means to recentre their accounts of practices.[40] They can explain the rise of a practice by reference to the intersubjective traditions and dilemmas that inform the changing activities of various clusters of political actors. They might even be able to relate the relevant dilemmas to what they conclude are facts about the world, although they also might conclude that some dilemmas were figments of the imagination of those who responded to them. Nonetheless, because the concepts of tradition and dilemma embody recognition of the contingency and particularity of social life, they can only do so much recentring. They certainly do not constitute mechanisms or large-scale social processes of which our practices stand as symptoms. Instead, they represent abstractions that do explanatory work only in so far as we can unpack them, at least in principle, in terms of contingent and intersubjective beliefs and actions. As abstractions, moreover, they characteristically enable us to recentre our accounts only at the cost of ignoring or marginalising those contingent beliefs, desires, and activities that fall outside the dominant patterns they capture. If we forgot this cost, we would neglect the critical perspective provided by interpretive approaches – a critical perspective to which I will return when evaluating New Labour.

Interpretivists can resolve theoretical problems in their approach, I believe, by allowing for situated agency even as they reject autonomy. Recognition of situated agency together with rejection of autonomy would suffice to sustain their criticisms of alternative approaches to political science. One target of interpretivism is the tendency within institutionalism to forsake the bottom-up stance of constructivism for a focus on allegedly given laws, rules, or norms. For some institutionalists, the beliefs and actions of individuals are defined by their social roles or by the norms that govern the institutions in which they participate. Institutionalists sometimes obscure the contingent and contested nature of social life by implying that the content and development of institutions are fixed by rules or a path-dependency inherent within them. To reject such institutionalism requires only a critique of autonomy. Once we allow that people's understanding of their world, including the norms that apply to it, is inherently theory-laden, we open up the possibility of different people grasping or applying a rule or norm in different ways, and we thus draw attention to the contest and contingency that institutionalists sometimes obscure. Another target of interpretivism is the behaviouralist tendency to reduce beliefs to intervening variables. A rejection of autonomy undermines this tendency much as it does the institutionalist use of laws, rules, or norms. Once we allow that people's understanding of the world, including the social categories to which they belong, is inherently theory-laden, we open up the possibility that people who fall within any given social category will hold diverse beliefs or even perform similar actions for distinct reasons, and we thereby make it necessary to unpack these reasons rather than relying on the social categories to act as markers for them. Yet another target of interpretivism is the account of the individual implicit within much rational-choice theory. Rational-choice theorists often imply that individuals are, or at least fruitfully can be treated as if they are, atomised units who possess nigh-on perfect knowledge of their preferences and situation and who act so as to maximise their utility. In most rational-choice models, neither traditions nor the unconscious interfere in the processes of belief-formation, deliberation, and action. To reject such rational-choice theory requires only a critique of autonomy. Once we accept that people's views of their interests and contexts are always infused with their particular, contingent theories, we undercut assumptions about individuals' pure and perfect knowledge of their preferences and their situation. A repudiation of autonomy suffices, finally, to distance contemporary interpretivism from the moralistic and evolutionary approaches that preceded the rise of modernist empiricism. Although interpretivists still seek to explain actions and practices within narratives, their denial of autonomy leaves little space in these narratives for the elder moralising ideas of reason, character, and progress. It prompts interpretivists to turn instead to decentred studies that highlight dispersal, difference, and discontinuity.

Interpreting New Labour

Throughout this chapter, I have been distinguishing various approaches to political science from one another. The content of these distinctions reflects contrasts that will run through the ensuing study of New Labour, notably that between objectified social categories and contingent practices, and that between scientific expertise and dialogue. On one side, we have those approaches – institutionalism, behaviouralism, and rational choice – that generally remain entangled with modernist empiricism or even positivism. These approaches often objectify aspects of human life: they treat contingent practices as institutions characterised by fixed laws, rules, or norms; or they treat fixed social categories as adequate markers for beliefs, perhaps even ignoring beliefs entirely; or they treat rationality as fixed in relation to assumptions about utility-maximisation. On the other side, we have social humanism and the interpretivism it inspires. Although the more structural forms of interpretivism sometimes slide towards objectifying beliefs and agency by suggesting they are given by ideologies or discourses, interpretivists rarely are entangled with positivism to the same extent as are exponents of other approaches to political science. Typically they explore contingent practices in relation to the meanings or beliefs embedded within them. They tend to practice critique and to promote dialogue.

Having defended an interpretive approach, I will go on to apply it to New Labour. As we have seen, however, the boundaries between interpretivism and other approaches, especially institutionalism, are fuzzy rather than clear-cut. As I pursue an interpretive study of New Labour, so I will further explore these boundaries. I thus combine a study of New Labour with explorations in political science in large measure because the ideas of political scientists often overlap with, and influence, those of political actors. When we looked at the history of political science, we saw how political scientists had objectified the poor, public opinion, public policy, and policy networks in ways that helped to make possible certain modes of governance. In the next chapter, we will find that New Labour has tried to establish a mode of governance that owes much to the new institutionalism. In Chapter 3, we will find that New Labour's self-understanding also overlaps with a type of interpretivism that gets perilously close to treating ideologies as objects whose contents derive from the relationships between the semantic units of which they are composed. These chapters will thus continue to explore the boundaries between different approaches to political science.

Chapters 2 and 3 also begin our interpretation of the beliefs, actions, and practices that characterise New Labour. Chapter 2 indicates how the new institutionalism has influenced New Labour's thought and policies. The Third Way is a response from within the social democratic tradition to dilemmas posed by the New Right, a response that also draws on developments within institutionalism in the wake of the rise of rational choice. New Labour reproduces institutionalist motifs in its attempts to reform the state and the economy. With respect to the state, New Labour promotes networks, partnerships, and zones as constitutive of a joined-up governance that is said to combine quality with efficiency precisely because it reflects our social being. With respect to the economy, New Labour promotes partnerships, civic entrepreneurialism, flexibility, and innovation as necessary to ensure our common prosperity within the new economy. Chapter 3 turns to the question of how New Labour's visions of the state and the economy have involved a redefinition of social democratic values. Chapters 4 and 5 add detail to this interpretation of New Labour by focusing respectively on the welfare state and the economy. Finally, Chapter 6 returns to explicit discussion of the contrasts that run through this study of New Labour. Whereas the Third Way exhibits the failings of New Labour's entanglement with the new institutionalism and communitarianism, an interpretive approach rooted in social humanism opens a vista onto alternative socialisms, notably the open community.

2   Institutionalism

Introduction

An interpretive approach to political science conceives of its objects of inquiry as contingent practices. These practices are the products of the actions, and so beliefs, of the relevant actors. We can explain beliefs, actions, and practices by reference to traditions and problems. This interpretive approach informs the ensuing study of New Labour. In broad terms, New Labour will appear as a response from within the tradition of social democracy to issues made salient by the New Right. Yet we need to invoke different issues and different features of social democracy depending on the particular aspects of New Labour we are trying to explain.

This chapter will begin to develop this interpretation of New Labour while also continuing the examination of different approaches to political science. New Labour intersects with, and draws on, the new institutionalism. To be more precise, New Labour has responded to problems made salient by the New Right in ways that overlap with, and are influenced by, the new institutionalist response to the rise of rational choice. What follows thus maps approaches to political science onto policy proposals and party agendas. One mapping is widely accepted: a neoliberal narrative promoted marketisation and the new public management as adopted by the New Right.[1] The other mapping has gone unnoticed: an institutionalist narrative promoted networks and joined-up governance as adopted by New Labour. Of course, these mappings represent broad conceptual and temporal conjunctures, not invariant ones: some neoliberals do not advocate marketisation and the new public management let alone support the New Right; and some institutionalists do not advocate networks and joined-up governance let alone support New Labour. Nonetheless, just as political scientists acknowledge such qualifications while recognising the reasonableness of the conjuncture often drawn between neoliberalism and the New Right, so we can do so while accepting the interaction between new institutionalism and New Labour.

Political scientists conjoin neoliberalism with marketisation and the New Right partly because of the conceptual overlaps between their ideas and partly because of temporal connections found in the lives of key actors. This chapter will point to a similar conjunction between the new institutionalism, its network theory, and New Labour primarily by drawing out the conceptual overlaps between them, arguing, for example, that institutionalism often inspires a focus on networks, that New Labour draws on institutionalist themes to counter the New Right, and that New Labour's vision of joined-up governance relies on network theory. Of course, these conceptual overlaps cannot establish that New Labour actually has been influenced by the new institutionalism – the connections could be merely fortuitous. To suggest influence, we need to point to appropriate connections, interactions, meetings, or events in the lives of leading actors. Although the conceptual overlaps at times will point towards such temporal connections, I will rarely pause to make the later explicit; so, because they make concrete the association of the new institutionalism with New Labour, I want to highlight some of them now.

The leading actors in this chapter are a diffuse, intersecting group of social scientists, policy advisers, and politicians. Together they effectively combine the Third Way, network theory, and institutionalism into a recognisable package. The main proponents of network theory are avowed institutionalists: we might think here of American social scientists such as Mark Granovetter, Paul DiMaggio, and Walter Powell as well as British ones including Rod Rhodes and Gerry Stoker.[2] Some of the British institutionalists, including Stoker, have provided policy advice to New Labour. Others have advised parliamentary bodies under New Labour governments, as Vivien Lowndes did the inquiry into innovations in citizen participation held by the House of Commons Public Administration Committee. More indirectly, New Labour's leading politicians, including Tony Blair, the Prime Minister, Gordon Brown, the Chancellor of the Exchequer, and Peter Mandelson, who held various offices of state, regularly appeal to social theories that are interwoven with the new institutionalism, such as communitarianism and social capital theory.[3]

The most important actors in my narrative are perhaps those employed in centre left think-tanks, such as Demos, the Foreign Policy Centre, and the Institute for Public Policy Research. These think-tanks constitute a conveyor belt that relays ideas and concerns back and forth between the new institutionalists and the government in much the same way as the Adam Smith Institute and the Centre for Policy Studies did between neoliberals and the New Right. Geoff Mulgan co-founded Demos in 1993. He was its first Director, and he is still Chairman of its Advisory Council. Earlier, he worked, from 1990 to 1992, as a Senior Policy Adviser to Brown. Today he works in the Prime Minister's Policy Unit, as Director of the Performance and Innovation Unit. Demos's current Director is Tom Bentley, and he took up the post after spending 1998 to 1999 working as a special adviser to David Blunkett, then Secretary of State for Education and Employment. Demos's former Deputy Director is Beth Egan, and she went on secondment to assist Brown during his time as Chancellor of the Exchequer.

Several of the researchers at Demos have also worked within New Labour: Charles Leadbeater authored a government White Paper entitled *Our Competitive Future*.[4] Perri 6 is a Demos researcher who straddles both the academy, where he defends neo-Durkheimian institutionalism, and government, where he provides New Labour with regular policy advice on holistic government. He also has close ties with Stoker with whom he collaborated on several projects for Demos. Similar connections within people's lives tie Demos to other centre-left think-tanks and these think-tanks to New Labour. Daniel Stedman Jones, a Demos researcher, previously worked in the Prime Minister's Policy Unit and also the Institute for Public Policy. Mark Leonard became the Director of the Foreign Policy Centre after having been a senior researcher for Demos; today he advises New Labour as a member of the Foreign and Commonwealth Office Panel.

There are, then, close personal connections between the new institutionalism and New Labour. Nonetheless, we should not assume that either institutionalism or network theory are inherently social democratic. In principle they can sustain all sorts of political positions, including, for example, Christian democracy and paternalist authoritarianism; indeed, because network theorists promoted their approach by using it to explain the successes of Asian economies, New Labour politicians at times have found themselves asking what British social democracy might learn from authoritarian states such as Singapore.[5] Nonetheless, the new institutionalism and network theory in practice have found a home in New Labour partly because of these personal ties and partly because of conceptual overlaps in their responses to the alliance between the New Right and neoliberalism. What is more, because conceptual and temporal connections map neoliberalism onto the New Right, and the new institutionalism onto New Labour, to champion an interpretive approach to political science against rational choice and institutionalism is to point towards a critique of the New Right and New Labour. From an interpretivist perspective, the New Right and New Labour seek to tame the contingency of human life in ways that mirror positivist approaches to political science. Their policies often rely at least implicitly on a reduction of contingent practices to an objectified rationality or objectified institutional arrangements.

The new institutionalism

Although the new institutionalism asks to be contrasted with an old institutionalism, we should take care not to caricature the latter.[6] The institutionalism of the 1950s and 1960s belongs within the modernist empiricism we explored in the last chapter. Modernist empiricists approached institutions as discrete units that were to be assembled into larger sets by means of comparison and classification across time and space as opposed to, say, narratives about character and reason. Although the Whig tradition continued to inform the objects that most political scientists chose to study – the institutions of an idealised Westminster model of government – the tools with which they did so became increasingly atomistic and analytical.[7] To some extent, moreover, the objects of study themselves changed as a result of the rise of modernist empiricism, so that by the 1950s and 1960s, British political science had come to include detailed accounts of electoral behaviour and the activities of parties and interest groups.

We have to look to America if we are to understand how and why the new institutionalists define themselves in contrast to this old institutionalism. Until the 1950s, American political science looked very like its British counterpart.[8] It too was dominated by a modernist empiricism that had arisen out of a break with history, law, and philosophy. It too retained aspects of an elder historical orientation, albeit one derived as much from German sources as from British Whiggism. It too had turned to atomistic and analytic modes of inquiry and also begun to shift its focus from legal structures to political behaviour. American political science became more obviously different from its British counterpart only with the behavioural revolution of the 1950s. Once we recognise that modernist empiricists often had begun to shift their focus from legal structures to the activity of voters, parties, and interest groups, however, we set the scene for a more nuanced account of the behavioural revolution than that with which most political scientists are familiar. Behaviouralism's novelty lay less in its focus on behaviour than in the rise of new techniques and systematic empirical theory.[9] The new techniques for collecting and analysing data included, most importantly, survey research as pioneered by the Survey Research Center at Michigan University. Survey research provided a means of creating new data and so making new aspects of human life, such as the attitudes of voters, available to quantitative analysis. New techniques of analysis included developments in content analysis, mathematical modelling, and statistical tests. The behavioural revolution also consisted of a range of systematic theories, such as structural-functionalism, which were said to be necessary in part precisely in order to make sense of the mass of factual data being generated on voting behaviour, parties, and interest groups. These systematic theories aspired to be universal, deductive, and predictive in a way that often reflected a debt to positivist philosophies of science.

The new institutionalism represents a response from within modernist empiricism to the techniques and systematic theory of behaviouralism and rational choice. Modernist empiricists already had begun to expand their horizons from legal structures to parties, interest groups, and voting behaviour, and many of them soon began to utilise the new techniques associated with the behavioural revolution. By the time we reach the new institutionalism, modernist empiricists had long recognised the importance of actors and behaviour that lie outside the formal legal arrangements of the state, actors that include social movements and think-tanks, and behaviour that includes economic exchanges and policy-making. Behaviouralism thus encouraged institutionalists to adopt looser, less formal, accounts of institutions. They began to stigmatise their predecessors for allegedly having concentrated solely on organisations that were associated at best with formal political practices and at worst with legal constitutions. They took themselves, in contrast, to be interested in the roles of less-formal organisations within society and the economy.[10] Their looser view of institutions sat snugly within their modernist empiricism. It further encouraged the shift from historical narratives of specific states to comparison and classification based on more atomistic analyses, for where the legalistic view of institutions had encouraged a focus on specific constitutional documents, the less formal view opened up a greater space for comparison as a means of identifying what aspects of an institution best accounted for its nature and its effects.[11] Modernist empiricists also incorporated, albeit more diffidently, cross-national quantitative studies and the analysis of aggregate data as means of pursuing their cross-national comparisons. In general, they had little difficulty accepting behaviouralist concerns and techniques as extensions of their own prior commitments to atomisation, analysis, comparison, and classification.

If modernist empiricists wanted to defend their cross-national comparisons, however, they had to fend-off the pretensions to universality of behaviouralist theory. After all, if any universal theory proved to be valid, it would apply to all countries, so it would render obsolete the idea that the study of particular states and comparisons between them was the best way to study politics. Behaviouralism thus threatened modernist empiricists even though they already had accepted the importance of examining less formal organisations and behaviour, and even though they quickly assimilated the new techniques; it threatened them in its adherence to universal and deductive theories. Hence political scientists such as Carl Friedrich and Sam Beer complained about the excessive abstraction of the purportedly universal theories.[12] Modernist empiricists argued either that universal theories could not apply to politics, or that when they did apply, they were too abstract to tell us anything of interest: some modernist empiricists even made both of these arguments, apparently unaware of the tension between them. Political scientists who challenged the universal pretensions of behavioural theories thus adopted history and comparison as their watchwords. In doing so, they lost sight of the contrast between their own modernist empiricism and the more genuinely historical narratives of the late nineteenth century.

Parallel developments within modernist empiricism occurred in many other social sciences. Among sociologists, Reinhard Bendix at Berkeley and Barrington Moore at Harvard challenged the pretensions to universality of behavioural theories by appealing to comparison and history, which thus came to define a space between universal theories and the study of behaviour, a space in which to pursue questions of class and state structures. These questions soon became increasingly prominent in comparative politics and comparative political economy. In these areas of study, behaviouralism took the form of a modernisation theory that had stumbled over the evidence that so many African and Latin American states had experienced coups d'état instead of becoming increasingly functionally differentiated and modern. It seemed that the state intervened in social development to resolve economic and social crises. Modernist empiricists were thus encouraged to draw on Marxist state theory to bolster their opposition to behavioural theory. However, while social scientists such as Theda Skocpol found Marxism inspiring – they thought it tackled the big issues about social change they believed the 1960s had raised – they developed their own state theory by drawing heavily on a modernist empiricism that had accommodated the techniques associated with behaviouralism.[13] Skocpol studied with Barrington Moore and, more especially, with Seymour Lipset, while Peter Hall did so with Beer. In responding to behaviouralism, these modernist empiricists helped to construct an emerging canon of sociological theory that consisted of authors and texts – from Karl Marx and Max Weber forward to Barrington Moore and Bendix – that they presented as the heritage of an analytic, comparative, and historical social science. This canon arose, like many others, as an attempt to establish a disciplinary identity with scant attention being paid to its historical accuracy. Does the canon suggest that our present concerns dominated when they did not? Does it imply that chains of influence existed where they did not?

Many characteristics of the new institutionalism arose as modernist empiricists and their students responded to behaviouralism. However, the new institutionalism flourished as a self-conscious movement only in response to rational choice. Rational choice, like behaviouralism, aspires to universality in a way that threatens modernist empiricism. Indeed, new institutionalists, with their roots in modernist empiricism, sometimes fixate on this similarity: although they allow there are differences between rational choice and behavioural theory, they emphasise their shared belief in 'One True and Unified Theory', at times getting so carried away they imply there are real temporal connections between the two so that the structural-functionalists become the 'forebears' of rational-choice theory, and rational-choice theorists become the 'successors' of the 'Grand Theorists of old'.[14] Modernist empiricists further modified their inheritance in response to rational-choice theory, albeit in ways already foreshadowed by developments in the wake of behaviouralism. For a start, because rational choice derives models from assumptions about individual motivation, it poses forcefully the question of what micro-theory can make sense of the analytic, comparative, and historical social science that arose from modernist empiricism.[15] New institutionalists typically attempt to fend-off a universal micro-theory by arguing that people's motives and actions depend on particular institutional settings. They argue that people and institutions alike are embedded in wider social contexts that structure their choices, behaviour, and development. However, to assert that 'the organisation of political life makes a difference' is not to answer, but only to displace, the question of the micro-level: as we have seen, it begs the question of how, and to what extent, context impacts upon conduct.[16] Some new institutionalists want to wish such awkward theoretical questions away.[17] They argue that to answer these questions would be to engage in navel-gazing upon matters that cannot be resolved, seemingly unaware that only a theoretical argument could show that empirical matters are not equally irresolvable. They argue that if we concentrated on these questions we would neglect empirical research into the big, pressing issues that really concern us, seemingly unaware that they thereby legislate from what happens to interest them to what ought to interest everyone else. And they argue that we can decide one theory is better than another only by doing research, seemingly unaware that what constitutes evidence for one theory being better than another is a theoretical question that can be answered only by theoretical means. However, let us not dwell on political scientists who mistake their own lack of theoretical curiosity for a justified dismissal of the role of theory.

Other new institutionalists have tried to respond to issues such as how context impacts upon conduct. We should distinguish here mainly between the responses of rational-choice and sociological institutionalists: although there are other strands to the new institutionalism, these are characterised by particular objects of inquiry more than by theoretical positions; so, for example, historical institutionalism concentrates on how institutions impact on their own and one another's development without any commitment to a particular micro-theory. Rational-choice institutionalists deploy the micro-theory of rational choice in order to explain how context impacts upon conduct. They argue that institutions structure the context, and so actions, of utility-maximising individuals by, for instance, providing information about other people's likely future behaviour or attaching inducements to actions. One source of this view lies within rational-choice theory itself: neoclassical economists and rational-choice theorists in political science had difficulties explaining the presence of stability, as represented by firms in markets or coalitions in democracies, without appealing to the ways in which institutions structure information and choices in repetitive situations.[18] Other rational-choice institutionalists are modernist empiricists who came to rely on the micro-theory of rational choice to fill out their accounts of the nature of institutions and how they change. Importantly, both of these groups of rational-choice institutionalists treat preferences as endogenous while exploring action as optimal within a relatively stable institutional environment. Sociological institutionalists promote an alternative to the micro-theory of rational choice. They take institutions to consist of the norms that determine or influence people's actions, so that individuals are not rational utility-maximisers but rather followers of rules or performers of roles.

Rational-choice theory also highlighted questions about the motor of change in the analytic, comparative, and historical studies that had emerged from the encounter of modernist empiricism with behaviouralism. New institutionalists conceptualise change in ways that mirror the preceding account of their intellectual history. In very broad terms, they update modernist empiricism by incorporating behavioural themes while renouncing the pretensions of universal theory in favour of mid-level analysis. They explain change by reference to critical junctures in a way that echoes the idea of critical elections that behaviouralists developed once they began to use longitudinal data to explore political developments over time.[19] Yet the vagueness of their broad concepts leaves them lacking the sort of micro-level sophistication that is demanded in the wake of rational choice. At this point, some new institutionalists again seek to avoid such awkward theoretical questions altogether. Others unpack concepts such as critical juncture and path dependency using the micro-theory of rational choice.[20] Sociological institutionalists, of course, have the most difficulty explaining change: if institutions fix the actions of individuals, how can individuals ever act so as to change the institutions? Perhaps we should not be surprised, therefore, that it is when they consider change that they are most likely to turn to meanings in a way that moves institutionalism closer towards an interpretive approach.

Although the new institutionalism remains a largely American phenomenon, it has been picked up by a number of British political scientists. Yet because modernist empiricists in Britain never faced such a strong challenge from behaviouralism or rational choice, they are less inclined to trumpet the newness of the approach and more inclined to portray it as old institutionalist wine in new bottles.[21] Just as modernist empiricists in Britain defined themselves against American positivism, so they now understand the new institutionalism as a movement in which the Americans have finally put such positivism behind them and returned to the sort of historical and comparative case studies of institutions that constitute the core of British political science. The new institutionalism is, they tell us, what they have been doing all along. In a sense, they are, of course, right, since, as we have seen, the new institutionalism retains many features of the modernist empiricism from which it emerged. Equally, however, the rise of the new institutionalism in Britain reflects modernist empiricist attempts to grapple with neoliberalism. British political scientists typically confronted neoliberalism as Thatcherism rather than rational choice, which has only a small presence among them. Thatcherism sought to transform many established institutions, including local government and the civil service, on the explicit grounds that the state, hierarchic structures, legal regulations, and fixed procedures were less efficient, and even less just, than the market. Economics replaced political science and public administration as the basis of public policy. Modernist empiricists sought a new narrative to counter the neoliberalism of Thatcherism. They found it in the new institutionalism.

Narrating the state

The new institutionalism arose as modernist empiricists responded first to behaviouralism and then to rational choice. Yet the issues involved were not solely matters of scholarly debate. On the contrary, many new institutionalists were motivated by the hope of countering those neoliberal policies that were widely associated with rational choice. Although our interest will be in the British case, similar motives inspired political scientists and political actors elsewhere. Peter Evans and John Stephens – two prominent new institutionalists – voiced them with respect to development studies:

> The problem goes beyond questions of theoretical progress. Development policy is currently dominated by models that privilege market rationality. They suggest that institutions or policies claiming to serve the common good through non-market means are 'covers' behind which individuals enhance their own power and pursue their own material self-interests. Efficiency in general and development in particular require aggressive expansion of the arenas governed openly and explicitly by market principles. Attempts to modify market outcomes in order to increase equity or generate a new distribution of factor endowments are viewed not just in practice but in principle as attempts at 'rent-seeking'. The work of the new utilitarians [rational-choice theorists] . . . has provided important theoretical legitimacy for this current policy and the unrestrained hegemony of the new utilitarianism is very likely to impede the emergence of future competitors.[22]

The new institutionalism is such a competitor. Many of its exponents believe that its analytic, comparative, and historical political economy inspires an alternative to the neoliberal narrative of our times.

Neoliberals treat social practices as the products of the actions of utility-maximising individuals. Doing so enables them to postulate the market as an inherently efficient form of social organisation. Hence their narrative of our times concentrates on the alleged problems inherent in the growth of the state and on the need for marketisation as a cure.[23] In their view, the hierarchic Keynesian welfare state was inherently inefficient, inflexible, and unresponsive, especially when compared to the market. Neoliberals told a story in which the state entered a time of crisis because of the inefficiencies of bureaucracy and the burdens of excessive taxation. Sometimes they suggested that these problems had become increasingly pressing once we entered a global age in which the increased mobility of technology, trade, and finance capital created a world market that underpinned an almost Darwinian selection process such that states had to liberalise their economies and public sectors or else they would perish. Because neoliberals postulated the market as an inherently efficient form of organisation, they unpacked this process in terms of states having to adopt neoliberal policies such as marketisation, contracting out, new management techniques, staff cuts, and stricter budgeting. In so far as neoliberals believed that these policies were necessary for any state to compete in the global market, they invoked an inexorable process of catch-up that guaranteed the spread of the minimal state, marketisation, and the new public management. The state might make decisions of policy but, instead of delivering services itself, it had to promote an entrepreneurial system based on market competition.

The neoliberal narrative inspired the New Right with its programme of public sector reform through marketisation and a corporate style of management. As Evans and Stephens suggested, the new institutionalism offered not only a restatement of modernist empiricism in the wake of rational choice but also a competitor to the neoliberal narrative. Although the new institutionalists generally acknowledge that the policies of the New Right led to changes in the nature and role of the state, they reject the neoliberal reliance on neo-classical economic theory and rational choice to explain these changes let alone to justify them. The institutionalist narrative relies, instead, on themes that reflect its roots in modernist empiricism. In general terms, this narrative relies on atomisation as a prelude to comparative and somewhat historical modes of inquiry. More specifically, it concentrates on the mid-level as a means of fending-off neoliberal claims about the inexorability of the turn to markets. Although institutionalists often are just as willing as neoliberals to appeal to global pressures impinging on states, they argue that the ways in which states respond to these pressures vary according to the nature of their inherited institutions. They reject the neoliberal belief that micro-level assumptions about utility-maximising agents show that neoliberalism itself will be a universal response to such pressures. They argue instead that the mid-level, which consists of relatively stable and unproblematic organisations, rules, and standard operating procedures, will result in different states responding differently. Hence, institutionalists seek to understand the impact of neoliberal policies in relation to these same mid-level factors, rather than in the terms offered to us by neoliberalism. Institutionalists, including Rhodes and Stoker, argue that marketisation and the new public management had unintended consequences as a result of entrenched institutional patterns and norms: neoliberal reforms fragmented service-delivery and weakened central control without establishing markets.[24]

Indeed, this institutionalist narrative now appears to dominate British political science, at least to judge by the broad consensus of those who contributed to the Whitehall and Local Government Programmes set up by the Economic and Social Research Council and spearheaded respectively by Rhodes and Stoker.[25] Most of the participants in these Programmes imply that the neoliberal reforms of the 1980s undermined the capacity of the state to act on its own without establishing anything like the neoliberal vision. The state now acts, they suggest, as one of a number of organisations and individuals who come together in diverse networks to deliver varied services.

The institutionalist narrative also draws heavily upon the looser view of organisations that has flourished among modernist empiricists since the behavioural revolution. In this view, institutions are best understood not as hierarchical structures governed by formal laws, but as networks characterised by informal norms and tacit agreements. Although institutionalists are often willing to agree with neoliberals that there are limitations to formal, hierarchic organisations, they do not think that these limitations extend to networks. On the contrary, the institutionalist narrative offers networks as the solution to a crisis of the state associated with both the failings of old hierarchies and the further damage wrought by neoliberal reforms. Granovetter and Powell and DiMaggio denounce the neoliberal policies of the New Right in part on the grounds that the state should turn to networks, trust, and diplomacy rather than markets, competition, and the new public management.[26] For institutionalists, then, the emergence of networks as an unintended result of neoliberal reforms is all to the good. The problems are the limited extent of these networks and the lack of awareness of them.

The concept of a network plays an ambiguous role in the institutionalist narrative. As well as denoting a superior mode of organisation, it also describes the inevitable nature of all organisations given our social embeddedness. Institutionalists want us to recognise that hierarchies and markets are in fact networks. Granovetter and Powell and DiMaggio invoke the concepts of embeddedness and network as an alternative to the neoliberal analysis of human action in terms of autonomous, utility-maximising individuals.[27] Human action is, they argue, always structured by social relationships. Typically, institutionalists, such as Perri 6, combine these two ways of conceiving of networks by suggesting that although all organisations take the form of embedded networks, those that best resemble the ideal-type of a network reap the benefits of so doing.[28] They argue that economic efficiency and success derive from stable relationships characterised by trust, social participation, voluntary associations, and friendship, at least as much as from markets and competition.

A final aspect of the institutionalist narrative derives from attempts to grapple with change, dynamism, and entrepreneurship in response to rational choice. New institutionalists typically accept that economic vibrancy now depends on flexibility, responsiveness, and innovation – virtues neoliberals ascribe to markets – at least as much as on trust and participation.[29] Yet they argue that these dynamic virtues are most prominent in networks, not markets, precisely because networks are in accord with our embedded autonomy. Institutionalism gained strength here from its apparent ability to account for what once seemed tremendous economic successes that were difficult for neoliberals to explain in terms of market competition, economic successes such as the computer and biotechnology sectors, especially in Silicon Valley and north-central Italy. What once looked like the cutting-edge, most prosperous parts of the new economy thrived, we were told, precisely because they were organised as networks. Some institutionalists suggest that the association of networks with economic success might be historically specific. In this view, hierarchies suited a Fordist era of mass production and routinised patterns of behaviour, but they are ill-suited to delivering the innovation and entrepreneurship that states now have to foster if they are to compete effectively in a new knowledge-driven global economy; today economic success requires the synergy and adaptability that characterise the looser organisational pattern of a network.

As we have seen, interpretivism entails a shift away from the broad styles and emphases of rational choice and institutionalism. It incorporates a critique of the role of objectification and expertise in these approaches to political science. The institutionalist narrative of our times often relies, explicitly or implicitly, upon just such objectification of contingent human practices. For example, institutionalists often accept that the state is subject to given, even inexorable, pressures that are hollowing it out. Institutionalist theories of networks, moreover, typically bypass meanings in search of typologies that seek to read-off the character of networks from social facts about them, such as their policy area, size, or resources.[30] Similarly, the difficulties that afflict institutionalist accounts of change reappear in their reduction of changes in networks to exogenous factors.[31] Our critique of the lingering effects of positivism in political science thus carries over to the two leading narratives of our times – neoliberalism and institutionalism.

An interpretive narrative would explain political practices by appealing to beliefs which it would explain in terms of traditions and dilemmas. It would decentre changes in the state by appealing to aggregate concepts not as natural kinds but only as abstractions that we postulate based on the contingent beliefs and actions of particular agents. It would portray change and conflict as endogenous to political practices, and it would highlight contingency and agency. When interpretivists disaggregate the state in this way, they problematise the idea that governance arises from given inputs – whether pressures or policies – as well as the idea that these inputs necessarily have the outcomes neoliberals expect. They draw attention to the fact that people construct various views of the pressures, and of the policies these require, depending on the traditions against the background of which they operate. Because people construct at least subtly different problems and responses from within different traditions, there arises a contest over various narratives and the policies they inspire. Exponents of rival political positions seek to promote their particular theories and policies. This political contest leads to a reform of the state, a reform that stands as the contingent product of a contest over meanings. Mind you, although we can distinguish analytically between the state and a contest over its reform, we rarely can do so temporally. The activity of governing continues during most contests, and most contests occur partly within practices of governing. The state contains a complex and continuous process of interpretation, conflict, and activity that generates the everchanging pattern of its own nature. We can begin to explain a state formation by taking an abstract snapshot of this process and relating it to the varied traditions and problems that inform it. The ensuing interpretation of New Labour aims to flesh out this alternative to the neoliberal and institutionalist narratives of our times.

A social democratic heritage

Changes within the state are products of the meanings that come to dominate in political contests. Interpretivism encourages us to explore these changes in relation to the contingent and contested beliefs that inform diverse policies and practices, and to explain these beliefs by reference to traditions and problems. In the case of New Labour's Third Way, we will find, first, that agents operating against the background of a tradition of social democracy generally constructed issues such as state overload in ways subtly different from the New Right. We will find, second, that their different responses to these issues reflect their tradition and their particular construction of the problems. And we will discover, finally, that New Labour conceives of the problems, and responds to them, in ways that are entwined with the new institutionalism.

To map New Labour's programme onto the new institutionalism is to draw attention away from the particular origins of the phrase 'Third Way'. This phrase rose to prominence only in 1998 when it was the title of a pamphlet by Blair and a book by the sociologist, Anthony Giddens.[32] The association of New Labour with a Third Way was cemented by the constant reiteration of the claim, made on the cover of Giddens's book, that he is Blair's 'favourite intellectual'. Even if this claim is true, we might get a better understanding of where New Labour is coming from if we look behind the phrase to the ideas and policies it covers. Perhaps the high profile of Giddens's theories acts merely as a retrospective systematisation and legitimation of ideas and policies that New Labour already had developed from other sources. Blair's pamphlet on the Third Way suggests as much when it describes the Third Way as 'the best label for the new politics which the centre left is forging in Britain and beyond'.[33] What is more, both Blair and the Labour Party more generally were promoting almost all the main themes of the Third Way before they adopted that label. Blair did so, for example, in an article on 'Why Modernisation Matters', which he wrote back in 1993 while still Shadow Home Secretary.[34] He argued there that both the left and right of the political spectrum had failed, notably in coming to terms with the new times created by rapid socio-economic change. He suggested that these new times required a reawakening of community through a greater emphasis on responsibilities. Labour Party documents also foreshadowed the main themes of the Third Way throughout the early 1990s. John Smith, Blair's predecessor as Party Leader, set up a Commission on Social Justice, which in its report of 1994 rejected the 'levelling' policies of the left and the 'deregulation' of the right in favour of a 'middle way', which it called 'Investor's Britain'. The Commission's report suggested that globalisation meant that prosperity now depended on 'high value-added production which requires skilled people using modern equipment in productive enterprises'.[35] It advocated a shift from redistributing income to redistributing opportunity, from a safety-net state to an enabling state, and a greater focus on education, training, and work as means of preventing poverty. Although the Commission was kept at arm's length from the Labour Party, similar themes soon appeared in policy documents coming out of the Party itself. The Party's Economic Commission declared in 1995 that the 'job of government is neither to suppress markets nor to surrender to them, but to equip companies and countries to succeed within them'; it argued that the 'new global economy' was such that 'technologies, raw materials and capital can be bought from just about anywhere' so now 'it is the level of skills in a company that makes the difference between success and failure', and 'for this reason, a policy of national economic renewal must mean enhancing individual economic potential as the route to rebuilding the industrial base'.[36] New Labour had adopted the content of the Third Way, then, long before it did the label. When New Labour did adopt the label, moreover, it ignored those of Giddens's ideas that it had not already accepted: it paid little heed to his call for global democratic institutions as a means of governing globalisation, while his commitment to active and reflective citizenship sits somewhat uneasily alongside its moralistic emphasis on duty.

The Third Way is a label for ideas and policies that New Labour already had adopted by the late 1990s. The origin of these ideas and policies lies elsewhere. Giddens himself emphasises the inspiration provided by President Bill Clinton and the New Democrats in America.[37] The Clinton government received regular visits from New Labour politicians, including Brown and Mandelson, and their advisers, such as Ed Balls and David Miliband. The New Democrats offered New Labour both electoral strategies – notably in dealing with the media – and specific commitments and policies, including the emphasis on employment as the solution to poverty, workfare schemes, and tax credits. Nonetheless, recognition of policy transfer from America to Britain does little to answer questions about the origins of the content of the Third Way. The whole point of the Third Way is, after all, that it highlights themes that weave these discrete policies together into some kind of package. Where do these themes come from? Why did some American policies – and not others – appeal to New Labour? What wider beliefs informed these policies even within America? To answer these questions, we might appeal to the new institutionalism as it overlaps with the social democratic tradition and also influences it.

Instead of fixating on the phrase 'Third Way', we should locate New Labour at the juncture where social democrats struggle to come to terms with issues raised by the New Right. Of course, the social democratic tradition contains competing strands – we should no more objectify it than we should institutions – so when we invoke it, or for that matter New Labour, Old Labour, or the New Right, we simplify complex patterns of beliefs and loyalties in order to interpret broad political movements.[38] In broad terms, however, we can identify a social democratic tradition for which the individual exists and attains the good only in the context of community. Blair often evokes this conviction, as when he insists we are 'citizens of a community' rather than 'separate economic actors competing in the marketplace of life'.[39] Social democrats thus join institutionalists in arguing – against the neoliberalism of the New Right – that sociality and solidarity are integral features of human life.[40] They believe that we are not isolated, interest-pursuing animals, but beings who make sense of the world, including our own interests, in the context of institutions that constrain us, enable our creativity, and bind us to one another in community.

In the next chapter, we will see how this belief in the socially embedded nature of the individual helped to justify the ethical commitments of social democrats to justice, citizenship, and fellowship. For now, we will concentrate on the welfare state, hierarchic bureaucracy, and Keynesianism as instruments by which social democrats have hoped to realise these values. Many social democrats wanted the state to create greater equality and prosperity through welfare provision, progressive taxes, and demand management. They unpacked our social nature and our responsibilities to one another in terms of universal social rights to a minimum standard of living, including adequate food and housing, as well as some protection from things such as ill-health and unemployment. The welfare state also embodied the command model of public service provision that became so popular with social democrats between the two world wars. Keynesianism then provided a way of financing the welfare state and promoting full employment. However, a number of problems appeared to confront this social democratic tradition during the 1970s and 1980s. Worries about an underclass challenged the welfare state. Worries about state-overload posed questions of the command model of the provision of public services. Worries about inflation and efficiency challenged a Keynesian approach to macro-economics. New Labour has responded to these issues in ways that draw on the new institutionalism and its narrative of our times.

The Third Way

New Labour is a response to problems highlighted by the New Right, but it has constructed the problems facing the welfare state, public services, and the economy in ways that differ from the New Right precisely because it has drawn on the social democratic tradition and new institutionalism. In the case of the welfare state, New Labour sometimes expresses fears about an underclass, but it generally portrays this class as trapped on welfare not because of psychological dependency, but because of institutional factors, such as the way in which welfare payments are reduced once claimants start to earn even modest wages. More particularly, New Labour's policy advisers suggest that the welfare state has trapped people in poverty because it has conceived of poverty in terms of wealth and income rather than social exclusion or 'network poverty'. Welfare dependency and even poverty are, in this view, results of insufficient or inappropriate social embeddedness. According to Perri 6, the most common way of finding work is through informal networks of friends, ex-colleagues, and acquaintances.[41] The welfare state traps people in unemployment by lumping them together apart from the employed and thereby undermining their ability to enter the social networks where jobs are to be found. The unemployed volunteer is treated as being unavailable for work, and yet, Perri 6 continues, volunteering is an important means by which they might make the sorts of contacts from which jobs flow. Likewise, training schemes for the unemployed are generally provided by specialist bodies as opposed to companies that might connect them to people who are in work. Perri 6 even criticises local councils for trying to keep local communities together when they design building projects. He suggests that they trap the unemployed and the poor in enclaves when they should be connecting them to other groups in the community. For New Labour, the problem of people being trapped on welfare is one of social exclusion from networks, not a psychology of dependency.

In the case of public services, when New Labour deplores the inefficiency and rigidity of the provision of goods by a hierarchic bureaucracy, it rarely describes such inefficiency and rigidity as inherent consequences of public ownership, as does the New Right. On the contrary, the Third Way offers a rebuttal of the New Right's attempts to reform the state. It implies that the New Right's exaggerated faith in markets failed to recognise the socially embedded nature of our being. New Labour believes that public services should reflect our innate sociality by embracing an ethic of mutual cooperation, even if they sometimes rely on market mechanisms to increase choice and promote responsibility. David Clark, then the Minister for Public Services, explained that policies such as market testing 'will not be pursued blindly as an article of faith' but they 'will continue where they offer best value for money'.[42] Although New Labour accepts that markets can be an appropriate means of delivering public services, it insists that markets often are not the most efficient way to deliver services because they can go against the public interest, reinforce inequalities, and entrench privilege, all of which can damage economic performance. For New Labour, the problem with public services is one of adapting them to new times, rather than of rolling back the state to promote market competition.

In the case of the economy, New Labour has rejected Keynesianism but it has adopted little of the monetarism associated with the New Right. New Labour follows the New Right in taking macro-economic stability, particularly low inflation, to be the leading pre-requisite of growth and high, long-term levels of employment; it, too, concentrates on supply-side reforms instead of demand management. Nonetheless, New Labour's supply-side vision reflects the new institutionalism – and the heritage of Wilsonian socialism – more than it does neoliberalism. Whereas the New Right attempted to remove barriers to market competition on the grounds that only by doing so could it ensure efficiency, New Labour follows the institutionalists in suggesting that the task of our times is to come to terms with the new economy. Leadbeater writes of a thin-air economy in which knowledge is all-important and in which the vital ingredients for success are flexibility and innovation.[43] Mulgan invokes a new 'connexity', produced by a revolution in communications and technology, which has brought a shift from both liberal individualism and old-style social democracy to new forms of interdependence.[44] For New Labour, the problems confronting the economy derive from a short-term outlook that has neglected investment in the supply-side as much as they do from inflation. New Labour thus opens up another space within which to criticise the policies of the New Right. This criticism, like the institutionalist response to rational choice, makes much of the dangers of neglecting social embeddedness and fetishising the market.

New Labour draws on the social democratic tradition to construct the problems that confront the state. It also does so to devise responses to these problems. While New Labour accepts aspects of the New Right's challenge to the Keynesian welfare state, it rejects the turn to markets and monetarism as inappropriate given our social embeddedness. It advocates instead networks of institutions and individuals acting in partnerships held together by relations of trust. New Labour does not entirely exclude bureaucratic hierarchy or quasi-market competition so much as advocate a mixture of hierarchies, markets, and networks, with the choice between them varying according to the nature of the service. As the government explains, 'services should be provided through the sector best placed to provide those services most effectively', where 'this can be the public, private or voluntary sector, or partnerships between these sectors'.[45] In general, however, New Labour deploys the new institutionalism to define an alternative to both Old Labour and the New Right.

In the case of the welfare state, a belief in our social embeddedness encourages New Labour to envisage a world of citizens who are linked together by reciprocal duties and responsibilities. These citizens collaborate with the state in a cooperative enterprise that aims to create an economically and socially vibrant nation. The state acts not as a safety-net but as an enabler and a partner. It provides citizens with opportunities to advance themselves, where it is up to citizens to take advantage of these opportunities. New Labour thus seeks to promote individual responsibility through cooperation. Blair has said, 'the modern welfare state is not founded on a paternalistic government giving out more benefits but on an enabling government that through work and education helps people to help themselves'.[46] The enabling state represents an allegedly new type of partnership – 'a new contract between citizen and state'.[47] The enabling state concentrates on overcoming social exclusion and network poverty. New Labour's New Deal for the Unemployed aims 'to make work pay' by eradicating the institutional disincentives to employment that are created by the rules that govern taxation and benefits. It also aims to connect the unemployed to the employed: the government offers a subsidy to employers lasting six months for each worker they recruit from among the long-term unemployed. New Labour appears to be acting on Perri 6's advice that welfare-to-work schemes should maximise the opportunities for the unemployed to make contacts with those in work.

In the case of public services, New Labour conceives of networks as peculiarly appropriate to the operation of the enabling state. The Service First programme promotes Quality Networks composed of locally organised groups of people, from all areas and levels of the public sector, who work together in partnerships based on trust. Blair himself talks of building relations of trust between all actors in society, where trust is defined as 'the recognition of a mutual purpose for which we work together and in which we all benefit'.[48] New Labour's model of service delivery differs from that of the New Right, although its emphasis on individual involvement overlaps with themes found in the New Right and although it embraces features of the new public management when it considers them appropriate. New Labour argues, indeed, that many features of the new public management, such as quasi-markets and contracting-out, maintained an unhealthy dichotomy between the public and private sectors. In this view, public bodies did not connect properly with private companies but merely contracted services out to them. The Third Way is supposed, in contrast, to develop networks that will enable public and private organisations truly to collaborate. In more concrete terms, the government has revived

Private Finance Initiatives in an attempt to provide various mechanisms by which public and private organisations can form partnerships and networks to finance and undertake collaborative projects.

The vision of the state as an enabling institution based on self-organising networks reappears in New Labour's response to the problem of economic efficiency. New Labour regards networks as ethical in that they reflect our social embeddedness within a community that gives us rights and responsibilities. It also regards them as the basis of economic efficiency and competitiveness. The economic prosperity of the community, as much as its social revival, depends on the creation of clusters of self-governing institutions, such as housing associations, schools, and local councils, all working together within networks. The models here are what once seemed to be the economic success stories then beloved of new institutionalists – the Asian Tigers, Silicon Valley, and north-central Italy. Leadbeater draws out, for example, the lessons to be learnt from California.[49] He argues that economic competitiveness now depends on a mixture of knowledge and entrepreneurship, especially in the areas of software, the Internet, and biotechnology. California succeeded, he tells us, because it has a culture of creative individualism that fosters the openness and experimentalism that are vital to knowledge and entrepreneurship. He argues, more particularly, that the hi-tech companies in Silicon Valley form networks that share information and collaborate on projects so that the local economy is characterised by cooperation and innovation rather than competition. What is more, Leadbeater continues, these hi-tech firms are models of stakeholding in that they are deeply embedded in the community: they have extensive schemes of employee-ownership, they focus on building loyalty among their employees and their customers, and they set high standards of corporate responsibility. In New Labour's view, the new knowledge-driven economy provides Britain with opportunities as well as constraints. It allows and requires us to foster innovative ideas and turn them into jobs and economic growth. Britain, New Labour explains, has to become an outward-looking, flexible, and creative centre. To do so, it has to develop networks, connexity, and social capital. Blair, following government advisers such as Leonard, even wanted to rebrand Great Britain as 'cool Britannia' – a people and a society characterised by 'know-how, creativity, risk-taking, and, most of all, originality'.[50]

An interpretive approach to New Labour suggests that the Third Way consists of a contingent set of beliefs adopted against the background of the social democratic tradition in response to a particular construction of the problems facing the welfare state, public sector, and economy. It also indicates the extent to which the Third Way overlaps with, and draws on, the new institutionalism and network theory. Of course, there are disagreements and debates among the politicians and policy advisers of New Labour: Leadbeater and Mulgan argue that the idea of stakeholding proposed by Will Hutton and John Kay is too cumbersome to meet the demands of the entrepreneurial, knowledge-driven economy of today; and Stoker points to tensions in New Labour's projects.[51] Nonetheless, these disagreements occur within a shared framework: Leadbeater and Mulgan allow that stakeholding remains a viable and popular idea; and Stoker suggests that politics is all about dealing with tensions. The elite of New Labour rely on an overlapping consensus common to the new institutionalism and Third Way. They speak a language of embeddedness, sociality, community, social capital, networks, and partnership.

Joined-up governance

New Labour's response to the perceived crisis of the state draws on the new institutionalism. It affirms social embeddedness, partnership, networks, and trust. Blair glosses the broad vision expressed by these ideas as, 'joined-up problems need joined-up solutions'.[52] Joined-up governance arises at the juncture where New Labour and the new institutionalism provide an alternative account of recent changes in the state to the neo-liberal one of the New Right. New Labour appeals to joined-up governance to resolve not only the crisis of the old-fashioned bureaucratic state but also the additional damage it suggests, following the new institutionalism, has been wrought on the state by the reforms of the New Right. The New Right, in this view, failed to recognise our social being and consequently fetishised markets in a way that damaged the efficiency, flexibility, and responsiveness of the public sector and the economy. This critique of the New Right suggests that its misguided policies led to failures of coordination and control.

   Joined-up governance is a response to problems of fragmentation and steering. A lack of coordination is one of the most widely invoked consequences of the public sector reforms of the New Right. Today public services are delivered by a combination of government departments, special-purpose bodies, the voluntary sector, and the private sector. There are well over 5,000 special-purpose bodies that spend at least £39 billion and to which ministers make about 70,000 patronage appointments. Marketisation has resulted, its critics say, in excessive fragmentation of the public sector. According to the new institutionalists, the fragmentation associated with the New Right merely exacerbates a lack of coordination that was also characteristic of bureaucratic hierarchies. Perri 6 argues that the organisation of government into separate departments, each with its own budget, undermines all attempts to deal with 'wicked problems' that cut across departmental cages.[53] The reforms of the New Right made it even harder, he implies, to deal adequately with these wicked problems; the reforms left this organisational pattern intact, and they also created a plethora of agencies that are only too willing to pass problems on to others in order to ensure that they meet the quasi-market criteria of success under which they now operate. Perri 6's examples include schools excluding difficult children who then turn to crime, and the return of the mentally ill to the community where they become a law-and-order problem. Government, he concludes, needs to be holistic; it needs to deal with issues in the round rather than through numerous different agencies.

A lack of control is another problem often associated with the reforms of the New Right. New institutionalists such as Stoker suggest that fragmentation has led to the involvement of an increasingly diverse set of organisations in the process of governance so that now even more than before the central core needs to provide leadership.[54] Once again the New Right stands accused of exacerbating a problem instead of resolving it. The New Right tried to reduce the size of the state by getting rid of functions through privatisation and regulation. According to institutionalists such as Rhodes, however, the unintended consequence of its so doing was a further loss of control by the central core – the state has been hollowed out.[55] New Labour echoes this institutionalist account of the problem of control. Its turn towards a more corporate approach, its attempts to strengthen horizontal policy-making, and the increased role it gives to the Cabinet Office all stand in part as efforts to increase the strategic capability of central government.[56]

New Labour draws on the social democratic tradition and new institutionalism to ascribe problems of coordination and control to the public-sector reforms of the New Right. It also draws on these sources to prescribe solutions to these problems. Joined-up governance tackles the problems using the tools championed by the new institutionalists with their appeals to social embeddedness and networks. These tools, New Labour suggests, can create a public sector that is flexible, entrepreneurial, and efficient – a public sector that is in tune with the new knowledge-based economy.

In response to fragmentation, the new institutionalists point to networks as offering a flexible and yet efficient mode of coordination. New Labour likewise claims that service delivery depends as never before on linking organisations. It says that its aim is not to create new hierarchic organisations but to establish responsive connections between organisations within a relatively unstructured framework. On the one hand, networks allegedly provide coordination between departmental cages. On the other, the coordination offered by networks allegedly does not produce a new system of cages since networks are purported to be decentralised and to rely on an indirect, diplomatic style of management. New Labour believes, then, that a major challenge facing the civil service is to improve 'collaborative working across organisational boundaries', and it suggests that the way to meet this challenge is by 'ensuring that policy making is more joined-up and strategic'.[57] Action zones represent one attempt to create networks that are capable of resolving the dilemma of fragmentation. New Labour has created a Social Exclusion Unit (SEU) to 'develop integrated and sustainable approaches to the problems of the worst housing estates, including crime, drugs, unemployment, community breakdown, and bad schools'.[58] The Unit has established employment, education, and health zones operating under a single regeneration budget. These zones are supposed to provide a way for the state to operate across departmental and regional cages when dealing with wicked problems.

Because institutionalists often champion networks as a superior form of organisation, they have paid considerable attention to the question of how best to control them.[59] Typically they concentrate on presenting those styles of management they believe best fit various types of network, where each type of network is defined by reference to allegedly objective social facts about it, such as the structure of the relations within it. Almost all the popular management styles seek to provide scope for central government to steer networks while promoting a culture of trust associated with diplomacy and negotiation. Stoker lists techniques of steering urban governance that clearly strive to avoid hierarchy: they include indirect management by cultural persuasion, communication, and monitoring, as well as more direct steering through financial subsidies.[60] New Labour too promotes a culture of trust while attempting to deploy various techniques to ensure central control. In the case of local government, for example, Mulgan and Perri 6 argue that local authorities have to show they can be trusted, but that, as and when they do, so central government should devolve greater powers and services to them.[61] In practice, New Labour's Local Government Act of 2000 considerably increases the powers of local government at the same time as the central government is intervening through persuasion and 'naming and shaming' in an attempt to ensure councils respond to its agenda in the way it thinks appropriate.[62] Elsewhere, too, New Labour combines a decentralisation that gives greater scope to other bodies with attempts to specify in great detail what these bodies should do, attempts to persuade them to do what is specified, and attempts to regulate them in relation to the specifications. In the case of employment, the government considers Action Teams to be a flexible programme based on local initiative, but it also relies on direct financial control to hold them to the three criteria it prescribes for judging them – a rise in the proportion of people in work, an improvement in the employment rates of disadvantaged groups, and the number of people employed through the direct efforts of the Team. In the case of health, the government suggests that local variations in standards of care can be overcome if organisations share principles of best practice with each other, but it also specifies national standards and preferred models for specific types of service, and it has created a National Framework for Assessing Performance that will assess the quality of services against criteria set by the centre.[63] In the case of education, even as schools have acquired more powers, so the centre has defined measures of literacy and numeracy and given a greater role to inspectors in the evaluation of individual schools.

According to New Labour, networks can resolve the problems of co-ordination and control that now beset the state. The government and its advisers equate networks with a flexibility and responsiveness that they portray as being peculiarly important in the context of the new economy. For Perri 6, the flexibility of networks means that joined-up governance will be able to identify and tackle problems before they become acute.[64] It means that government agencies will be able to work in partnership with private-sector ones so as to acquire additional finance and expertise. The alleged responsiveness of networks implies that joined-up governance will be able to tackle issues in the round instead of through numerous, separate agencies. It implies that the state will be able to focus on changing cultural habits through information and persuasion rather than on changing behaviour through coercion and control. More generally, networks are portrayed as organisations peculiarly conducive to the growth of what Leadbeater calls a 'civic enterprise culture'.[65] Just as new institutionalists believe that networks inspire a dynamic entrepreneurialism, so New Labour appears to think that the flexibility and responsiveness of joined-up governance will encourage an innovative, people-focused culture that will attract civic entrepreneurs. Civic entrepreneurs are defined here as visionary individuals whose skills lie in building networks and establishing trust. We are thus presented with the prospect of moving away from a world of risk-averse static organisations staffed by bureaucrats towards a brave new one of complex networks staffed by social entrepreneurs who create synergies and virtuous cycles.

An interpretive approach to New Labour suggests that joined-up governance is the product of a contingent set of beliefs adopted against the background of a social democratic tradition in response to particular constructions of the problems of coordination and control. It also indicates the extent to which joined-up governance overlaps with, and draws on, the new institutionalism. Of course, here too there are disagreements and debates among the politicians and policy advisers of New Labour: Perri 6 and other Demos researchers call on the government to learn from its early mistakes and to devolve more.[66] Yet these disagreements occur, once again, within a shared framework: Perri 6 elides his concept of holistic government with joined-up governance while also appealing to Action Zones and Single Regeneration Budgets as concrete examples of what he has in mind.[67] The elite of New Labour rely on an overlapping consensus common to the new institutionalism and the Third Way. They speak a language of networks, zones, steering, partnership, trust, and civic entrepreneurship.

Conclusion

An interpretive approach leads us to clump together New Labour, joined-up governance, and the new institutionalism in much the same way as

political scientists already clump the New Right, the new public management, and neoliberalism. In Chapter 1, I offered an interpretive critique
of the very institutionalism that we have now associated with New Labour.
Some political scientists have responded to interpretive approaches by
suggesting that they are compatible with positivism since the two examine
very different objects. They say that interpretive approaches enable us to
understand people's views of the world, whereas behaviouralism or institutionalism allow us to explain the nature or development of the world
itself, say, political parties or the state. This response fails to recognise
that many interpretive approaches take our social world to consist of
practices and actions that embody the beliefs of the relevant actors so
that political scientists have to refer to beliefs if they are to explain objects
such as political parties or the state. To interpret people's beliefs is not
to offer additional information to that provided by positivists, but to give
an account of the world that rivals those of positivists.

Institutionalists tend to suggest, due to their lingering positivism, that
there is just one story to tell. They focus on institutions as transmission
belts between social pressures and policy outcomes. They imply that the
social pressures, the institutions, and the policy outcomes are given as
natural facts, so that the only story to tell is that which relates these facts.
An interpretive approach emphasises that different people construct
pressures, institutions, and outcomes differently depending in part on the
tradition against the background of which they so do. It tells a story
based on various stories, all of which have historical significance. For
example, the narratives that institutionalism and New Labour offer of the
crisis of the state reflect their debts to specific traditions of modernist
empiricism and social democracy, and these accounts coexist with others
that owe a debt to rather different traditions. From an interpretivist
perspective, the institutionalist story is not the only one; it is not an
account of a given history so much as an historical event with its own
problematic genealogy.

One alternative story presents New Labour and the new institutionalism, as I have in this chapter, as intersecting movements situated at the
juncture where social democracy and modernist empiricism struggle to
come to terms with issues raised by the New Right and neoliberalism.
Perhaps someone might ask: could a refashioned institutionalism have
revealed the links between institutionalism and New Labour, and the
contingency of their constructions of the crisis of the state, or would such
a refashioning have to emphasise meanings, agency, and contingency to
such an extent that it would no longer be recognisably institutionalist?
Such questions are spurious, however, since they imply that institutionalism and interpretivism are natural kinds when really they are names we
use to clump together diverse beliefs and practices. Such questions imply
there are rigid divisions where really there are only shifting patterns of
differences and similarities.

Interpretivism certainly has much in common with institutionalism. It too entails a belief in social embeddedness. It too points to the importance of institutions – though these are conceived as practices and traditions – as contexts in which agents respond to the world. Interpretivism even encourages a belief in networks as a ubiquitous form of social organisation: all social life is about interdependent actors engaging in interactions predicated on interpretations of one another. Nonetheless, interpretivism challenges two related tendencies widely apparent in both the new institutionalism and New Labour. First, interpretivism undercuts the tendency to objectify institutions by marginalising questions about the diverse actions and beliefs of the agents within them. Institutions should be seen as practices that are constantly being recreated and modified through the actions of agents, actions that usually create and also embody a conflict over meanings. Second, interpretivism thus undercuts the assumption of predictability and control based on scientific expertise. Politics does not arise from fixed rules or norms that political scientists might take for granted and that the state might establish. It is constructed from the bottom up, beginning with the contingent actions of innumerable individuals.

3 Communitarianism

Introduction

'The ethical basis of socialism is the only one that has stood the test of time', argued Tony Blair in 1995.[1] The emergence of New Labour has been characterised by two rhetorical moves found in this utterance. To begin, social democracy is equated primarily with moral values as opposed to public policies. Next, the relevant values are held up as the enduring core of social democracy so defined. An interpretive approach suggests that these rhetorical moves are contingent, historical acts. A survey of Labour Party Members of Parliament in 1906 found that the authors and books that had influenced them most were John Ruskin, *The Bible*, Charles Dickens, Henry George, and Thomas Carlyle. By 1962 these influences had changed to George Bernard Shaw, H. G. Wells, G. D. H. Cole, and Karl Marx, a list indicating a more economic and less religious outlook. The direction of change continued through 1975, when Marx topped the list, followed by R. H. Tawney, Shaw, Nye Bevan, and Wells. Then a survey in 1994 indicated a return to religious and ethical influences. Robert Tressell's, *The Ragged-Trousered Philanthropist* was mentioned by 20 per cent of respondents, after which there came Tawney, *The Bible*, Marx, and John Steinbeck, with George Orwell making a first appearance. As the commentary on this last survey observed, 'some notion of a new ethical socialism is clearly the answer that an increasing number of Labour MPs have begun to turn to in response to the political malaise of the left in the late 20th century'.[2]

New Labour's representatives often suggest that the Third Way retains core social democratic values while adopting new ways of realising these values to suit the new times in which we live. Gordon Brown and Tony Wright, a Labour MP, write, for instance, of 'fundamental socialist values' that possess 'an enduring quality' even as 'particular policy applications ... change, in the light of new problems, knowledge and circumstances'.[3] New Labour's representatives here objectify social democracy. They portray a contingent and changing practice as a fixed entity defined by given values. New Labour thereby gains rhetorical advantages: it can claim both to be true to its inheritance and to have ditched the policies that critics allege had made the Party unelectable. Yet the rhetoric also embodies a widespread theory of ideology that attracts some interpretive political scientists. Indeed, it inspires, whether explicitly or implicitly, most attempts to explain New Labour's ideas. An appreciation of the limitations of such accounts will help us both to understand New Labour and to identify an adequate political science.

Theorising ideologies

Objectified accounts of ideology remain remarkably common. At their least sophisticated, these accounts imply that ideologies are rooted in ahistorical human needs. Proponents of ideologies are particularly inclined to give weight to their beliefs by claiming that they reflect universal facts of human nature. Social democrats from Max Beer to Tony Benn have traced their ideas back to a primitive communism tied to universal values originally embedded in religion.[4] At a more sophisticated level, these objectified accounts allow that ideologies arise in particular contexts that explain the salience of the problems they address and the values they defend, but from the moment they arise, they allegedly contain fixed accounts of human nature and fixed ethical commitments against the background of which particular policies are formulated, tried out, and rejected. While political scientists sometimes allow for ethical debate within an ideology and for overlaps between ideologies, they thus, as in the example of Andrew Heywood, 'seek to identify a common core of values and principles which are distinctive to the ideology'.[5] Numerous studies treat ideologies as objects based on static values, concerns, or debates. Andrew Vincent discusses the historical origins of socialism only then to define it in terms of stable, abstract views and debates about 'human nature', 'equality and liberty', 'state and democracy', and 'markets and the economy'.[6] Perhaps such discussions can provide useful ways of introducing people to themes that recur in complex political traditions. Undoubtedly problems arise when political scientists mistakenly ascribe explanatory power to them.

One such problem appears in Vincent's account of New Labour. Vincent contrasts New Labour with an earlier state socialism: New Labour exhibits a greater acceptance of markets, a more jaundiced view of the state, and a stronger moral tone. Thereafter he compares New Labour's ideas with various strands of new liberalism before concluding, 'what is called New Labour is a redrafting of components of the new liberalism which has, in fact, recovered some of the pre-1914 "new liberal" language'; New Labour has reinterpreted 'a fecund liberal vocabulary'.[7] Surely new liberalism can explain New Labour's ideas, however, only if the former influenced the agents of the latter? Vincent's use of new liberalism to explain New Labour's ideas also appears to preclude his appealing to other traditions such as social democracy. Indeed, when he considers social democracy, he effectively assimilates it to new liberalism. He does so, moreover, not by a historical investigation of influences, but by again pointing to similarities. He says, 'purportedly socialist theorists, such as Harold Laski, G. D. H. Cole and R. H. Tawney, employed theoretical frameworks which were remarkably close to those of the new liberals'.[8] Surely we could establish that new liberalism by itself can explain New Labour, however, only by showing that other ideological traditions had not influenced the latter's leading actors? Vincent's objectified account of ideology informs his account of New Labour. Because he reifies ideologies, he seeks to establish which ideology an instance belongs to by comparing it with the values and debates that allegedly are constitutive of different ideologies: New Labour exhibits the characteristics of new liberalism, so we should explain it by reference to that ideology. Moreover, because he reifies ideologies, he tends to see them as mutually exclusive: New Labour exhibits the characteristics of new liberalism, so we cannot see it as an example or development of socialism.

Objectified accounts of ideologies contrast with a disaggregated approach that refuses to ascribe to them any existence independent of the particular beliefs and actions of individuals. A disaggregated approach recognises that ideologies are ideas and practices that people produce through their ongoing activities. They are contingent, changing traditions in which no value or debate has a fixed, central, or defining place. We can describe them adequately only by tracing how they develop over time as their exponents inherit beliefs and actions, modify them, and pass them on to others. Because ideologies are not fixed entities of which specific instances partake, we cannot locate people in one by comparing their ideas and actions with its allegedly constitutive features. Rather, we must trace the relevant historical connections to identify the ideology against the background of which people adopted the beliefs they did. To explain New Labour's ideas, we must explore a historical process as opposed to comparing the result of this process with objectified ideologies; after all, the fact that the process ended in views similar to new liberalism does not mean that new liberalism played a role in the process, and, if it did not, it would be irrelevant to an explanation of New Labour.

Michael Freeden provides perhaps the most sophisticated attempt to avoid the first problem we have found to beset objectified accounts of ideology.[9] Freeden argues that ideologies are 'morphological', a biological metaphor that seems to disavow the static analyses that often characterise the more structuralist varieties of interpretive political science. Ideologies consist, Freeden tells us, of central and peripheral concepts that exist in complex, dynamic relations with one another. To elucidate an ideology, he says, we have to explore the diverse ways in which the relevant concepts are combined at different times and in different places. Freeden's theory has much in it that we might admire – a refusal to segregate ideology from political thought, a recognition of the dynamic relationship between concepts, and an account of 'decontestation' as a feature of dominant ideologies. Freeden deploys his subtle theory to describe New Labour as an 'amalgam' of 'liberal, conservative, and (how could it be otherwise!) socialist components'.[10] His recognition of the dynamic relationships between concepts informs an admirable refusal to box New Labour 'in a hermetically sealed ideological family'.[11] Instead he refers to ideas from different ideologies so as to cover many of the important ideas that characterise New Labour.

Freeden's morphology does not seek to slot particular instances into one exclusive ideology. Nonetheless, although we get a fuller account of New Labour's ideas, his account of ideologies still exhibits problems. For a start, because he defines ideologies by sets of concepts, he concentrates on matching different bits of New Labour's programme with the core bits of various ideologies. The theoretical problem of explanation thus remains unresolved even though the flexibility of his model allows for a subtle and complex description of New Labour. Surely we cannot just assume that New Labour took the bits of its amalgam from the traditions that he highlights? We also might raise here a second problem with objectified accounts of ideology. Even if we assumed that New Labour took its ideas from the ideologies identified by Freeden, we still would not know why it had adopted this amalgam rather than some other. Because Freeden defines an ideology as a set of concepts that can be combined in diverse ways, he concentrates on describing the ways in which they have been combined. Because the concepts themselves are static, albeit contested, they seem to determine – or at least to limit – the possible ways in which they might be combined. Surely, however, people can reject concepts, modify old ones, and create new ones in unlimited ways?

A disaggregated account of ideology suggests that people inherit ideologies but that they then might modify them in unlimited ways. Ideologies are not constructions that combine static, albeit contested, concepts or debates. They are contingent and changing practices that people produce through their utterances and actions. They are inherited beliefs and patterns of action that people apply, modify, and transform for reasons of their own. We can elucidate them adequately, therefore, only by tracing the processes through which their exponents apply, extend, and modify them. Because ideologies are not composed of concepts with a given range of meanings, we cannot explain their development by showing how people or organisations combined such concepts. We explain them, rather, by tracing the historical processes of reflection and contestation in which people deployed them in response to various problems. To explain New Labour's ideas, we have to explore a historical process instead of describing how the result of this process combines objectified concepts or ideologies; after all, the fact that the process led to New Labour adopting ideas often held by liberals and conservatives does not tell us why it did so.

To explain New Labour's ideas, we have not only to locate it in the tradition from which its leading actors set out, but also to grasp how they then modified this tradition in response to specific issues.

A third problem with objectified accounts of ideologies appears if we return to the self-understanding of New Labour. Objectified accounts suggest that ideologies consist of a protected set of concepts or values that remain static, albeit subject to debate, while the policies associated with them develop in response to changing circumstances. However, if we define some values or concepts as protected, we are in danger of being insensitive to ways in which they might be extended, modified, or even rejected. Alternatively, if we recognise that these values or concepts have changed, we will be tempted to talk of a rejection or betrayal of the ideology. David Marquand tells us, for example, that New Labour 'is not socialist ... it has abandoned the tradition once exemplified by such paladins of social democracy as Willy Brandt, Helmut Schmidt, Ernest Bevin and Hugh Gaitskell'.[12] If we mistakenly define an ideology in terms of core concepts, we will be liable to conclude that either these concepts must remain unchanged or the ideology will have been deserted. We will be unlikely to recognise that the ideology can develop in ways that transform the allegedly core concepts.

A disaggregated model of ideologies conceives of them as webs of interconnected beliefs that map onto a perceived reality at various points. At times, changes in ideologies will begin with concepts a long way from points in the web that map onto external reality. At other times they will begin with concepts close to such points. Either way, no concept can stand alone, so the content of any concept depends on those around it, which means that the initial change will cause further changes throughout the ideology. No part of the web remains immune from revision. On the contrary, when people change their views of what policies are appropriate, the change will influence their values. Even if the impetus for ideological change in the Labour Party derives from grappling with altered circumstances, we should expect the effects of this process to appear in the Party's ethic.

Martin Seliger provides perhaps the most sophisticated attempt to avoid this third problem with an objectified account of ideology.[13] He distinguishes between the fundamental and operative levels of ideology, where the fundamental level is that of ethical principle, and the operative level is that at which ethical principles are compromised by the demands of action. Yet because he allows for the fundamental level being modified as a result of operational factors, he opens up the possibility of describing changes in the allegedly core values of an ideology. Nonetheless, once we recognise that ethical principles and policy commitments thus change alongside one another, we have no reason to take the former as fundamental in any significant sense. Principles and policy commitments appear instead as mutually dependent in a way that precludes our conceiving of

the former as basic or fundamental and the latter as derivative or operational. At best Seliger's concepts are misleading metaphors; they suggest
a hierarchical, dependent relationship where there is actually a reciprocal
one. At worst they are indicative of a mistaken belief in the protected
nature of ethical values within objectified ideologies.

When interpretive approaches drift towards an objectified concept of
ideology, as do those of Vincent, Freeden, and Seliger, they overlap with
those of other political scientists, notably behaviouralists and institutionalists. One reason for this overlap lies precisely in the objectified nature
of their concepts and the ways in which these thus facilitate claims to
expertise. Another reason is that objectified concepts of ideology typically
inspire modes of inquiry resembling those of modernist empiricism. They
encourage an analysis that builds on atomised concepts and proceeds to
classify and compare ideologies by reference to such atomised units. One
last reason why other political scientists generally favour objectified
concepts of ideology is that they can easily treat ideas so conceived as
just one variable within their larger theoretical frameworks. In such frameworks, beliefs become atomised attitudes to be correlated with behaviour,
ideals in contrast to interests, or rules that govern speech as opposed to
actions and practices. Institutionalists can contrast ideational, environmental, and organisational factors that influence the ways in which parties
change as if the latter two were not at least in part ideational constructs.
And behaviouralists can locate party manifestos along an objectified ideological spectrum running from left to right as a prelude to looking for
correlations between their ideological content and things such as voter
behaviour.[14]

We have found aspects of objectification not only in behaviouralism,
rational-choice theory, and institutionalism, but also in the interpretive
theories of Vincent, Freeden, and Seliger. We have done so in spite of the
fact that they explicitly oppose essentialist accounts of ideology. To oppose
essentialism is, of course, not necessarily to avoid it. Nonetheless, it is
worth pausing to ask why their theories exhibit aspects of objectification
despite their avowed hostility to essentialism. One possible explanation
would be that we simply have to abstract from particular thinkers if we
are to identify patterns and so ideologies. Vincent, Freeden, and Seliger
might argue that their theories do not postulate objectified ideologies but
merely ones that exhibit necessary features of generalisation and abstraction. They might portray their abstractions as contingent and historicist
rather than essentialist. We should not dismiss this argument too quickly:
it is, after all, this very contrast that explains why their theories represent comparatively sophisticated attempts to avoid objectification. What
we should do, however, is ask whether they undertake the necessary tasks
of generalisation and abstraction in the most appropriate manner.

Vincent, Freeden, and Seliger abstract in order to set up general models
of ideologies. Typically they decide upon the synchronic and diachronic

content of an ideology by relying on standard categories, such as liberal and socialist, together with their sense of the dominant strands within each category. Aspects of objectification appear here because they have no adequate criteria by which to define what does and does not belong within each ideology. Rather, they construct abstract models, and then proceed to describe or classify particular cases by their similarity to these models. Aspects of objectification appear again here because they thus give priority to the abstract models in locating particular cases within their categories. The models effectively act as prior, given objects in terms of which to understand particular cases.

While a disaggregated approach to ideologies does not preclude classification in terms of ideational similarities, it might make us ask whether such classifications serve any useful purpose, particularly when, as seems likely, we can find similarities, at some level of abstraction, between any two clusters of ideas. The purpose of any classification usually resides in its explanatory power. However, with ideologies, the similarities and classifications lack explanatory power. Just because certain instances of political thought share some characteristics does not imply they have a historical relationship such that one explains the rise of the other, or that these characteristics explain why they manifested themselves at the particular moments they did.

A disaggregated concept of ideology prompts us to conceive of the necessary tasks of generalisation and abstraction in a different manner from Vincent, Freeden, and Seliger. We concentrate not on classifying particular cases in relation to abstract models, but on tracing relevant historical connections. We explain particular cases by exploring the processes by which people inherited and modified certain ideas and patterns of action. Thus, we abstract in order to postulate an ideology as that which captures the inheritance of the particular case in which we are interested. We trace historical connections back through the immediate influences on the case we are explaining to the beliefs and actions that constitute the inheritance of these immediate influences. By doing so, we define ideologies not by reference to a given content – whether perennial or contingent – but, rather, pragmatically in relation to that which they explain. Moreover, we give priority to the particular case as the grounds on which we identify the synchronic and diachronic content of an ideology. We appeal to an abstraction derived from the historical influences on the case we are studying, not one established prior to that case. And we justify doing so on the grounds that these influences help explain the historical character of that case, not because that case happens to bear similarities to the abstraction.

Socialist ethics

An objectified theory of ideology fails to recognise that the process of change is continuous. It encourages us to compare New Labour's ideas

with accounts of the allegedly constitutive features of abstract constructions. In contrast, a disaggregated theory draws our attention to the ways
in which people inherit traditions and practices, modify them, and pass
them on to others. If we are properly to explain New Labour's ideas, we
must provide an account of such a historical process. Although a complete
account of this kind would be a considerable undertaking – one requiring
us to unpack various strands within New Labour – we can highlight
three aspects of this process corresponding to the three problems already
highlighted in objectified accounts of ideology. First, when considering
Vincent's work, we found that we should begin by locating New Labour
in the tradition from which its actors set out. Second, when considering
Freeden's work, we found that we should proceed by showing how these
actors modified this tradition in response to specific problems. And, finally,
when considering Seliger's work, we found that we should show how their
responses to these problems led them to modify the Party's values.

To begin, we should locate New Labour's Third Way in the ideological tradition from which its adherents set out. Competing positions coexist
within New Labour, and they derive in part from different traditions,
some of which overlap with traditions that also inform other political
parties. Yet we can aggregate most of these positions in a broad social
democratic tradition without too much simplification. As we saw, Brown
and Blair explicitly identify themselves with the ethic of this tradition.
Mandelson and Roger Liddle, a member of the Downing Street Policy
Unit, similarly tell us that New Labour stands for 'an ethical socialism
which draws on the ideas of Tawney and Ruskin'.[15]

Ethical socialism emerged as a potent force in the 1890s, although it
had clear predecessors among the Owenites, romantics such as Ruskin,
and Christians such as F. D. Maurice. The most important themes within
ethical socialism were: an idealist philosophy, immanentist theology, or
evolutionary theory that established the social nature of our being; an
analysis of brotherhood or fellowship as the moral expression of our social
nature; a faith that human instincts were leading us towards an ethic
of fellowship; a call for this new ethic to take hold of our personal lives
in a process of individual regeneration; a belief that individual regeneration would lead inexorably to social transformation; and a social ideal
conceived in terms of a moral economy and cooperative community.[16]
In the first half of the twentieth century, social democrats such as R. H.
Tawney, John Macmurray, and William Temple continued to express
many of these themes. In the 1950s and 1960s, ethical socialists, like
many others, became more and more committed to Keynesian economic
planning and the welfare state as the practical means of realising their
moral ideals.

The values of social justice, citizenship, and community dominated social
democracy during the 1950s, 1960s, and 1970s. Although there were
debates about the exact content of all of these values, we can identify widely

shared beliefs about them. Social democrats believed that justice rested on a notion of moral equality that required substantial movement towards economic equality. They thought that the distribution of wealth ought to be based on principles of need and welfare, rather than the dictates of market efficiency. They often described the market as immoral in that it placed material prosperity over the moral equality of human beings, whereas a moral economy would give every person her due. Social democrats who accepted Fabian or Keynesian economic theories could combine this vision of a moral economy with notions of efficiency but, even when they did so, they generally thought that the state should act to promote social justice even if necessary at the expense of efficiency. As Tawney explained, 'the essence of all morality is this: to believe that every human being is of infinite importance, and therefore that no consideration of expediency can justify the oppression of one by another'.[17]

Social democrats commonly deployed citizenship as an inclusive concept that entailed social and economic rights as well as political ones. In the welfare state, these rights became embodied in universal entitlements to things such as education, housing, and unemployment protection. Social democrats believed that as citizens we participate in a common life, so the state, as the moral expression of this life, has a duty to provide us with a minimum standard of living. Temple famously argued, for example, 'every citizen should be secure in possession of such income as will enable him to maintain a home and bring up children'.[18] Although some political theorists wrote of an 'invertebrate residuum', the members of which lacked the capacity to be full citizens, social democrats rarely paid much attention to such a residuum, and even when they did, they suggested that the residuum would be brought to full citizenship by the welfare state, or else that we owed a duty to provide even for the residuum. When social democrats argued that wealth should depend on service and so be denied to those who did not fulfil their social obligations, their target was almost always the idle rich – who they saw as merely exploiting the workers – not the unemployed.

Most social democrats unpacked community in terms of cooperation and social – or, at times, class – solidarity. Social democracy was defined principally against competitive individualism, not capitalism. To social democrats, the moral economy and the rights of citizenship were expressions of a cooperative community. Many ethical socialists had a mystical vision of fellowship as expressing a divine unity found in all things. Edward Carpenter wrote, for example, of a 'region of Self' in relation to which 'the mere diversities of temperament which ordinarily distinguish and divide people dropped away and became indifferent, and a field was opened in which all were truly equal'.[19] While social democrats might express the unity of all in these mystical terms, or as a corollary of our brotherhood under God, or in terms set by idealist philosophy, for almost all of them it required a fellowship in which people would cooperate for a common good.

Social democracy has a long association with the ideals of social justice, citizenship, and community as well as the means represented by Keynesianism and the welfare state. New Labour represents a descendent and modification of this tradition. No doubt a full account of social democracy would qualify such a broad picture by looking beyond public pronouncements and iconic texts to Cabinet discussions and public policies. Perhaps doing so would show that Labour governments often were ambivalent about universal welfare, full employment, and higher taxes, in part because of economic and electoral concerns. Still, we are identifying a tradition against the background of which Blair and others set out rather than comparing New Labour with our own understanding of the Party's past.[20] Thus, the explicit appeals of Blair, Brown, and Mandelson to the ethical moment in social democracy as that which has most influenced them provides us with a justification for focusing on the values of social justice, citizenship, and community.

As we saw in the previous chapter, social democrats broke with many of the policies associated with the Keynesian welfare state as a consequence of accepting the reality of various problems. They have come to believe that such policies no longer provide a viable means of realising their moral ideals. In the rest of this chapter, we will see how this reformulation of policies has entailed a modification of the values of social democracy. In the 1980s a range of issues posed problems for social democrats but, to simplify the analysis of changes in the social democratic ethic, we might focus on three of them – inflation, the underclass, and changes in the working class – and the ways in which the responses to them have altered, respectively, the content that social democrats ascribe to social justice, citizenship, and community.

Social justice

Throughout the 1950s, 1960s, and 1970s, the Labour Party took an extension of state control to be the primary means of promoting social justice. At the very least the state was to create greater equality through progressive taxation and the provision of welfare benefits. By 1980 these policies were threatened, as we have seen, by a growing concern with inflation, bureaucratic inefficiency, and government overload. Inflation in particular was seen as a major problem for the economy when at the end of the 1970s the Labour Government, under pressure from the International Monetary Fund, agreed to introduce strict monetary controls. The neo-liberalism of the New Right typically conceived of inflation in terms defined by the monetarist critique of Keynesianism. Monetarism encouraged a shift from demand management to supply-side reforms, notably those aimed at creating a more effective labour market. And it co-opted the values of choice and freedom by portraying the state as unresponsive to individual wants in comparison with the market.

During the 1980s and 1990s, social democrats increasingly accepted the supply-side emphasis of the economic theory of the New Right. Labour Party documents suggested that economic recovery would bring unacceptable inflation unless it was pursued in the context of a 'commitment to macro-economic stability' and 'supply-side policies to boost investment in industry'.[21] Brown, as Chancellor of the Exchequer, often has expressed New Labour's reluctance either to raise taxes or to boost demand by increasing public expenditure. An emphasis on the supply-side of the economy has led the Labour Party to modify its stance towards marketisation. Mandelson and Liddle tell us that New Labour has renounced the statist policies once associated with the Party in favour of an increased concern with efficiency and good management.[22] Even privatisation has a place in government thinking, as both Blair and Brown first indicated during the 1997 election campaign.

As New Labour has turned to supply-side economics, so it has modified the social democratic concept of social justice. Three changes stand out as particularly significant. The first is a shift in the relative importance of equality and efficiency. Whereas social democrats used to stress the importance of a moral economy even at the expense of efficiency, they now argue in favour of redistributive measures only when these do not damage industrial competitiveness. The important contrast here is not that between what social democrats say they want to do and what they actually achieve or the sorts of policies they adopt when they are confronted with hard choices, but rather that between their past and present ideological commitments. In the past, social democrats typically defended social justice as the first call on the economy. Gore argued that the Biblical doctrine of stewardship implied that individuals possessed wealth only as a trust for the social good, so the first charge on industry had to be living wages for the workers.[23] Today New Labour emphasises instead the overriding importance of securing an efficient and competitive economy as the context within which moves towards social justice then might be made. Blair even told a meeting of European socialists that minimum standards of social provision were vital only if they did not hinder job creation.[24] When New Labour thus ascribes greater importance to efficiency, it alters the content of distributive justice. It implies that if things like high wages or less progressive taxation are necessary for efficiency, they are acceptable: it implies that people can earn or merit greater wealth than others as a result of their role in the economy rather than for reasons of welfare or need. 'New Labour's belief in the dynamic market economy', Mandelson and Liddle tell us, 'involves recognition that substantial personal incentives and rewards are necessary in order to encourage risk-taking and entrepreneurialism.'[25]

A second significant change in the social democratic concept of social justice is an increased emphasis on individual choice. Whereas social democrats typically used to stress the needs and welfare of producers and the political participation of citizens, they now pay as much attention to the freedom and choice of consumers. In the past, social democrats usually understood social justice primarily in terms of a minimal level of welfare for the citizen and a fair deal for the worker. New Labour still believes in a minimal level of welfare, but the concern with a fair deal for the worker is matched, and at times replaced, by a concern to empower the consumer. Mandelson and Liddle tell us, for example, that public services should be provided in ways that suit the citizen rather than the provider.[26] No doubt New Labour developed this concern with the consumer in part because of a widespread perception that the public sector is unresponsive to those it is meant to serve, and perhaps we should not assume that New Labour takes the same view of the relation between consumers and producers in the private sector. Nonetheless, public-sector workers are still workers, and a more suspicious attitude towards public-sector unions almost inevitably has spill-over effects upon the view one takes of the private sector. New Labour certainly has sought both to distance itself from the trade unions and to emphasise the need for consumer choice in the private sector.[27] The important point here is, however, that the new emphasis on choice entails a shift in the social democratic view of distributive justice. If individuals are to be free to choose things such as the schools their children go to or who is to manage their state-pensions, then we must accept the inequalities that result from some of them making good choices and others making bad ones. New Labour thus appears to be committed to allowing distribution to reflect the merits of the choices people make as well as their needs or welfare.

The final change in the social democratic concept of social justice derives from the ways in which the previous ones have transformed the content of equality. In the past, many social democrats conceived of equality in terms of outcome: redistributive policies sought to transform outcomes, even if there was rarely a sense that the result would be literal numerical equality. Today New Labour explicitly disavows a primary concern with redistribution, at least in part because its elevation of efficiency at the expense of equality combines with its increased emphasis on choice to set clear limits to redistribution. Equality now consists primarily in the equality of opportunity to make certain choices or to participate in the quest for efficiency. When Brown gave the Anthony Crosland memorial lecture – named after a leading revisionist of the Gaitskell years – he vigorously asserted the importance of such a focus on equalising people's opportunities over their lifetimes.[28] Likewise, David Blunkett, as Secretary of State for Education and Employment, described the welfare to work programme as a way of 'tackling social exclusion' by promoting 'opportunity for all', which is, of course, very different from the elder social democratic belief in tackling social exclusion by providing goods, such as pensions, homes, and education, to everyone, or, at least, everyone in need.[29] New Labour emphasises opportunities, not substantive benefits. In addition, we might distinguish here between different ways of unpacking a belief in equality of opportunity. New Labour does not advocate a literal equality of opportunity, as if all pupils should have an equal chance of going to Eton or all graduates should have an equal chance of getting the job they want. Rather, it unpacks equality of opportunity in terms set by its focus on network poverty. For New Labour, equality applies to little more than a minimal opportunity defined in terms of the avoidance of social exclusion. At times New Labour even appears to be interested solely in the opportunity to get a job. It exhibits little sense, for example, of the need to address the fact that richer people typically can more easily afford tuition fees and other costs associated with self-improvement or with enhancing their employment prospects. Whereas social democrats used to believe in a right to a minimum quality of life, New Labour only defends access to the possibility of such a minimum.

Obviously we should not over-emphasise the changes in the social democratic ethic. New Labour remains keen to reduce inequalities between a privileged minority and the underprivileged, and its greater stress on the choices of consumers does not mean that it no longer worries about the limitations of markets as a means of securing a just distribution. Nonetheless, New Labour's response to the dilemma of inflation – and also those of bureaucratic inefficiency and government overload – has resulted in a clear modification of the Party's concept of social justice. As early as 1985, Bryan Gould, then a leading presence in the Party, wrote, 'Mrs Thatcher has succeeded to a considerable extent in changing the terms and meaning of the debate so that the emphasis is more on freedom than equality.'[30] Today, New Labour has put equality in a more subsidiary relationship to efficiency, modulated the principles of welfare and need with those of choice and desert, and shifted from an emphasis on redistribution to one on equality of opportunity to the limited resources needed to avoid social exclusion.

Citizenship

The Labour Party traditionally stood for a concept of citizenship that entitled all citizens to political, social, and economic rights. The state, as the moral expression of community, was to provide a guaranteed minimum standard of living to all of its citizens. Social democrats generally believed that we had a duty to care and provide for the less fortunate members of society, and the welfare state was one way of our fulfilling this duty. For many of them, the provision of universal benefits was also a way of creating virtuous and independent citizens: the welfare state provided people with the prerequisites they needed to become responsible citizens. During the 1980s, growing worries about an underclass suggested that these later social democrats had been overly optimistic. Social scientists began to argue that the welfare state had created a class of people who were dependent on benefits and had neither the means nor the incentive for self-improvement. They suggested that when the state provided benefits that did not carry obligations, it undermined the responsibility of those who received these benefits: the welfare state had eroded virtue and so indirectly promoted crime, drug-abuse, and other ills that were corroding the moral fabric of society. The Conservative governments of the 1980s were, once again, the first to address the problem posed by belief in an underclass. They altered the range and conditions of many welfare benefits in ways that the Labour Party initially condemned outright.

As we have seen, New Labour too now talks of an underclass, albeit in somewhat different terms. New Labour accepts, in Mandelson's and Liddle's words, that 'the complex web of means-tested benefits weakens incentives' so that 'today's welfare state too often traps people in long-term dependency'.[31] Simply by accepting the existence of an underclass, a part of which is taken to be in a condition of welfare dependency, New Labour has committed itself to devising new policies designed less to alleviate poverty than to enable people to break free of the welfare-trap. Blair has said, for example, 'Labour's modern welfare should not just recommend increased benefits but . . . [also] reduce dependency and get rid of disincentives to paid work.'[32] The Labour governments have put welfare-to-work programmes at the forefront of their agenda. Under the New Deal, the government now provides the unemployed with training, education, or subsidised places on employment schemes, rather than simple cash payments, while the unemployed in return have to take up these opportunities or they risk losing some benefit. The first part of the New Deal to be put into practice was that for young unemployed people. Young people who have been out of work for over six months are offered a job with a private or public sector employer, a job in the voluntary sector, a place on an environmental task force, or else full-time education or training, and all these options now include a minimum of one day's training a week to provide recipients with the skills they need to remain in employment. Nonetheless, the 'New Deal is not a soft option', the government explains, because the recipients have 'to take up those opportunities'; 'staying on benefit will no longer be an option'.[33]

As New Labour has responded to the underclass, so it has modified the social democratic concept of citizenship. Three changes stand out as especially significant here too. The first is a shift of emphasis from the citizen as a recipient of rights to the citizen as a bearer of duties. The rights ascribed to citizens have altered somewhat as the concept of social justice has shifted from entitlements to benefits to entitlements to opportunities. In addition, the relationship between even these latter rights and duties has been rethought in response to issues such as that of the underclass. The combined effect of these shifts appears in Blair's assertion, 'for every new opportunity we offer, we demand responsibility in return'.[34] Whereas earlier social democrats invoked the idea of duty primarily to denote the obligation of the well-to-do to improve the lot of the less privileged, many now talk at least as much of the duties that those on welfare owe to society, and even of the need to instil virtue within them. The Commission on Social Justice flagged this change in the Party's thinking as early as 1994. Its report defended the rights to health, education, and housing, but explicitly tied these rights to the performance of duties by the recipients.[35] It argued that the state should enable citizens to improve themselves while compelling them to fulfil their responsibilities.

More recently, Blair has explained that 'we accept our duty as a society to give each person a stake in its future', but in return 'each person accepts a responsibility to respond' – 'to work to improve themselves'.[36] New Labour's appeal to duty carries beyond the sphere of employment: so, for example, the right to housing carries an obligation to abstain from anti-social behaviour, while the right to an education for one's children entails an obligation to ensure they attend school. At first, New Labour postulated a reciprocal relationship between rights and duties, but since the mid-1990s it has begun to invoke a more hierarchical relationship in which duties appear to be fundamental with rights as their pale reflection – a mirror opposite of the dominant view among social democrats through the 1950s, 1960s, and 1970s. Blair told the Labour Party Conference, 'a decent society is not based on rights' but 'on duties', and elsewhere he explained that this implies that duty 'defines the context in which rights are given'.[37] Similarly, when the Labour Party adopted a new Clause Four as part of its constitution in April 1995, this declared, 'the rights we enjoy reflect the duties we owe'. For New Labour, rights now appear to be justified mainly by their role in enabling us to fulfil duties that have a more inherent value in that their performance is constitutive of a good community.

The second change in the social democratic concept of citizenship is the aspect of exclusion that follows from the new stress on the obligations of the recipients of social rights. It even seems that those people who do not fulfil the duties ascribed to them by the state are no longer seen as full citizens, for their exclusion is implicit in the fact that they are to be denied some of the rights given to other citizens. Blair points to such exclusion when he insists, 'if we invest so as to give the unemployed the chance of a job, they have a responsibility to take it or lose benefit'.[38] Under the New Deal, 'young people who refuse or fail to take up a place in one of these options will be required to take up a place identified for them by the Employment Service', and, more significantly, if they then 'refuse or fail to take up [these] places . . . benefit sanctions will be applied'.[39] When earlier social democrats such as Sidney Webb invoked parasites or idlers, they had in mind those rich profiteers who lived off the rent and interest produced by other people's labour. When New Labour expresses similar concerns, it refers either to a general decline in the moral fabric of society or to specific groups from among the underclass, such as the young unemployed or single mothers.

A final change in the social democratic concept of citizenship concerns a change in the location of responsibility from society to individual. When New Labour presents rights not as entitlements but as things we earn by fulfilling our duties, it implies that when the duties are not fulfilled, the failing lies with the individual, or at least it will do so once New Labour's other policies are in place. Surely it would be unfair, after all, to penalise people – say, by cutting their welfare benefits – for failing to do something they could not do largely because of social factors? New Labour thus downplays the constraining effect on people of the consequences of complex patterns of action. We can see this neglect of the social in New Labour's remarkable reluctance to ask whether or not the economy is providing enough jobs to absorb the unemployed. Indeed, New Labour's reluctance to sign a European Charter of Rights, which includes the right to work, might make us suspicious that it doubts that the economy is in fact able to absorb the unemployed. If such suspicions are correct, we might judge New Labour's individualisation of certain responsibilities to be disingenuous.

Community

Social democrats have always made much of the value of community. William Morris famously wrote, in his utopia, *News from Nowhere*, 'fellowship is heaven, and lack of fellowship is hell: fellowship is life, and lack of fellowship is death'.[40] As Morris's utopian vision illustrates, social democrats typically unpacked fellowship in terms of an egalitarian and cooperative society in which individuals identified with the commonwealth at least as much as with their own material advantage, although more often than not the intention was to challenge any clear distinction between the two. In practice, fellowship came to mean, above all else, heavily progressive taxation such that the well-to-do sacrificed a degree of personal prosperity in order to contribute to society. Community thus underlay the traditional social democratic values of justice and citizenship. The ideal of community inspired the tax system that financed the redistributive measures associated with the social democratic concept of justice and the socio-economic rights associated with citizenship.

During the 1980s historians and social scientists such as Eric Hobsbawm spread the idea that the nature of the working class had changed significantly.[41] They argued that technologies and affluence had combined to change the aspirations of the group of voters on whom Labour most depended; if workers had not fallen into the underclass, they had risen into the lower middle class. Hobsbawm interpreted these changes within a Marxist historiography according to which post-Fordism brought to a halt the forward march of labour. In this view, changes in the mode of production, including the rise of computer technology, produced a new set of social relations, notably a decline in manual labour, and so eroded electoral support for the Labour Party. A range of such theses about new times flour-ished largely because of their apparent ability to explain Thatcherism in other than neoliberal terms: the rise of new types of workers with different aspirations appeared to underlie, for example, the popularity of Con-servative policies such as the selling-off of council houses.[42] More generally still, numerous electoral pundits and left-wing theorists came to believe in the 1980s and early 1990s that the Labour Party had to bring itself into line with new economic patterns and the social groups these had created if it were ever to emerge from the electoral wilderness in which it seemed to find itself.

Successive election campaigns and meetings with focus groups certainly convinced New Labour that the Party's association with higher rates of taxation was a major electoral milestone. Most people just were not willing to contribute more to the community, or so it seemed. New Labour tried desperately hard to distance itself from a policy of increased taxes for the lower middle class and the working class; these classes were no longer expected to forgo additional comforts for the sake of the community. Mandelson and Liddle reiterate this message throughout their account of what New Labour stands for: they tell us that New Labour does not believe in 'big tax rises for the hardworking majority', that 'a fairer tax system ought to be about rewarding hard work', and that 'it would be illogical for Labour to oppose a relief in the tax burden on ordinary families'.[43] New Labour's determination to avoid increased taxes was so strong that even before the 1997 election the Party agreed to stick to the spending limits set by the previous Conservative government. In addition to this reluctance to raise taxes, New Labour has responded to the changing structure of the working class largely with the same policies by which it has dealt with inflation and the underclass, for these policies are intended not only to help keep government spending down but also to make govern-ment more responsive and to give people more choice; they are supposed to meet people's aspirations as identified by Frank Field, a Minister of State for Social Security from 1997 to 1998 – the aspirations to enjoy the satisfactions of ownership and choice and to spend for oneself 'the gains of increased earnings'.[44]

New Labour makes much of its faith in community, as when Blair insists that people are 'citizens of a community', not 'separate economic actors competing in the marketplace of life'.[45] Although it does so in part to reinforce the simple but effective contrast between it and a harsh and uncaring New Right, its leading actors really do seem to be inspired by an idea of community. Indeed, community appears in New Labour's discourse as both an inspiration for conversion and a New Jerusalem much as it did for earlier ethical socialists such as Philip Snowden with his come-to-Jesus rhetoric. Blair's 'political awakening', for example, apparently followed his discovery of 'MacMurray's interpretation of the social commitment of Christianity through the idea of community'.[46]

Even as we can recognise that many of the leading actors in New Labour genuinely believe in an ideal of community, however, so we might highlight the ways in which they have modified this ideal. Their acceptance of the legitimacy of the new aspirations of the working class has led them to ascribe a greater role to competition and materialism. They have come to advocate what Wright calls 'collective individualism'.[47]

In the past, social democrats usually defined community in terms of co-operation and in opposition to self-interest and competition. New Labour eulogises, in contrast, a community that encompasses these latter things. Blair has said, for example, that the 'final destination is a society where you combine that strong and competitive and enterprising sense of achievement with a sense of decency and compassion'.[48] Field too appeals to a tradition of ethical socialism only then to call for policies that recognise that 'self-interest is one of the most powerful of human characteristics'.[49] Social democrats used to think of the welfare state as a practical expression of interdependence and fellowship. Today, New Labour believes in restructuring the welfare state so as to create more space for individualism and competition. Field has written of the importance of 'channelling self-interest and self-improvement in a manner which enhances the common good'.[50] The main ideas behind New Labour's welfare reforms, given its reluctance to raise taxes, seem to be just such an appeal to self-interest together with the emphasis on duties that we noted earlier. The Labour Party's vision of community no longer consists, we might say, of individuals who undertake cooperative activity for a common good that subsumes their particular selves. It consists, instead, of citizens who are united by having a stake in a shared enterprise, and who are thus required to fulfil certain duties, but who otherwise are encouraged to compete in order to advance themselves in their own ways and by their own merits. According to Blair, community requires us to acknowledge 'an obligation collectively to ensure each citizen gets a stake in it', but the purpose of this stake appears to be less to unite us around a common good than to create a society within which 'opportunity is available to all, advancement is through merit, and from which no group or class is set apart or excluded'.[51] New Labour's Third Way is one of competitive individualism within a moral framework such that everyone has the chance truly to compete. It feeds hefty doses of individualism, competition, and materialism into the traditional social democratic ideal of community.

In the past, social democrats also usually understood community as an inherent form of solidarity that was disrupted by capitalism but that still found expression in the working class. New Labour represents community, in contrast, as the fragile and contingent achievement of people acting ethically so as to fulfil their duties to others. Indeed, New Labour often implies that community has been lost or at least endangered by social developments since the 1960s, especially by the excessive individualism of the New Right: we have lost our sense of having responsibilities for one another; we have become selfish, atomised beings insistent only upon our own rights. One effect of this change in the ideal of community is that New Labour's spokespeople sound moralising when they urge people to fulfil their duties so as to renew the community. Although some commentators talk of a new authoritarianism, this charge is, of course, false, exaggerated, or vague. Nonetheless, even when Blair repudiated this charge, he tellingly appealed to the need for just that type of moralising that I am suggesting is more or less inexorably linked to New Labour's vision of community. He said, 'we are about wanting to encourage people to make good and valuable choices whether in terms of their own behaviour or their actions toward others', which 'is not "new authoritarianism"' but 'common sense', for while 'people want tolerance', 'they also want rules'.[52] A related effect of this change in the ideal of community is that New Labour places great emphasis on volunteering and other forms of active participation within local communities. The Active Community Unit is meant to promote just such participation, since, as a working group attached to this unit wrote, 'volunteering and community activities are central to the concept of citizenship and are the key to restoring our communities'.[53]

Communitarianism

New Labour has modified social democratic values even if only as an unintended consequence of reformulating policies. In fact, its leading spokespeople often give the impression that they deliberately modified these values. Sometimes they imply that the social values that thrived through to the 1950s have been eroded by the emergence of a rights-based culture during the 1960s and 1970s. 'The Left got into trouble', according to Blair, 'when its basic values became divorced from . . . ethical socialism'.[54] The present task thus appears to be to return to the ethic of socialism's golden age as represented by the Atlee governments. At other times they suggest that even the ethic of this golden age requires modification if it is to serve our present needs. 'What is required today', thus appears, in Blair's words, to be 'a new relationship between citizen and community for the modern world'.[55] Whether New Labour promotes a return to an elder ethical socialism or new values, its proposed ethic draws extensively on communitarianism. Indeed, if we are properly to understand New Labour, we need to explore not only changes in its policy commitments but also its debt to communitarianism, for the new policies are as much a consequence of the impact of new ethical theories as these ethical theories are a consequence of the reformulation of policies.

We have to turn to the United States again in order to trace the roots of the communitarian theories that inform the ethical shifts associated with New Labour. At first 'communitarian' was a label applied to political philosophers who were hostile to the liberal philosophy of John Rawls.

Despite their differences Alasdair MacIntyre, Michael Sandel, and Charles Taylor all opposed Rawls's thin concept of the self and the priority he ascribed to the right over the good.[56] In the early 1990s this same label was used to cover a group of social scientists, most notably Amitai Etzioni, but also others such as Robert Bellah and Robert Putnam, who concentrated less on philosophical analysis than on a diagnosis of the ills of contemporary society and corresponding prescriptions for the good society. It is this latter group who have influenced New Labour. Once again, we can identify connections in the lives of key actors that help to make concrete the conceptual influences at play here. Elaine Kamark, a special adviser to President Clinton, introduced both Blair and Brown to the ideas of Etzioni, who himself served as Senior Advisor to the White House from 1979 to 1980 and later wrote a pamphlet on the Third Way for Demos.[57] Putnam was invited to address Blair and others among the elite of New Labour when he visited Britain in April 2001.

Communitarians often deploy a temporal narrative closely parallel to that of New Labour. Etzioni appears, for instance, to invoke American society in the 1950s as an era of stable values and so a viable community. A widely shared set of values, based to some degree on the dominance of Christianity, gave people 'a strong sense of duty to their families, communities, and society'.[58] Although the society based on these values involved coercive breaks on autonomy, especially for groups such as women and ethnic minorities, it had an admirable moral vitality. For Etzioni, moral vitality is the foundation of social order and so of great importance even though it involves a loss of autonomy. As he explains elsewhere, we need a balance 'between community and autonomy, between the common good and liberty, between individual rights and social responsibilities'.[59] If the 1950s exhibited an admirable community, the 1960s and 1970s brought an excess of autonomy as evidenced by a growing sense of entitlement, a neglect of responsibilities, a decline in respect for authority, and consequent social problems, including the type of dependency widely associated with the underclass. 'We are not talking simply about nostalgia for the 1950s', according to Putnam, but rather about issues of public policy, since:

> school performance, public health, crime rates, clinical depression, tax compliance, philanthropy, race relations, community development, census returns, teen suicide, economic productivity, campaign finance, even simple human happiness – all are demonstrably affected by how (and whether) we connect with our family and friends and neighbours and co-workers.[60]

Communitarians often identify the source of our excess of autonomy in the rise of counter-cultural movements in the 1960s, which undermined values such as hard work and thrift, and encouraged new socio-economic patterns such as the entry of women into the labour market, which limited the time they could devote to family and voluntary action in the community. The consequent excess of autonomy appeared, Etzioni argues, in both welfare liberalism and the neoliberalism of the New Right.

The communitarians typically conceive of community as a fragile product of virtue as best manifested in the family and voluntary associations. Community thus retains in their writings many of the features ascribed to it by the long line of social theorists who contrasted it with society – *Gemeinschaft* not *Gesellschaft*. Typically, they unpack community in terms of local traditions, shared values, face-to-face relationships, and a close connection between private and public virtue. Historically, social theorists have contrasted these features of community with those of a civil society that they characterised in terms of individualism, rationalism, contractural relationships, and the rule of law, and that they thereby portrayed as being the setting for, or even part of, the spread of modern market economies. In contrast, communitarians often fuse civil society with community in opposition to both the state and the market. Civil society appears, in their view, as the site of families and voluntary associations that embody a spirit of community that is at odds with the individualistic rationalism of the market as well as the impersonal bureaucracy of the state. The dubious fusion of community and civil society enables communitarians such as Etzioni to operate with three sharply distinguished categories – the state, the market, and communities in civil society – while also facilitating a neglect of the particularity and exclusion that historically have been associated with community. Many communitarians go so far as to present their ethic as socially inclusive on the grounds that all members of society can participate in the processes of collective decision-making.[61]

Invocations of inclusive communities are surely in tension with advocacy of strong communities based on shared values. How can we be sure nobody will reject the shared values on which our communities are based? And if we cannot be sure of this, how can we include such people in our communities? In spite of the tensions highlighted by such questions, communitarians typically insist on the importance of reasserting strong values in order to stop the moral drift that they believe has occurred in society since the early 1960s. These strong values are associated, they suggest, with religion and, perhaps more importantly for our purposes, with work and family. In this view, work and family teach responsibility, self-reliance, and involvement; they bolster self-esteem, purpose, and the sense of contributing to a community; they encourage people to relate their individual choices to their collective responsibilities. The communitarians thus have advocated welfare-to-work programmes and measures to support families. William Galston argues that the state should promote marriage actively while also making divorce more difficult for couples with children.[62] This emphasis on the family and work is, communitarians argue, vital for any adequate attack on poverty since stable, intact families provide 'the best antipoverty program for children', and paid employment provides the best solution to the adult poverty of the under-class.[63]

Communitarians advocate policies to promote family and work in an attempt to bring about a more general shift away from autonomy towards community. In their opinion, we need a greater stress on responsibilities and duties as opposed to rights. Etzioni promotes, more specifically, 'a moratorium on the minting of most, if not all, new rights; re-establishing the link between rights and responsibilities; recognizing that some respon-sibilities do not entail rights'.[64] Part of the value of family, work, and other institutions in civil society derives precisely from the fact that, in the view of the communitarians, they are where we learn and practise exercising responsibility, in contrast to the state from which we tend to demand rights. It is at this point that the communitarians seek to resolve the tension between their invocation of strong values and their idea of an inclusive community. At times, they elide inclusion with the activities through which we fulfil our duties: the unemployed are socially excluded so to bring them into the workforce is to enable them to participate in the economy. At other times they suggest that the community consists of umbrella institutions that bind together people within civil society.

New Labour's reworking of social democratic values derives as much from communitarianism as from the consequences of its reformulation of public policy. New Labour deploys communitarianism and ethical social-ism against the statism of Old Labour and the individualism of the New Right, both of which it accuses of promoting excessive autonomy rather than a balance between rights and duties. Blair argues that Old Labour's emphasis on rights 'had very little to do with any forms of left-of-centre philosophy recognisable to the founders of the Labour Party': 'for too long', he complains, 'the demand for rights from the state was separated from the duties of citizenship', when really 'the rights we enjoy reflect the duties we owe'.[65] New Labour's debt to communitarianism does not stop at a general insistence on duties; it also includes specific emphases on family and work. Blair believes, 'it is largely from family discipline that social discipline and a sense of responsibility is learned', while Brown thinks that the task for government today is 'to revitalise the work ethic in our society'.[66]

The communitarian themes adopted by New Labour – responsibility, family, and work – inform many of the changes we found in the values of social democrats. Consider the reformulation of the ideal of community. Communitarianism provides a source for the role of community as an inspiration for conversion and a vision of the New Jerusalem. It also espouses the concept of community as a fragile achievement of ethical action in civil society, an achievement that has been undermined in recent years, rather than as the inherent solidarity of a people or class. Consider next the changes in the ideal of citizenship. New Labour's insistence that we need a greater emphasis on duties mirrors the best-known theme of communitarianism. Similarly, the shift of the locus of responsibility from society to the individual reflects the communitarian promotion of self-reliance and the personal performance of duties. Here, too, the aspect of exclusion we noted in New Labour derives in part from the communitarian concern to promote strong values, a concern we saw to be in tension with the ideal of an inclusive community. Consider, finally, the shifts in the social democratic ideal of social justice. Many of these can appear now as corollaries of New Labour's emphasis on individual responsibility and work. The greater emphasis on individual choice seems to be more or less entailed by an emphasis on people learning to take responsibility through the effects on them of their actions in civil society. Likewise, the new ideal of equality as referring to access to opportunities reflects the communitarian shift of the locus of responsibility from society to the individual: it is up to the individual to take up the opportunities that society makes available to him or her.

Communitarianism, like institutionalism, has reinforced and influenced themes in New Labour's thought. To recognise this is to raise questions about how and why communitarianism and new institutionalism can be brought together in this way. To some extent we can answer such questions by showing, as I have tried to do, that they embody overlapping responses to the New Right and the dilemmas it posed for alternative intellectual and political movements. To provide a more complete answer, we might turn to the historical and conceptual links between communitarianism and new institutionalism viewed as related products of modernist empiricism as it evolved in response to behaviouralism.[67]

Within anthropology and sociology, modernist empiricism often took on a functionalist hue, as indeed it did in political science albeit to a lesser extent.[68] This functionalism was a broad one that overlapped with, but also stood in contrast to, the structural-functionalism associated with the systematic theories of behaviouralists. It arose primarily as anthropologists and sociologists addressed much the same problems as those that gave rise to modernist empiricism in political science. Anthropology and sociology too had been dominated for much of the nineteenth century by moralistic and evolutionary approaches.[69] Then in the early twentieth century anthropologists and sociologists adopted functionalism partly in response to more analytic conceptions of science and partly in response to a loss of faith in reason and progress following the First World War. Although we can read back aspects of functionalist reasoning into nineteenth-century theorists, including Auguste Comte and Herbert Spencer, it was only later that social scientists, such as Emile Durkheim, Bronislaw Malinowski, and A. R. Radcliffe Brown, distinguished between functional explanations, which they saw as scientific, and those that either searched for historical origins or examined individual motivations. Functionalism sought to explain social facts by showing the contribution they made to social order. As such, it entailed an interest in the interconnections between elements in a social whole – the ways in which the elements support or reinforce one another – that might appear to be at odds with the atomisation and analysis that characterised modernist empiricism. However, the social or cultural whole typically appeared less as a product of an at least partly unique historical process, than as a framework that possessed sufficient universality to facilitate the comparison and classification of the more atomised aspects of varied wholes. The social whole was thus little more than a site of postulates – such as the requirements of all social orders or the needs of all individuals – that served to make possible comparison between what otherwise might have appeared to be the radically different products of radically different cultures. The functionalists explained objects in terms of their synchronic roles in a social order, with history being at most a way of showing what objects were and were not available to fulfil a given role. They sometimes made an explicit contrast between their forms of explanation and the more conjectural histories of the nineteenth century.[70] Functionalists conceived of the whole, then, in a way that resembled the concept of 'a system' in the systematic theories of the behaviouralists, and they did so in spite of their use of organic metaphors.

To equate early functionalism with the theories of the behaviouralists would be anachronistic, however. Apart from anything else, functionalism arose in France and Britain, only really arriving in America in 1931 when Radcliffe Brown took up a post at the University of Chicago and Talcott Parsons, who had turned to Durkheim under the influence of Malinowski, began to teach at Harvard. Even then, moreover, functionalism remained part of an American modernist empiricism, which in so far as it sought philosophical inspiration tended to do so not in the almost unknown work of the Vienna Circle but in the highways and byways of an indigenous pragmatism that G. H. Mead infused with the social psychology of Wilhelm Wundt. This modernist empiricism characterised the Harvard Circle who adopted overlapping themes in social psychology, pragmatism, functionalism, and systems theory, a circle that included sociologists such as Parsons and Robert Merton, management theorists such as Chester Barnard, and those industrial psychologists, including Fritz Roethlisberger and Lloyd Warner, who were pioneers in the human relations movement as it emerged from the Hawthorne Experiments at the General Electric Plant in Chicago.[71] Warner was a social anthropologist who had been influenced by Radcliffe Brown while doing fieldwork with Australian Aborigines. Although he thought his research contributed to the comparative sociology championed by Radcliffe Brown, he also tried to bring aspects of social psychology into it so as to develop a broader approach to processes and functions within systems. He was typical of the members of the Harvard Circle, who characteristically combined systems theory, functionalism, and social psychology.

We should distinguish, then, between a narrow structural-functionalism that was picked up in the systematic theory of the behaviouralists and a broad functionalist strand within modernist empiricism. Just as Parsons inspired some behaviouralists, so Merton and others such as Philip Selznick inspired social scientists who wanted to tie systems theory or functionalism to mid-range theories. Selznick studied with Merton at Columbia University. He combined a functionalist approach to organisations with the idea, which he took from the human relations movement, that community is an integral aspect of human behaviour. He thereby developed what has been called the 'natural systems' approach to organisations.[72] Barnard, Selznick, and others all thought of the executive as a cooperative system, and more generally of organisations as communities. It is at this point that we reach Etzioni.

Etzioni is, let us remember, a sociologist of organisations who was inspired by a jumble of systems theory, functionalism, and social psychology that was almost ubiquitous in American social science. After completing a doctoral thesis on the organisation of kibbutzim, he turned to comparing and classifying organisations from a functionalist perspective.[73] Of most interest to us are the continuities between his early functionalism and his later communitarianism. Etzioni approached organisations against the background of the broad functionalist concern with social order. He classified formal organisations as coercive, remunerative, or normative, according to the primary mechanisms by which they maintained social control and the corresponding functions they fulfilled for members. Coercive organisations have to ensure compliance through force since the people within them tend to resist them. Remunerative organisations get individuals to conform to their norms or requirements by paying them so to do. Normative organisations manufacture conformity out of the feelings of obligation and shared standards of their members who join them in order to pursue a goal that they believe to be morally worthwhile. Etzioni's communitarianism reproduces just this analysis of organisations at the macro-level of society. He tackles the functionalist concern with social order by means of a threefold classification. 'All forms of social order', he writes, 'draw to some extent on coercive means (such as police and jails), utilitarian means (economic incentives generated by public expenditures or subsidies), and normative means (appeals to values, moral education).'[74] Society thus appears to be akin to other organisations, notably in being preoccupied with its own maintenance, that is, with social control. Communitarianism adds to this broad functionalism an explicit commitment to certain modes of social control. Although Etzioni believes a good social order will balance the coercive, utilitarian, and normative, he argues that to achieve such a balance today we have to pay more attention to the normative. Interestingly this argument reproduces themes that emerged in his response to the effusion of neoclassical economics, much as the new institutionalism flourished as a response to rational-choice theory. Etzioni's socio-economics restates his general analysis of the problem of social order so as to point to social groups and communal determinants of behaviour that he believed were neglected by the individualism and stress on rational self-interest that char-acterised neoclassical economics. Competitive action occurs in a particular subsection of the totality of social relations, he argued, a subsection that is defined by contextual factors such as ethical norms, social ties, and state regulation.[75] Efficient and well-ordered societies require a normative dimension that has almost vanished, he implies, from contemporary society, and especially business, which is dominated instead by an excessively utilitarian ethos.

Once we recognise the ubiquity of various combinations of systems theory, functionalism, and social psychology within American sociology, we can highlight yet other ways in which communitarianism and the new institutionalism interweave with one another. For a start, some strands of the new institutionalism draw on much the same organisational theory we found in Etzioni's early work. While Selznick was developing a 'natural systems' approach to organisations, Herbert Simon was taking the systems metaphor in a more cybernetic direction; he conceived of organisations as akin to a computer program that was itself a simple version of how brains process information. Simon then collaborated with his student James March to examine how such processing works under conditions of bounded rationality. March collaborated, in turn, with Johan Olsen to develop the 'garbage-can model' of decision-making in organisations before then drawing on their work on bounded rationality to provide an influential statement of the new institutionalism.[76] We should not be surprised to discover, therefore, that when March and Olsen later contrast a rational-choice model with the one they prefer, the latter reproduces many themes associated with a cybernetic approach to organisations – limited informa-tion, routine, rule-following, cognitive heuristics.[77] Other strands of the new institutionalism also derive from the broad functionalism that informs communitarianism. Barrington Moore, in particular, situated much of his work in relation to a 'functional school' in anthropology that he associated with Sir Raymond Firth, a student and later a colleague of Malinowski at the London School of Economics, who opposed structural-functionalism from a broad functionalist perspective. When new institu-tionalists such as Theda Skocpol portray themselves as Moore's disciples while berating functionalism, we thus might take them to be opposed to structural-functionalism but not the broader functionalism that constituted such a powerful presence within modernist empiricism.[78]

Communitarianism and the new institutionalism also interweave with each other in that some communitarians draw directly on modernist empiri-cism within political science. Putnam studied, for example, with David Butler and Donald Stokes – the pair who introduced behavioural tech-niques into the Nuffield Election Studies – before completing his graduate studies at Yale University. His early work on Britain and Italy combined the types of comparison and classification so characteristic of modernist empiricism with attention to the types of data then being generated by behavioural techniques; it did so, moreover, to look at one of the behavioural topics – the beliefs of politicians – that modernist empiricists had began to explore prior to the behavioural revolution.[79] Putnam's work stands less as a way of developing or testing the grand theories of behaviouralism and more as a way of approaching the types of questions that have since come to define the new institutionalism, notably the links between social, institutional, and economic vibrancy. In this context, he concluded that the quality of civic life informs the effectiveness of democratic institutions. The quality of civic life acted, he suggested, as 'social capital', where 'social capital refers to the connections among individuals – social networks and the norms of reciprocity and trustworthiness that arise from them'.[80] He delivered a communitarian message, finally, by arguing that America was becoming an excessively individualistic society lacking the associational life and civic engagement that constituted the social capital that was so important for a well-ordered and prosperous democracy.

Social capital theory, communitarianism, and the new institutionalism inspire overlapping narratives that have arisen out of modernist empiricism. They postulate a type of organisation – a network or normative system – that embodies social capital, trust, and civic engagement, and that is characteristic of civil society or community. They present this type of organisation as both economically and morally superior to both the bureaucracies that characterise the state and the excessive individualism of the neoliberal market. And they thus prescribe associations and partnerships as the source of civic spirit, responsibility, mutuality, reciprocity, an entrepreneurial spirit, social order, and, it is tempting to add, any other good anybody might care to mention. New Labour draws on these overlapping narratives to define its policies and its ethic in large part because of the way in which they chime with its own concern to update social democracy in response to the New Right.

Conclusion

Accounts of New Labour's ideas typically compare them with reified ideologies – new liberalism, revisionist socialism, the New Right. We should ask what we gain from such comparisons. Of course, if we are familiar with an ideology but not New Labour, they might help to introduce us to New Labour's ideas, for any comparison of an unfamiliar object with a familiar one can help acquaint us with the former. Yet the comparisons purport not only to familiarise us with unfamiliar ideas, but also to provide a deeper understanding or explanation of New Labour's ideas. This they do not do. To find similarities between two sets of ideas is not to establish that they stand in an informative or explanatory relationship to one another. To explain New Labour's ideology, we have rather to trace a historical process in which its adherents inherited a set of beliefs and then modified them in response to salient issues. Although New Labour contains competing ideas that we should draw using fine brushes to evoke different traditions and different responses to varied problems, we might sketch the broad outline of this picture by depicting a tradition of social democracy that faced difficulties following the rise of the New Right. The role of the social democratic tradition and the New Right in this process explains the similarities of New Labour's ideas to those of Crosland and Thatcher. But, because we are trying to trace a historical process of change, rather than just discovering similarities, to assimilate New Labour's ideas too closely to earlier modernisers would be to neglect the impact of recent dilemmas, while to assimilate them too closely to the New Right would be to neglect the impact of the tradition of social democracy.

Much energy has been spent debating whether or not New Labour remains truly social democratic. This debate provides a setting in which commentators can commend or oppose New Labour but it has little other value. Contributors to the debate propound definitions of social democracy, exhibiting different degrees of historical sophistication, before then comparing New Labour with these definitions. But the results of their comparisons tell us only whether or not their view of New Labour fits under their definition of social democracy. Moreover, because ideologies are contingent and changing entities, their static definitions are arbitrary. Their definitions can express only their values or their account of what has characterised most social democrats up until now. Their definitions cannot capture the essence of social democracy or its legitimate historical trajectory, for there is no such thing. Because ideologies are contingent and changing entities, New Labour necessarily exhibits both continuities with its predecessors and changes from them. We can say that New Labour has adopted new policies in response to problems such as inflation, welfare dependency, and the changing structure of the working class, and the process of devising new policies has led it to modify the values of social democracy. Equally we can say that it has accepted a communitarian narrative that instantiates a new ethic that has required it to devise new policies. Of course, we can define ethical concepts at a level of abstraction such that they embrace the values espoused by both earlier social democrats and New Labour; we can refer abstractly to social justice, citizenship, and community. Even so, the fact remains that New Labour has transformed the content of these ethical concepts. The notions of 'choice and responsibility' espoused by New Labour are not implicit in the tradition of social democracy in the way Jack Straw, the former Home Secretary, has suggested.[81] Rather, New Labour brings a greater concern with choice to the ideal of social justice, a greater concern with duty to the concept of citizenship, and a greater concern with competition to the ideal of community. It does so, moreover, in part because of its overlap with, and debt to, communitarianism, which intersects with the new institutionalism as two contemporary descendants of modernist empiricism. In so far as an interpretive approach stands in contrast to modernist empiricism, therefore, we might expect it to prompt ethical positions somewhat at odds with those of New Labour. Chapter 6 will explore this expectation in greater detail.

4 The welfare state

Introduction

The previous two chapters used an interpretive approach to explore the traditions and problems that inform New Labour's ideas. All too often political scientists assume that interpretive approaches aim solely at an understanding of ideas as opposed to an explanation of actions and practices. In their view, interpretation enables us to understand the meanings that bubble up on the surface of politics, but, if we want to explain these bubbles, we need to invoke the deeper currents of interests, economic forces, or institutions. This view implies that interests, economic forces, or institutions are given, objective facts as opposed to subjective beliefs. Typically it also equates subjective beliefs solely with values and identities. I have argued, in contrast, that interests, economic forces, and institutions can influence actions only by way of people's beliefs about them, for all of our experiences are constructed in part by our prior theories. When people act on interests or institutional norms, they still act on their beliefs; it is just that the relevant beliefs are those they hold about their interests or institutional norms rather than about values or identities. Any adequate explanation of people's actions has to invoke their beliefs even if only implicitly. An interpretive study provides us, in other words, with an explanation – as well as an understanding – of the relevant actions and practices. When we point to the traditions and problems against the background of which people formed their beliefs, we explain why they hold the beliefs they do, and when we unpack people's beliefs and desires, we explain their actions and the practices to which these actions give rise.

The foregoing interpretation of New Labour represents not only an attempt to chart some of the sources of its ideas but also the beginnings of an explanation of its practice. Although interpretive studies often have explanatory intent, we should not assume that the ideas governments express always correspond to their practice. Gaps arise between the two because politicians dissemble and because their actions typically have unintended consequences.[1] When politicians dissemble, they express beliefs other than their actual beliefs. For example, they might say that new welfare policies have helped to bring down unemployment when they actually believe the fall in unemployment has been due to economic growth.[2] When interpretive studies seek to explain actions and practices, they thus have to try to unpack the actual beliefs of the appropriate actors as well as their expressed ones. Nonetheless, the question of dissembling need give us little concern because I have been describing what I take to be the actual beliefs of the elite of New Labour. Gaps between professed beliefs and actual practice can also arise because governments have limited control over how people implement and respond to their policies. For example, the fact that government policies create an opportunity for the unemployed does not guarantee that it will be adequately delivered to them or taken up by them. An interpretive study of the beliefs of New Labour can provide an explanation only of government policies, not of how these policies then operate, for to do the latter we would need also to study the beliefs of civil servants and citizens. The practice of interest to us is, in other words, that of the Labour governments.

Whereas the previous two chapters concentrated on the beliefs of the elite of New Labour, I want now to explore how these beliefs have been enacted in various policies, focusing on the welfare state and the economy. One reason for this focus is the widespread conviction within New Labour that social fragmentation and economic decline are the two main issues confronting Britain today.[3] Another reason is that the welfare state and the economy are the two areas of policy that are of most importance for alternative accounts of New Labour.

What is New Labour?

Before we examine government policy, we might usefully compare the broad contours of the preceding account of New Labour with the main alternatives.[4] I have portrayed New Labour as a social democratic response to issues made prominent by the New Right, where its conceptions of these issues, and its responses to them, have been influenced by new institutionalism and communitarianism. New Labour follows the tradition of social democracy in asserting a social concept of the individual against what it regards as the excessive individualism of neoliberals. It draws on the tradition of social democracy and communitarianism to argue that recognition of our social nature is a prerequisite of resolving the social fragmentation that now besets us. And it draws on the tradition of social democracy and new institutionalism to argue that recognition of our social nature will lead, in addition, to increased economic vitality and prosperity. Although the tradition of social democracy provides an important context for New Labour, the issues that New Labour seeks to resolve are ones first highlighted by the New Right's diagnosis of the ills of the Keynesian welfare state. The New Right prompted New Labour to offer a parallel diagnosis of the failings of its own past, although it then did so in terms drawn from communitarianism and new institutionalism. Old Labour is accused here, as communitarianism suggests, of falling prey to a rights-based culture that neglected individual responsibility. And it is associated, as new institutionalism suggests, with inflexible hierarchies, when networks and partnerships allegedly are far better suited to meet the demands of the new economy. New Labour holds out a vision of a welfare state that, first, requires individuals to fulfil their duties in return for receiving their rights and, second, delivers these rights through networks based on relations of trust.

One alternative account understands New Labour as a capitulation to the New Right. This account often draws on rational-choice theories of party competition. It is particularly common among political scientists who focus on economic policy, as we shall see in the next chapter.[5] The argument, in brief, is that political parties, at least within two-party systems, tend towards a bipartisan convergence; each adopts those practices and policies that have enhanced the electoral performance of the other. So, as this tendency would suggest, New Labour has adopted the policies of the New Right in an attempt to accommodate itself to the preferences of the electorate. An interpretive approach suggests that because New Labour often has been responding to issues made salient by the New Right, there are indeed overlaps between their respective worldviews. They overlap, for example, in rejecting the bureaucratic hierarchies and rights-based culture that they associate with Old Labour. Perhaps the most significant similarity is, however, the way New Labour conceives of the global economy, at least implicitly, as a competitive setting that renders economic efficiency a prerequisite for almost everything else. When institutionalists invoke costs of learning to explain the persistence of inefficient institutions, or when New Labour represents flexible labour markets and welfare reform as economic imperatives of the global economy, they tacitly accept the neoliberal idea of a universal, unavoidable, and tyrannical economic rationality, a rationality that operates at the micro-level so as to create structural constraints to which we have no option but to bow. Yet, despite such overlaps, we should be wary of understanding New Labour as a capitulation to the New Right, or, for that matter, of describing the new institutionalism as a capitulation to neoliberalism. A recognisable gap separates New Labour from the New Right, and, if we interpret the former as a capitulation to the latter, we risk neglecting the constructed and contingent nature of social life in a way that would leave us few resources with which to explain this gap. The gap exists because even though New Labour and the New Right have conceived many of the problems confronting Britain in broadly similar terms and so adopted overlapping polices, they have done so against the background of competing traditions, the continuing influence of which has led to differences in their ideas and policies.

Another alternative account of New Labour understands it as a response to economic constraints on social democracy.[6] This account is particularly common among institutionalists and those who focus on the reform of the welfare state, as we shall in this chapter. The argument, in brief, is that globalisation, inflation, and the like constitute constraints on states, but these constraints still allow states to take various paths, and the path they take depends on their inherited institutions. New Labour thus illustrates how Britain and other social democracies represent a distinct world of welfare, a particular variety of capitalism, with a different trajectory from American neoliberalism. An interpretive approach suggests that because New Labour has responded to problems against the background of social democracy, it is indeed a development of this tradition in response to things such as globalisation and inflation. New Labour draws on the tradition of social democracy, for example, in its continuing emphasis on improving the lot of the poor through the welfare state. It also extends the shift in macro-economic thinking that occurred in the Party in the late 1970s when the goal of full employment was abandoned as part of a shift towards proto-monetarist policies. Yet, despite New Labour's debt to the tradition of social democracy, we should be wary of understanding it as a response to economic constraints on this tradition. Such an understanding appears to imply that the relevant constraints are given so that social democrats have no option but to respond to them in a limited set of ways. Interpretivists might argue, in contrast, that even if these constraints are real, they still influence the behaviour of political actors only if these actors hold appropriate beliefs about them. By using terms like 'dilemma' and 'issue', we draw attention to the fact that these constraints are not given as pure experiences; they are constructed in part against the background of particular theories. In doing so, we encourage questions about whether New Labour has understood them aright and what alternative responses to them might have been available.

If New Labour is neither a capitulation to the New Right nor a path-dependent development of social democracy, perhaps it really is a new, path-breaking political paradigm.[7] An interpretive approach suggests that there is something new about New Labour. It differs from earlier social democratic politics in having responded to at least partly novel issues such as the underclass. And it differs from earlier responses to these issues in being informed by the tradition of social democracy. Nonetheless, accounts of New Labour as a new paradigm typically rely on just that tendency towards objectification that bedevils so much political science. The very idea of a Third Way, for example, invokes capitalism and socialism as fixed and independent categories for, if they did not have given boundaries, we could not identify a Third Way that lay outside of them. An interpretive approach suggests, in contrast, that capitalism and socialism are diverse practices with neither true content nor fixed boundaries; they have also interacted with one another so as to influence each other's development.[8] An implicit objectification appears again within other accounts of New Labour as path-breaking or a new political paradigm since these accounts presuppose an objectified path or paradigm – a given trajectory or set of concepts and values – from which New Labour has departed.

The whole debate about New Labour's novelty is misconceived, like that over whether or not it remains authentically socialist, in large part because it embodies the objectification that characterises so much political science. These debates engross so many only because political science – and perhaps our political culture – has come to take for granted the objectification associated with the atomisation and classification of modernist empiricism. Once we fully recognise contingency and agency, we will allow that novelty and change are inherent, ubiquitous features of human life: we always confront slightly novel situations, and because traditions do not fix their own application, our responses to such situations are inevitably open-ended sites at which we modify and develop inherited traditions. New Labour is inevitably a novel development of tradition precisely because all political parties are perpetually remaking themselves as novel entities. The only appropriate questions are, therefore, those that concern the content, and possibly the extent, of such novelty. If political scientists address the different question of whether or not New Labour is new, they are being seduced by objectified concepts; they make sense of this latter question only by assuming, explicitly or implicitly, that New Labour might or might not have broken with a set of objectified norms, rules, values, or concepts that they mistakenly take to have been constitutive of the Party.

In what ways and for what reasons has the Labour Party remade itself? How has it responded to which issues against the background of what patterns of thought? While the broad contours of my account of New Labour overlap with several others, its specific focus on novel responses to issues made salient by the New Right brings to the fore New Labour's debt to new institutionalism and communitarianism. New Labour has combined these two strands of social science with ease in part because both of them arose out of modernist empiricism as it confronted behaviouralism and rational choice. Indeed, New Labour's debt to communitarianism not only overlaps with its debt to new institutionalism, it also reinforces the suspicion, discussed in the previous chapter, that New Labour deploys the phrase 'Third Way' to describe ideas that it already had adopted from other sources, for, while New Labour accepts much of the communitarian agenda, Anthony Giddens complains, 'strong communities, duties, obligations – this is the traditional stuff of conservatism, not socialism'.[9]

New Labour owes a debt to the contemporary descendants of a sweeping modernist empiricism. The very sweep of modernist empiricism means that in some contexts it is too broad a category to do much explanatory work. For example, we might disaggregate it into an old institutionalism in political science and a diffuse functionalism in sociology if we want to explain the development of certain strands within it. In other contexts, its wide sweep and the conceptual and temporal overlaps between its different strands are precisely what make it so useful. Its wide sweep certainly enables us better to grasp how and why communitarianism and new institutionalism coexist in the ideas and policies of New Labour. Communitarianism and new institutionalism alike embody two later developments of modernist empiricism. To begin, they embody the development that occurred when modernist empiricists began to associate themselves with mid-level theory as opposed to the grand theories of some behaviouralists. Robert Merton introduced the notion of mid-level theory to contrast his approach with structural-functionalism, while, at least in Britain, many political scientists began to contrast their approach with a positivism they associated with behaviouralism. Modernist empiricists argued that theory was applicable only in certain contexts or only to certain cases. They even defined their approach as historical on the grounds that it allowed for greater particularity than did behaviouralism, although, of course, they typically continued to disavow narratives in favour of atomisation and analysis as preludes to comparison and classification. In addition, communitarianism and new institutionalism embody a second development that occurred when these mid-level theorists confronted the challenge of rational-choice theory and other extensions of neoclassical economics. Amitai Etzioni extended his organisational theory into a critique of a society that had been led to an excessive individualism by neoclassical economics, while Peter Hall and others constructed the new institutionalism by combining similar strands of organisational theory with the comparative and historical social science of mid-level theorists. The descendants of modernist empiricism thus began to blur the question of whether social theories could aspire to universality with that of whether explanations of social phenomena should give priority to individuals or institutions. In more general terms, they associated their approach to social science with opposition to individualism and neoliberalism. They tied mid-level theorising to the suggestion that an excessive individualism fails to allow adequately for the role played within society by things such as community, civil associations, and networks. Much of their appeal to New Labour derives precisely from the suggestion that community, civil society, networks, and partnerships provide a better alternative to both the state action associated with Old Labour and the markets associated with the New Right.

The breadth of modernist empiricism is also useful in that it highlights the dominance within contemporary social science and public policy of certain modes of objectification as a basis of claims to expertise. All too often, modernist empiricists and their descendants dismiss the pretensions of behaviouralism and rational choice to offer a universal science of politics while remaining complacently unaware of the very similar tendency to objectification found in their faith in mid-level theorising. For a start, when they defend a focus on institutions against the micro-level theory of rational choice, they imply that we can treat institutions, at least to some degree, as given objects; after all, if we have to unpack institutions in terms of the actions of individuals, we cannot dismiss the micro-level concerns of rational-choice theory as rapidly as communitarians and new institutionalists seem to do – institutions might matter, but they would need to be understood in terms of some kind of micro-level theory. In addition, when modernist empiricists reject the grand theories of the behaviouralists in the name of history or the particular case, they rarely intend also to repudiate mid-level theories that rely on comparison and classification to reveal cross-temporal and cross-spatial correlations and regularities. When they objectify organisations, institutions, and the like, they typically seek mid-level theories that provide them with an alleged expertise that legitimises their recommendations for public policy.

We can explain much of New Labour's reform of the welfare state by appealing to the communitarianism and new institutionalism on which it has drawn to respond to issues highlighted by the New Right. On the one hand, communitarians and new institutionalists have been all too ready to suggest that they possess an expertise that can guide public policy. On the other, New Labour has been all too ready to accept this proffered expertise as a source of alternatives to the policies associated with Old Labour and the New Right. We have already seen in outline how this alliance has conceptualised the reform of the welfare state. New Labour wants the state to become an enabling partner that works through networks so as to tackle social exclusion and promote individual responsibility as well as guaranteeing rights. For a start, New Labour has sought to promote social inclusion and individual responsibility by altering the benefit and tax systems so as to make the state less of a 'safety net' and more of a 'springboard' that bounces people into work. As Mandelson and Liddle explain, New Labour wants a welfare state that is 'universal in its reach but no longer uniform in what it offers', a welfare state that provides 'services that offer people a hand-up, not just cash payments to give them a hand-out', a welfare state that 'guarantee[s] access for all to a decent minimum quality of life and fair life chances, while permitting greater individual freedom of choice'.[10] In addition, New Labour has sought to establish joined-up governance by promoting networks based on trust and diplomacy, and it has sought to overcome problems of fragmentation and control by introducing new styles of partnership and regulation. As Mandelson and Liddle explain, New Labour wants to emphasise the importance of 'building a relationship of trust between purchasers and providers' and thereby of promoting the efficient and coordinated networks that are needed for a 'modernizing' transformation of 'the administrative machine'.[11]

The general direction of New Labour's reform of the welfare state embodies its beliefs that the state should be an enabling partner that promotes responsibility as well as guaranteeing rights and that it should do so through networks based on trust. Of course, government policies reflect other beliefs, notably those concerning what is and is not politically feasible and those about short-term considerations. Equally, however, these other beliefs themselves are not simply given; rather, they are informed by a tradition of social democracy, issues raised by the New Right, and communitarianism and new institutionalism. In what follows, I thus will consider only how the general direction of welfare reform relates to two aspects of my account of New Labour. First, New Labour has a distinctive public philosophy that explains its policies towards the welfare state and the delivery of public services. Second, this public philosophy draws on communitarianism and new institutionalism, so it differs in crucial respects from those associated with Old Labour and the New Right.

Welfare to work

New Labour has modified the Party's traditional ideas about welfare so as to promote a vision of the state as an enabling partner that promotes responsibility and social inclusion. The New Right highlighted issues associated with an underclass and spiralling public expenditure, arguing that these required that we 'roll back the state'. New Labour accepts that these sorts of issues bedevil what it regards as the vision of Old Labour. Yet it argues that the New Right's attempts to roll back the state have eroded community values. On the one hand, New Labour marks a distinct shift within social democracy, a shift that owes a clear debt to the New Right's concerns about the underclass and individual responsibility. It complains that Old Labour turned the state into a paternalistic provider of universal benefits to passive recipients. Welfare policies reduced recipients 'to passive dependency instead of helping them to realise their full potential'.[12] On the other hand, New Labour does not seek to dismantle this state but rather to transform it into a vehicle for promoting individual responsibility through active intervention. Blair insists, 'the modern welfare state is not founded on a paternalistic government giving out more benefits but on an enabling government that through work and education helps people to help themselves'.[13] The state can best fulfil this enabling role, according to New Labour, if it cooperates with people in an allegedly new type of partnership; Blair evokes 'a new contract between citizen and state'.[14] This contract requires the enabling state to accept responsibility for providing suitable opportunities for all its citizens. It requires citizens in turn to accept a duty of utilising these opportunities. A government policy paper lists in more detail the duties of the government and citizens.[15] The duties of government include providing assistance in finding work, making work pay, and supporting those who are unable to work. The duties of citizens include seeking either training or work, taking up opportunities, being independent, saving for their retirement, and not engaging in welfare fraud. The duties of everyone include helping people to realise their full potential, promoting economic independence, and building a cohesive society.

This list of duties rightly suggests that New Labour places great emphasis on work. 'Work', Blair tells us, is 'the best form of welfare – the best way of funding people's needs and the best way of giving them a stake in society.'[16] The government takes work, as do communitarians, to be a leading tutor of responsibility, and, as do communitarians and new institutionalists, to be the solution to poverty. It believes that the welfare state should tackle social exclusion by bouncing people into work where they will learn responsibility and gain self-esteem as well as becoming able to support themselves. Thus, the government's flagship welfare reforms – the New Deals – are intended to move people from welfare to work. Under the New Deals, the government accepts the responsibility to create opportunities for work and training, while the citizen, if capable, must accept the reciprocal responsibility to seek and accept opportunities. As we saw, for example, the New Deal for Young People requires those aged between 18 and 24 to accept work, undertake full-time education or training, undertake voluntary work, or join an environmental task-force where they get little more than they would on benefit. When Gordon Brown introduced the New Deal he emphasised that it was 'something for something, not something for nothing', since 'there will be no option of simply staying at home on full benefit'.[17] Mind you, those who refuse jobs or fail to appear for work will have their benefit cut not indefinitely, but only for two weeks for a first offence and four weeks for later ones. The state also provides employers with a subsidy of £60 a week for each worker they recruit through the New Deal as well as a grant to provide New Deal employees with training towards a recognised qualification. In addition, each young person who registers for a New Deal scheme gets assigned to a personal adviser who can give them expert advice on things such as training programmes and searching for jobs and who can provide support to ease their transition into working life after they leave the scheme. A similar New Deal scheme targets the long-term unemployed – people aged over 25 who have been out of work for more than two years. If they fail to find a job in six months, they must choose between subsidised employment, with the government paying a small amount to employers for up to six months for each worker they recruit from this group, or full-time vocational training for a year.

Of the total planned expenditure on New Deals, 73 per cent was allocated to that for young people, and a further 13 per cent was allocated to that for the long-term unemployed.[18] Yet, while these two compulsory schemes thus have received most resources, there are also voluntary schemes for lone parents, the disabled, and others. The scheme for lone parents mainly targets those whose children are of school-age although it is also available to those with younger children. Lone parents who sign up to the New Deal receive information and support from personal advisers, and they can benefit from expanded child-care services. Their sole duty is to attend a biannual interview to discuss their employment prospects. The New Deal for the disabled provides them with personal support and expertise from an adviser, while requiring them to take a reformed 'All Works Test': whereas the old incapacity test used to focus on what disabled people could not do, the reformed one is supposed to identify their skills and so training and work that is appropriate for them.[19] Yet another New Deal scheme targets older claimants of benefits. It offers help to people who are aged over 50 and who have been out of work for more than six months. If they return to work, the government gives them a tax-free 'employment credit' on top of their wages. The scheme also offers training grants and special assistance to those who want to set up their own business. Finally, there is a New Deal for the partners of people who are claiming benefit. Although this scheme does not provide cash payments, it offers training programmes and advice about things such as searching for a job, interview technique, and the availability of benefits while in work. The government hopes it will reduce the number of households in which nobody has employment. Collectively all these New Deals now cover a majority of those who are neither employed nor in full-time education.

All new benefit claimants now enter a 'Single Gateway' that operates alongside the New Deals.[20] They receive an initial assessment during which they have to explain their plans. They then move on to one of the four options offered under the New Deal only if they still have not found work after four months. In the interim, they now pass through a new intensive Gateway; they have to attend every day during working hours to receive assistance with soft skills, including communication, personal appearance, and punctuality, and they get an adviser who helps them with an intensive job search. The Single Gateway packages a range of initiatives that attempt to make it easier for them to find work or training. In particular, it promotes single sources for access to personal advisers, information, and benefits in relation to work, training, education, housing, and tax credit. New Labour claims that it will make people more responsible for their economic independence by providing them with the information they need to become so. As with the New Deals, so here government policy has a punitive feature in that the state can withhold benefits until claimants participate satisfactorily in work-focused interviews. The Single Gateway further signals to citizens 'the linkage between rights and responsibilities'.[21]

The Single Gateway and the New Deal aim to reduce dependency by providing opportunities for people to work or train. The government also aims to ensure that employment pays by eradicating disincentives to work created by the tax and benefit system. Perhaps the most important measures reduce the burden of tax upon those who take low-paying jobs. The government has introduced a minimum wage and also a lower, ten-pence tax band. Families now pay no income tax if their weekly income is less than half the national male average earnings. Other measures seek to add to the financial benefits gained through being employed. The 1998 Budget introduced a new Working Families Tax Credit, which supplements earnings from paid employment with cash benefits so that every family with a full-time worker has a guaranteed minimum income of £190 a week, and a Childcare Tax Credit, which allows working parents who earn up to £20,000 a year to offset up to 70 per cent of the costs of childcare up to a ceiling of £100 a week for one child or £150 for two or more children.[22]

The latter tax reforms rightly suggest that New Labour has adopted some of the communitarian focus on the family as well as its overriding stress on work. The government usually defends its support of families on the grounds that they provide a bulwark against poverty or social exclusion. But Blair also believes, 'we can not be morally neutral about the family' as 'it is in the family that we first learn to negotiate the boundaries of acceptable conduct and to learn that we have responsibilities'.[23] The government has thus introduced other policies to benefit families, especially those with children. Child benefit is, for example, one of the very few benefits to have risen above the rate of inflation. In the 1998 Budget, Brown raised child benefit for the first child from £11.45 a week to £14.40. In the 1999 Budget, he again increased the rate for the first child, this time to £15 a week, while also raising the rate for the second child from £9.60 to £10 a week. Then in 2001 he introduced an additional Baby Tax Credit for families with a child born in any given tax year. Likewise, the Employment Relations Act increased maternity leave for all employees from 14 to 18 weeks, and it established a statutory right to three months of parental leave for all employees.

New Labour has adopted a range of policies targeted at the underclass in an effort to bounce them back into work. These policies are meant not only to encourage individual responsibility but also to promote social inclusion and thus tackle poverty as it is conceptualised by many communitarians and institutionalists. Arguably, then, we should understand the government's welfare-to-work policies not simply as a way of promoting labour market attachment, but rather as one piece in a larger jigsaw of policies that tackle what it believes to be the root causes of unemployment, poverty, and other such ills.[24] No doubt getting welfare recipients into work quickly remains a priority, especially for those who already have the skills they need to find a job. As we have seen, for example, the intensive Gateway period emphasises soft skills such as personal appearance and punctuality rather than long-term education and training. Nonetheless, New Labour also promotes policies designed to improve human capital, that is, to improve people's skills so that they can stay in work and make more of their lives. These latter policies include the supply-side economic policies that we will consider in the next chapter, and a range of social and educational policies that tackle so-called wicked issues, policies such as trust funds for children in care, the National Childcare Strategy, and Individual Learning Accounts.

In December 1997, the government created the Social Exclusion Unit (SEU) within the Cabinet Office to coordinate policies that tackle network poverty across a range of departments and agencies. While the SEU covers only England, the Scottish Office has set up a Social Exclusion Team, which places greater emphasis than does its English counterpart on rural areas, and Wales and Northern Ireland now have similar strategies for the renewal of excluded communities. The SEU concentrated initially on what the government believes are the four main social problems: drugs, homelessness, truancy, and the worst housing estates. New Labour hopes that by tackling these problem areas the SEU will enhance people's life skills and thereby enable them to get and retain jobs. The government has also created Employment Zones in an attempt to tackle the wicked issues that it believes perpetuate social exclusion in the particular form of unemployment. These Zones provide local areas with greater flexibility to deal with specific problems than does the New Deal. They allow local partnerships to put together diverse funding packages to provide people with 'personal job accounts' to support diverse types of employment, volunteering, and training. The SEU and Employment Zones are intended to complement the New Deal and the Single Gateway as means of tackling unemployment and social exclusion in the context of New Labour's rejection of demand-management as a technique for promoting full employment.

While New Labour places great emphasis on welfare-to-work programmes, it has adopted broadly similar policies in other areas of social security, including, for example, pensions. As Blair says, 'we believe that those who can save for their retirement have the responsibility to do so, and that the State must provide effective security for those who cannot'.[25] During a long process of consultation, Frank Field outlined plans for 'stakeholder pensions', while Mandelson and Liddle proposed mutual pension funds.[26] Legislation to create stakeholder pensions was then included in the Welfare Reform and Pensions Bill of 1999. Field wanted to retain the Basic Pension, but to scrap the State Earnings-Related Pension (SERPS) in favour of a system in which all people in work would be compelled to contribute to second pensions organised by the private sector. In fact, the government drew back from compulsion. It provides all pensioners with a guaranteed minimum income that will be updated regularly in line with earnings, though not with inflation, and it also intends to be pro-active in encouraging pensioners to take up Income Support if they are entitled to it. Then it will replace SERPS with a new state-sponsored second pension for those earning less than £9,000 a year so that their income apparently will be doubled, while, for those earning between £9,000 and £18,000, it will introduce extra rebates on National Insurance as an inducement to join funded second pension schemes. Stakeholder pensions will be available to workers whose employers do not provide occupational pensions.

Although pension reform is a response to demographic and financial dilemmas, the scheme for stakeholder pensions embodies the public philosophy discussed earlier. For a start, stakeholder pensions point towards a new conception of the relationship between rights and responsibilities. They are meant to encourage people to take more responsibility for their retirement by offering provision on top of the limited state pension, and they are meant to promote mutuality since members retain any profits as either lower premiums or higher pensions. They are supposed to promote, in Field's words, 'a new welfare era where collective provision is achieved through individualised ownership and effort'.[27] In addition, the state again acts as an enabling partner. It establishes and regulates a framework within which stakeholder pensions operate, and it does so in order to enable individuals to provide for their own retirement. Within this framework, it sets standards that the operators of stakeholder pensions have to meet. Stakeholder pensions must have an 'approved governance structure' that acts in the interests of members: the Welfare Reform and Pensions Bill requires funds to be established within existing trust law and to be run by a board of trustees, while allowing for other governance structures to be approved in the future. Finally, the government hopes that stakeholder pensions will promote social inclusion. Hence the funds must accept low minimum contributions and allow members to stop and restart contributions without any penalty. These regulations aim to ensure that everyone can join a fund: people in low paid, part-time, or irregular work – many of whom are excluded from existing pension schemes – are supposed to have better opportunities to save for retirement. Field even suggests that these new pensions might act as agents of social cohesion since 'they are inclusive bodies, thriving on participation, co-operation and partnership'.[28]

The welfare state includes, of course, not just social security but also health, education, housing, and personal care. When New Labour talks about welfare reform, however, it typically refers almost exclusively to social security. Its targets are the benefits paid to adults who for one reason or another are not in paid work or do not have sufficient incomes in their retirement. It does not appear to regard benefits paid to people in work as anything like so problematic, and it has left intact the principle of universal provision to health and education. We should not assume, though, that New Labour believes these other areas of the welfare state operate satisfactorily. It is just that the perceived problems with them lie with the delivery of services more than their content. The Party pledged in its election manifesto of 1997, for example, to abolish the internal market in the National Health Service (NHS) and to do more to ensure that money was spent on patients not bureaucracy.

Service delivery

Just as New Labour has reformed social security in ways that reflect its debt to a communitarian emphasis on responsibility and work and an institutionalist one on network poverty and social inclusion, so it has reformed the welfare state as a whole, including health and education, in ways that reflect its debt to an institutionalist faith in the benefits of networks and a communitarian one in the voluntary sector and civil society. The SEU and Employment Zones provide examples of a widespread quest for networks. They are meant to promote joined-up policies and thereby tackle wicked problems in the round. Similarly, stakeholder pensions provide an example of the widespread quest for civil society. They are meant to encourage both mutuality and partnerships with the voluntary and private sectors. All of these policies illustrate how the government has acted on the idea, expressed here by Field, that 'much of today's welfare ills' arose from 'the replacement of those [nineteenth-century] self-governing guilds and societies by top-down state provision'.[29]

The New Right, too, challenged top-down provision, arguing that it was excessively bureaucratic and so both inefficient and antagonistic to individual freedom. Conservative governments attempted to make public services more efficient through privatisation, marketisation, and the new public management (NPM). They promoted a concept of the citizen as a consumer who should be free to choose from an array of services. New Labour has responded to the dilemma of bureaucratic inefficiency, in contrast, by attempting to open-up established hierarchies so as to create a variety of networks governed by relations of trust. The government praises networks for offering a flexible and effective alternative to both the bureaucracy associated with Old Labour and the markets favoured by the New Right. New Labour tries to distance itself from Old Labour by saying, 'we must not assume that everything government does has to be delivered by the public sector', while also criticising New Right policies such as Compulsory Competitive Tendering (CCT) for over-emphasising the private sector and so improving efficiency, when they did so at all, only at the expense of quality.[30]

Officially, the Labour governments have replaced market testing and CCT with the idea of Best Value in government services. The Best Value initiative reviewed all central and local government services so as to identify the most appropriate supplier in each case.[31] Best Value suppliers were defined as those that delivered the highest quality services in relation to costs thereby balancing efficiency with quality. Unlike CCT, Best Value does not necessarily require privatisation or competitive tendering of services, but only that 'competition will be considered seriously as an option in every case'.[32] New Labour insists that the choice of deliverer should depend on which sector provides a particular service with most efficiency and quality. 'Services should be provided through the sector best placed to provide those services most effectively', where 'this can be the public, private or voluntary sector, or partnerships between these sectors'.[33]

New Labour believes that many areas of the public sector are not amenable to competitive markets. One clear example is the NHS where the government is abolishing the internal market. New Labour criticises the internal market on a number of grounds. Most importantly, it claims that the internal market fragmented health services, creating thousands of organisations, such as Health Authorities, General Practitioner Fundholders, and NHS Trusts, which often were in competition with one another when their activities should have been coordinated more closely.[34] In addition, it suggests that the internal market forced organisations to compete even when cooperation was more appropriate; organisations were unwilling to share principles of best practice for fear of losing competitive advantage.[35] Finally, the government believes that the internal market generated new tiers of bureaucracy, raised administrative costs, distorted performance by measuring purchasing efficiency rather than service quality, and created instability through short-term contracts that in some instances were agreed only on a day-to-day basis. Far from promoting quality and efficiency, marketisation often undermined standards of service.

Although New Labour believes that marketisation is often inappropriate in the public sector, it criticises 'one-size fits all' services for stifling innovation and putting the needs of institutions ahead of those of the users of services. It insists, 'there will be no return to the old centralised command and control systems of the 1970s'.[36] Indeed, New Labour has extended several of those initiatives of the New Right that sought to bring into the public services a greater business orientation and an increased focus on the customer. The government has continued the Next Steps programme with its shift of managerial responsibilities to agencies – which now employ almost 80 per cent of all civil servants – albeit with an allegedly greater emphasis on the improvement of the performance of agencies.[37] Within this context, the government has also maintained a range of initiatives that seek to extend private sector practices to the public sector. It has expanded the Public Sector Benchmarking Project (PSBP), which the Conservatives launched in 1996: the PSBP seeks to improve the public sector by developing principles of best practice, derived from a Business Excellence Model, for nine areas, including efficient use of resources, customer satisfaction, and effective policy-making.[38] Likewise, New Labour has persisted with the Charter Mark scheme as a way of encouraging improvement in the delivery of public services: Charter Marks reward public-sector organisations that focus on customers as indicated by their success in meeting criteria such as access, choice, fair treatment, and accessible and effective procedures for complaint and redress.[39] More generally, the government committed itself to market-testing and contracting-out when they offer best value in spite of having given a pre-election pledge to a moratorium on such practices for the duration of an independent review.

Few people would object to the idea that government should deliver services so as to ensure it gets best value. The difficult questions are obviously about how this is to be achieved. New Labour thinks that the answer lies principally with networks on the grounds that they are especially conducive to efficiency because, for example, 'by working together with other services, each organisation can make more effective use of its resources'.[40] New Labour characteristically promotes networks composed of several interdependent actors who cooperate to deliver public services. Although it accepts that both markets and flexible, customer-focused hierarchies have a place within the public sector, its primary commitments are to joined-up government and Public–Private Partnerships (PPPs).[41]

The search for joined-up government begins in Whitehall and Westminster. The Cabinet Office now houses a number of new units, such as the SEU, the purpose of which is to tackle issues that cut across the boundaries between departments. The Women's Unit and the Anti-Drugs Coordination Unit were established in 1997, and moved to the Cabinet Office in 1998, to coordinate activity on their respective topics. Although there are earlier precedents for such Units within the Cabinet Office, those of New Labour are more active and more open to participation by people from outside the civil service. What is more, the Performance and Innovation Unit was established in October 1998 with the specific task of promoting joined-up government throughout Whitehall. New Labour also pursues joined-up government by means of task forces, which are arguably the most distinctive feature of its style of governance for, during Blair's first hundred days alone, the government established over 40 task forces, advisory groups, and policy reviews.[42] These task forces, too, provide a way of bringing outsiders into Whitehall. Beyond Whitehall, the government has introduced various initiatives to create flexible frameworks for cooperation and to encourage departments and agencies to participate within them. The Invest to Save Budget (ISB) scheme provides extra funding, for example, to projects in which two or more public bodies collaborate to deliver more efficient services.[43] Typical ISB projects include 'one-stop shops' that give users access to multiple services at one location: the one-stop shop in Camden, London, provides a single location at which lone parents can deal with their Income Support, Child Support, Housing Benefit, and Council Tax Benefit. Similarly, the Single Gateway scheme provides, as we have seen, access at one location to services offered by the Benefits Agency, the Child Support Agency, the Employment Service, and the benefits departments of Local Authorities.[44] Sure Start and the Single Regeneration Budget are yet other examples of 'cross-cutting' initiatives that seek to transcend traditional departmental and administrative boundaries. The number of these initiatives appears to be set to rise yet further given that the government has created Integrated Service Teams to explore ways of improving collaboration between service providers.[45]

Local government and the NHS are major providers of welfare services. It is here that New Labour trumpets most loudly 'best value', which it associates with joined-up government as opposed to markets or the 'old culture of paternalism'.[46] Networks have superseded the internal market within the NHS. The government has created 'a new statutory duty for NHS Trusts to work in partnership with other NHS organisations' so that all the actors that are involved in the delivery of healthcare services – General Practitioners, NHS Trusts, and Local Authorities – work together to develop integrated systems of care based on Health Improvement Programmes.[47] The Health Improvement Programmes specify standards for healthcare that have been mutually agreed upon by the relevant actors in consultation with one another. Joined-up government and diplomacy have thus replaced markets and competitive contracts as the perceived means of promoting quality and efficiency within the NHS.

New Labour's advocacy of networks extends from joined-up government within the public sector to partnerships between public and private organisations. It actively encourages 'Partnership Networks' between local authorities and the private sector. Perhaps the most important links to the private sector arise, however, from the government's resurrection and expansion of Private Finance Initiatives (PFIs), or, as they are called now, PPPs. These schemes allow for the private sector investing in capital projects in the public sector and then leasing the new constructions back to the state. Under the Conservatives, PFIs often maintained a clear division between public organisations and private companies. Private companies planned, designed, and constructed buildings or roads and then sold them to the public-sector organisations that provided the relevant service. Under the Labour governments, PPPs have become a means of encouraging public and private organisations to form deeper partnerships that involve collaboration at all stages of a joint venture; the private sector brings management and expertise as well as finance. The overall scale of PPPs under New Labour is simply vast. During its first term in office, some 150 contracts were signed, covering four prisons, five hospitals, and 520 schools, and with a total value of over £12 billion.[48]

The government envisages individuals relating to one another through trust, negotiation, and agreement within networks, rather than through the competition and contracts of the market. We have already seen how various special units and task forces embrace 'outside experts, those who implement policy and those affected by it'.[49] The government also hopes its networks, especially those at the local level, will encompass front-line service providers and citizens. In the NHS, it has set up a National Taskforce on Staff Involvement, the membership of which includes nurses, doctors, and a hospital porter.[50] More generally, New Labour has modified the Citizen's Charter of earlier Conservative governments to establish Service First. The Service First charter programme encourages 'Quality Networks' composed of local groups, the members of which should come from all areas and levels of the public sector. They are intended to contribute to the development and dissemination of principles of best practice, the sharing of troubleshooting skills, and the building of new partnerships between appropriate organisations. The government thus aims to encourage public services to work together to ensure that services are effective and coordinated. This shift from the Citizen's Charter to Service First appears even more significant when we locate it alongside the introduction of Public Service Agreements (PSAs).[51] PSAs publish and demand measurable improvements from all central government departments and agencies.[52] Each organisation specifies its general aims and objectives, the resources available to it, its performance targets, and information about how it intends to increase its operational efficiency.

Citizens participate in this brave new world of networks not only as 'clients' but also through increased avenues for consultation and involvement in the planning and delivery of services. A government document tells us that 'people should have a say in what services they get and how they are delivered'; indeed, public services are more or less required to 'consult and involve' present and potential users.[53] The government recommends a wide array of methods for meeting this requirement; these include interviews, focus groups, citizen juries, and citizen panels. Citizen juries consist of a small number of lay people who scrutinise specific proposals; they hear evidence from experts and interested parties over several days and then report their conclusions. Citizen panels consist of a larger representative sample of the population; they discuss specific proposals and also develop broader ideas about future services. The flagship citizen panel in Kirklees, West Yorkshire, consists, for example, of 1,000 local residents who three times a year receive surveys from the local authority and the local health authority. New Labour has even established an omnibus People's Panel made up of 5,000 members, representing a cross-section of the population, who are consulted about all sorts of issues, including, to date, transport, local democracy, new technology, and care in the community.

New Labour believes that high-quality public services are best achieved through cooperative networks based on negotiation and trust. Blair describes such trust as 'the recognition of a mutual purpose for which we work together and in which we all benefit'.[54] The government promotes trust between organisations through the Quality Networks programme: organisations provide information about their practices to one another so as to facilitate better cooperation. It promotes trust within organisations through 'management within boundaries': individual responsibility and discretion increasingly will replace hierarchical structures so that individuals are trusted to make decisions and implement policy without being constrained by strict procedures. And it promotes trust between organisations and individuals through Service First: citizens rely on organisations to provide appropriate services, and organisations rely on citizens to use these services appropriately. Trust arises, in turn, according to New Labour, from a balance between rights and responsibilities. The Service First programme is explicitly based on a partnership between users and providers in which both parties have rights and responsibilities. The rights of the users include those to clear information about what is on offer, well-defined procedures for complaint, and fair treatment. Their responsibilities include extending courtesy to staff and promptly providing accurate information when asked for it.

Although the promotion of networks allows New Labour to embrace novel styles of service delivery, it also fragments parts of the public sector, leaving the state with fewer means of direct control. The government thus can appear janus-faced in its simultaneous promotion of local initiatives and reassertion of central control through inspection and regulation. Alongside the creation of decentralised Action Zones for Health and Education, for example, we have new organisations designed to impose the will of the centre; these include the National Institute for Clinical Excellence (NICE) and the Commission for Health Improvement, the Office for Standards in Education and the hit-squads that take over failing schools. More generally, the remit of the Regulatory Impact Unit, formerly known as the Better Regulation Taskforce, has been extended from the private to the public sector. It introduced, as part of the wider initiative to 'modernise government', a programme of 'public sector regulatory efficiency' that applied the principles that the government takes to be constitutive of good regulation – namely, transparency, accountability, targeting, consistency, and proportionality – to domains such as healthcare, education, social services, and the police. New Labour seeks to retain central control not only through inspection and regulation, but also, when it is deemed necessary, through direct intervention. Here the government has developed various schemes of 'earned autonomy' that distinguish 'green' and 'red' local authorities or agencies. The 'green' organisations are given increased powers and even allowed to test new ways of delivering services. When regulatory agencies discover bad 'red' ones, however, these can be subject to various types of government intervention, including takeovers, in order to remedy their failings.

Even as New Labour seeks to undercut old hierarchies in which the state operates through direct commands, so it has adopted a regime of regulation to reassert the centre's control of public services in an attempt to guarantee standards of quality and efficiency. This new regime of inspection and regulation once again reveals the government's faith in networks. The regulators are themselves meant to operate through networks characterised by diplomacy and trust, or at least they are meant to do so unless direct intervention is deemed necessary. In personal care, for example, the government looks to networks to counter a fragmented system within which regulation had been 'piecemeal' and 'divided'.[55] New regional Commissions for Care Standards (CCSs) will regulate care services in line with national standards developed by the government in consultation with relevant groups and individuals.[56] The CCSs will be independent of government and composed of representatives from local government, health authorities, service providers, and service users. A General Social Care Council will regulate the training of social workers, help to set standards of good conduct, and recommend principles of best practice for all who work in social services.[57]

A similar invocation of networks characterises New Labour's regime of regulation and inspection in the NHS. The government hopes to overcome problems of fragmentation and steering, including 'unacceptable variations' in the standards of health service, by building networks in which the deliverers of services can compare their performance and share principles of best practice.[58] NICE will regulate frontline healthcare.[59] It will aim to ensure high and consistent standards of clinical practice throughout the NHS by drawing on a partnership of health professionals, academics, economists, and representatives of patients, and by forming networks alongside NHS organisations at all levels, including local providers of care, regional bodies, and national groups such as professional associations and the Department of Health. NICE will operate alongside a range of regulatory procedures. For a start, a National Framework for Assessing Performance, covering all organisations within the NHS, will assess the quality of services against the criteria of improvement of health, fair access, effective delivery of appropriate care, efficiency, the experiences of patients and carers, and outcomes for health.[60] Each of these criteria has detailed performance indicators: for example, fair access refers to the socio-economic and demographic characteristics of patients, the mean time from diagnosis to operation, and the patients' evaluations of their experiences. National Service Frameworks will also specify national standards for specific types of service: for example, the Calman-Hine Cancer Service Framework defines the arrangements that are deemed appropriate to high quality and comprehensive cancer care.[61] In addition, a Commission for Health Improvement will provide independent scrutiny of healthcare providers such as NHS Trusts.[62] It will monitor the implementation of the National Service Frameworks and the guidance provided by NICE. It will have the power to investigate and to intervene when performance is deemed unsatisfactory. Finally, the government will introduce an annual National Survey of Patient and User Experience to enable NHS organisations to measure their performance against the aspirations and experiences of patients, to compare their performance with that of other organisations, and to identify trends in performance over time.[63] The Survey will address issues such as waiting times, ease of access to services, the availability and clarity of information, the privacy and dignity of patient care, and the courtesy and helpfulness of staff. The outcome of each survey will be published, and NHS organisations will be required to take action to rectify any problems indicated by the results.

Conclusion

New Labour has a distinctive public philosophy that is indebted to both communitarianism and new institutionalism. In this chapter, we have seen how this public philosophy explains the broad contours of its welfare policies. New Labour seeks to tackle social exclusion and network poverty. It does so following communitarianism by promoting individual responsibility especially in relation to work and the family. And it does so following new institutionalism by taking on the role of an enabling partner within networks based on trust. New Labour's welfare reforms also illustrate how its new policies entail changes to social democratic values such as social justice, citizenship, and community. In the case of social justice, for example, to give skills to the poor – whether these be soft skills or not – is to do nothing to alter the fact that the market then determines the value of these skills; it is to do nothing to change the patterns of social justice produced by the market as opposed to enabling the excluded to be included within these patterns.

How should we judge New Labour's welfare policies? One possibility is to examine how they measure up against the Party's values. As we have seen, though, these values are not as clear as they might be. At times New Labour defends values such as opportunity and responsibility that derive in part from communitarianism. These values do indeed appear to inform many of its welfare policies. At other times New Labour identifies with elder social democratic ideals of equality and citizenship. Not surprisingly its policies seem far less redolent of these values. Thus, critics from within and without the Party often emphasise the punitive elements of the New Deal schemes, viewing them mainly as a withdrawal of benefits, and they then suggest that such withholding of state assistance sits awkwardly alongside the Party's commitment to social justice. These critics argue that even if the New Deals offer some people a way out of poverty, they are unacceptably harsh for others, and even if they help to reduce future poverty, the most vulnerable groups in society still need traditional cash benefits to alleviate their poverty right now.[64] Other critics argue, similarly, that the government's overwhelming stress on paid employment both overlooks the value of unpaid work such as parenting and fails to address inequalities among the working population.[65]

Another way to judge New Labour's policies is in terms of their effectiveness in meeting their stated objectives. Official statistics provide some evidence of a genuine reduction in the level of unemployment. It is unclear, however, whether this is due to the welfare reforms or simply a by-product of an economic boom. Doubts also surround the ability of the reforms to sustain any reduction for which they might be responsible. Critics complain that the New Deals emphasise cosmetic, short-term measures: because the subsidies they provide are only temporary, typically lasting for two years, we might expect that many of those involved will fail to find permanent employment once the subsidy ends. In addition, critics point to problems that beset all such schemes of subsidised employment: there are problems of displacement – subsidised workers merely taking jobs that otherwise would have gone to others – and of deadweight effects – the state gives unnecessary financial assistance to people who would have found employment anyway. Several critics argue, in more general terms, that long-term reductions in unemployment depend on the creation of permanent jobs, rather than on motivating or compelling people to work.[66]

Other doubts concern the effectiveness of New Labour's approach to the delivery of public services. For a start, the government encourages competition where appropriate while remaining vague about the nature of suitable competition and the circumstances in which it is appropriate, and some critics take this vagueness as evidence that the practice of Best Value barely differs from CCT, or even that Best Value represents an extensive privatisation agenda.[67] Furthermore, although networks are intended to promote a collaborative, joined-up approach to the delivery of services, they themselves can be arenas of conflict. Problems can arise, for instance, if different actors in the local partnerships that deliver health-care want to commission services contrary to each other's priorities.[68] While a greater role for the state might help to resolve such conflicts, New Labour's regime of regulation is itself a site of significant tensions. The government's aim of devolving powers to the local providers of services surely conflicts with the imposition of centrally defined targets and standards.[69] Centrally defined targets also can erode partnership in so far as they force local providers to attend to the wishes of government rather than the needs of their communities. In some cases the heavy-hand of the centre might seriously undermine the possibility of collaborative networks. Finally, some critics claim that New Labour's regime of regulation damages efficiency and effectiveness because it imposes extra costs and bureaucratic constraints.[70] Beneath many of these tensions, there lurk issues of accountability; whereas hierarchical models of service delivery generally contain vertical decision-making structures that have clear lines of accountability, networks typically contain more horizontal links that can blur lines of responsibility.[71]

Judgements about the effectiveness of New Labour's welfare policies often rely in part upon other judgements about its economic policies. Any welfare-to-work programme surely requires, for example, that the economy is robust enough to provide jobs to those who pass through it. Some communitarians thus argue that the state should combine welfare-to-work schemes with a right to work or at least with policies that manage economic demand, especially within particular regions, so as to generate appropriate jobs. New Labour appears, in contrast, to place its faith in supply-side economic policies. Of course, it follows the new institutionalism in suggesting that its reform of the welfare state will foster the networks, skills, initiative, and dynamism that allegedly are so important for economic success today. 'Globalisation means', according to Blair, 'that we will only succeed economically if we create a society of opportunity for all': the Third Way is, then, a 'modernised social democracy' that seeks to create such a society by managing change in a way that 'overcomes insecurity and liberates people, equipping them to survive and prosper in this new world'.[72] Equally, however, New Labour suggests that its economic policies will ensure the macro-economic stability and supply-side vigour needed to create permanent jobs and to fund welfare programmes.

5   The economy

Introduction

New Labour's welfare reforms are supposed to improve Britain's competitiveness and prosperity as well as to tackle social exclusion. Just as
communitarians and new institutionalists argue that social cohesion and
networks lead to more committed and dynamic companies that are capable
of a stronger and more competitive performance, so New Labour evokes
a society in which morally empowered individuals promote social cohesion and so an economically vibrant nation. However, the main policies
by which New Labour seeks to improve the country's competitiveness and
prosperity are, of course, economic ones. As we saw in the last chapter,
some political scientists assimilate these economic policies to those of the
New Right. They deploy rational-choice theories of party competition to
argue that New Labour has pursued a politics of catch-up in which it has
adopted the economic policies of the New Right in order to compete with
the electoral successes of the Conservatives. An interpretive approach
suggests, in contrast, that we should explain New Labour's economic
policies as a product of a contingent process in which it has modified the
tradition of social democracy in response to issues highlighted by the New
Right, where its response to these issues reflects the influence upon it of
communitarianism and new institutionalism.

The economic policies of New Labour enact the belief that we live in new
times that apparently require social democrats to update the means by
which they seek to realise their ideals. In this view, the increased mobility
of capital and the rise of new technologies have undermined not just the
hierarchic welfare state but nationalisation, planning, and Keynesianism:
because capital is increasingly mobile, and because demand increasingly
depends on factors beyond a state's borders, governments no longer can
manage demand; instead, they must ensure that the economy is attractive
to international investors. Following the new institutionalists, New Labour
suggests that these new times require post-Fordist flexibility based on
skills, innovation, partnership, and networks. Governments today should
act, in this view, both to create a stable macro-economic environment and

to revitalise the supply-side of the economy through the promotion of training and networks.

After globalisation

Historically, many social democrats believed in Keynesian demand-management as a means of securing nigh-on full employment. In their view, government intervention through fiscal policy and public spending could stimulate demand and thereby create jobs and generate economic growth. During the 1970s, Keynesian policies became associated with chronic inflation and even with rising unemployment and stagnant growth. While doubts about Keynesian policies surfaced in the Labour Party, its leaders still generally believed in a trade-off between unemployment and inflation such that the state should address the former by stimulating demand even if doing so created a bit of inflation. Gordon Brown appealed to Keynesian ideas in 1984 when he praised the American and French governments for giving greater priority to employment than to low inflation, and again in 1986 when he complained, 'the [Conservative] Government refuse to spend enough money' in spite of the 'employment benefits' of so doing.[1] The New Right, in contrast, espoused a provocative critique of Keynesianism through its use of monetarist ideas. The New Right argued that economic growth depended less on high rates of employment and demand than it did on stable economic conditions characterised by low levels of inflation. The key to stability and low inflation lay, they suggested, in tight regulation of the money supply, with the key monetary lever being interest rates rather than taxation or public expenditure. Stability also required, they added, that the state conduct monetary policy in accord with rules, rather than discretion, so as to maintain credibility. Finally, the faith of the New Right in the market led to a widespread belief that once the state ensured stability, it needed only to withdraw from the economy for the market to work its magic and bring prosperity and growth; left to its own devices, the market would secure an efficient supply-side and so enable British industry to compete successfully in the global economy. Demand management thus gave way to deregulation of the supply-side, in the particular forms of labour market reforms and tax cuts for industry, which were supposed to reduce the costs of production and thereby generate an internationally competitive economy.

The failure of the economic policies of the French socialist government led by François Mitterand appeared in the eyes of many in the Labour Party dramatically to mark the end of any lingering Keynesian aspirations. It seemed that Keynesian policies could not survive the responses they elicited from finance capital, which had become increasingly mobile thereby undermining the viability of the protectionist and exchange control measures that once might have provided some insulation from such responses. Today New Labour accepts that many of the problems highlighted by the

New Right did indeed beset Keynesianism. Nonetheless, New Labour has conceived and addressed these problems in ways that reflect both its social democratic inheritance and its debt to the new institutionalism. Whereas the New Right believed that problems akin to those afflicting Keynesianism are inherent in state intervention in the economy, New Labour portrays them as products of new times; it is 'the new international economy that has greatly reduced the ability of any single government to use the traditional levers of economic policy', or so Mandelson and Liddle argue.[2] The new international economy requires us, in New Labour's opinion, to adopt macro-economic policies akin to those of the New Right together with very different policies towards the supply-side.

Although the new times often get described in the bold terms of globalisation, we would do well to disaggregate them into the increased mobility of capital and the rise of new technologies. It is the increased mobility of capital that appears to undermine the old Keynesian policies. Governments can no longer manage demand because it now derives in no small measure from beyond the borders of the state. What is more, if governments fail to keep the confidence of investors, capital now will flow out of the country to places that the financial markets regard as more profitable. In New Labour's view, the increased mobility of capital thus gives force to four of the leading tenets of the macro-economic theories of the New Right. First, low inflation should be at least as important a goal of economic policies as low unemployment. Second, the key monetary lever should be interest rates, not fiscal policy. Third, government should develop monetary policy in accord with rules, not discretion. And, finally, the supply-side of the economy is more significant than the management of aggregate demand. Brown echoes themes from the New Right when he says, 'stability, long-term prudence, and a dynamic supply side are key building blocks for prosperity'.[3] But, for New Labour, they are the building blocks for prosperity because of new times rather than because of the inherent limitations of state intervention in the economy. New Labour does not believe that state intervention is inherently damaging to the economy. On the contrary, it rejects the New Right's belief that the government should withdraw as much as possible from the supply-side of the economy through deregulation and tax-cuts. It believes that the other facet of our new times – the rise of new technologies – requires government to act so as to transform the supply-side of the economy in such a way as to enhance international competitiveness. Government should play an enabling role by forming networks and partnerships to ensure the quality and efficiency of things such as the labour force and the infrastructure. Blair expressed many of the differences that thus set New Labour apart from the New Right when he said, 'governments can best improve economic performance by addressing supply-side weakness', associating the Third Way with 'active government working with the grain of the market to ensure a highly adaptable workforce, good education, high levels of technology, decent infrastructure and the right conditions for high investment and sustainable non-inflationary growth'.[4]

'The driving force for economic change today', Blair tells us, 'is globalisation.'[5] Globalisation constitutes, for New Labour, a fixed context within which the increased mobility of capital means that states have to ensure a stable macro-economic environment if they are to avoid excruciating punishment from the financial markets. New Labour believes that many of the macro-economic theories of the New Right are valid at least in this new context. Its leading lights now believe, in the first place, that Keynesian policies will produce unacceptable levels of inflation, which, in turn, will undermine growth and so actually end up fuelling unemployment. For Peter Mandelson, 'inflation leads to recession as night leads to day', while, for Gordon Brown, the 'supposed long-term trade-off between inflation and unemployment will simply not work'.[6] In this view, the state no longer can tackle unemployment, if it ever could, by stimulating demand. New Labour has even portrayed the battle against inflation as one fought on behalf of social justice by suggesting that inflation particularly harms those who depend on low or fixed incomes. New Labour often reasserts, 'the government's central economic objective is to achieve high and stable economic growth and employment'.[7] However, it believes that low inflation and stability, rather than demand management, are the ways to realise these goals. As Blair explains, the long-term battle against unemployment 'demands a hard line against inflation'.[8] Low inflation and stability are crucial here because they encourage, in Brown's words, 'the long-term investment on which high levels of growth and employment depend'; they allow companies to make reasonable assumptions about future economic conditions and so to invest with greater confidence.[9] In addition, New Labour implies that low inflation and stability have added importance within the new global economy since they provide competitive advantages in attracting what is now highly mobile investment capital.

In the second place, New Labour accepts that the best way to foster low inflation and stability is to use interest rates to control the supply of money. Keynesian policies typically stimulated demand through government expenditure and other measures that increased the amount of money available within the economy. They led to inflation because they reduced the value of money in comparison with that of commodities. New Labour thus concludes that the control of inflation depends on a tight money supply to ensure that the value of money does not fall in relation to commodities.

Here New Labour also suggests, in the third place, that monetary policy best controls inflation and best promotes stability when it is conducted in accord with rules rather than being left to governmental discretion. We are told that rules are necessary in order to insulate monetary policy from short-term manipulation for political advantage and to promote stability more generally. Both Blair and Brown invoked, in this context, an explicit 'target' for low and stable inflation.[10] Ironically they criticised the Conservatives for constantly shifting their target and creating uncertainty and instability. 'During the last two decades,' Brown complained, 'governments have adopted and then abandoned a succession of monetary targets' so that 'far from [their] delivering monetary stability, Britain has suffered the most volatile inflation record of any G7 country in the last ten years.'[11]

In New Labour's view, monetary policy is not the only precondition of low inflation and macro-economic stability, let alone of growth and high employment. The control of inflation also requires a prudent fiscal policy, while growth depends on suitable supply-side measures. Fiscal policy should seek to avoid, in particular, the inflationary effects of excessive tax-cuts. Blair, Mandelson, and others criticise the New Right for introducing tax-cuts that fuelled consumer spending and inflation thereby pushing up interest rates at a time when a tight monetary policy meant that these rates were already high.[12] Instead of cutting taxes, we are told, governments should pursue a responsible programme of expenditure designed to modernise the supply-side of the British economy and thus fulfil the other preconditions of growth and rising employment. New Labour often invokes rules again here, albeit in a less literal form, as a way of stabilising fiscal policy. Brown argues, for example, that 'rules for fiscal policy' can lock governments in to good practice; he refers especially to a 'sustainable investment rule', according to which government should stabilise public debts at a prudent level, and a 'golden rule', according to which governments should borrow money only for purposes of investment.[13] Fiscal policy and public spending are not to be renounced in the name of the market, but rather used as tools for investing in the supply-side of the economy so as to promote growth and employment.

Although New Labour thus accepts, fourth, a focus on the supply-side of the economy, the content of its supply-side vision differs from that of the New Right in ways that reflect the new institutionalist analysis of the impact of new technologies on the economy. These technologies imply that, as Blair explains, 'our economies and our workforces have got to become more adaptable, more innovative, more dynamic'.[14] The new economy requires a transformation of the supply-side of the economy. New Labour insists that the state can play an active role in promoting this transformation. A belief in the importance of supply-side intervention dominates New Labour's critique of the economic policies of the New Right. As early as 1995, the Labour Party explained Britain's slow growth rate by pointing to an investment gap between Britain and her principle competitors: Britain had invested a lower proportion of its national income than any other G7 country, and less than all but 2 of the 24 OECD countries.[15] Conservative governments had not invested enough in infrastructure and skills. They had not even done enough to encourage the private sector so to invest.

The New Right sought to create a stable macro-economic environment within which the market could work its magic. The ineffectiveness of state action meant, in its view, that government should restrict itself to deregulating labour markets and reducing taxes as a means of stimulating supply-side activity. New Labour argues, in contrast, that deregulation and tax cuts generated inflationary pressures and also encouraged a short-term outlook that hindered economic growth. Blair complained of the then Conservative government, 'everything is geared up to the short-term'.[16] New Labour suggests, for a start, that companies did not use the capital released by reduced labour costs and tax rates to invest in the supply-side; they retained it as either increased profits or share dividends, putting 'short-term profit making before long-term considerations'.[17] What is more, New Labour continues, such short-term attitudes run directly counter to those required for success in the new knowledge-based global economy. Whereas the New Right sought competitiveness in the cheap labour that deregulation was supposed to produce, the new economy actually rewards initiative, motivation, flexibility, skills, and knowledge. The new institutionalism thus provides New Labour with a means of tarring the New Right with the brush of economic incompetence, and with an alternative economic policy based on skills and partnerships. As Blair argues, 'in global markets, where products can be made anywhere and shipped anywhere . . . we cannot base our future prosperity on the traditional blocks of the old industrial economy – raw materials, land, machinery, cheap labour'; instead, 'we must base our competitiveness on distinctive assets which our competitors cannot imitate – our know-how, creativity and talent'.[18] As Brown too argues, 'in a world in which capital, raw materials and ideas are increasingly mobile, it is the skills and ability of the workforce which define the ability of a national economy to compete'.[19] The moral is clear: as Mandelson and Liddle put it, 'governments can best promote economic success by ensuring that their people are equipped with the skills necessary for the modern world'; or as New Labour later put it, 'the government has a key role in acting as a catalyst, investor and regulator to strengthen the supply-side of the economy'.[20]

New Labour believes, then, in supply-side socialism.[21] The government should not leave matters to the market within a stable macro-economic environment. Instead, it should intervene actively in the supply-side so as, in Blair's words, to 'promote long-term investment', 'ensure that business has well-educated people to recruit into the workforce', and 'ensure a properly functioning first-class infrastructure'.[22] Intervention in the supply-side allegedly can promote economic dynamism and also serve to make Britain more attractive to investment capital. It just needs to be conducted within the context of a stable macro-economic environment.

The manner and substance of the envisaged intervention in the supply-side reflects New Labour's debt to the new institutionalist analysis of our times in that it focuses on training and the creation of networks as opposed to industrial planning in the context of a hierarchic bureaucracy. The commitment to training also draws in part on 'post-classical endogenous growth theory'. According to this theory, economic growth depends in large measure on supply-side factors, notably human capital or skills. Hence public expenditure on such factors can be justified in terms of its beneficial impact upon growth in addition to any contribution it makes to social justice. Social measures appear, then, to be an integral part of economic policy. The new institutionalist account of the new economy reinforces this post-classical endogenous growth theory by implying that a skilled workforce has become even more important due to changes in the global economy.

New Labour associates economic vitality, following the new institutionalism, with skills and technology and also with networks based on collaboration, trust, and negotiation. 'Collaborate to compete' has become something of a mantra within the Department of Trade and Industry (DTI). The role of the state, Blair explains, 'is not to command but facilitate, and to do so in partnership with industry': the state should be, as Brown says, a 'catalyst', 'co-ordinator', 'partner', and 'enabler'.[23] The government seeks to work in partnership with other organisations in networks so as to create the conditions in which companies can become more competitive and successful through their own activity. It believes, 'successful businesses depend upon strong team work – with suppliers, customers, joint-venture partners, universities, and between managers and employees'.[24] What is more, New Labour sometimes implies that if businesses are left to their own devices within the market, they typically develop a short-term outlook that fetishises competition and quick profits at the expense of the long-term benefits to be reaped from collaboration. Hence, the argument goes, 'the government has an important practical role in helping to promote partnerships'.[25] New Labour envisages an enabling state that actively intervenes in the supply-side of the economy so as to enhance the preconditions of competitiveness in the new global economy, where these preconditions are those highlighted by the new institutionalism – knowledge, skills, and dynamism as fostered by partnerships and networks. In this view, the state should enter into networks in order to promote quality and efficiency in the supply-side and thereby nurture growth and employment. New Labour thus claims that its strategy for economic competitiveness eschews both 'state intervention' and 'a naive reliance on markets'.[26] It relies instead on partnerships between the state and companies, partnerships in which the state establishes an appropriate macro-economic context within which companies can be competitive, and in which the state also invests in supply-side capabilities when companies are unable to do so by themselves. Let us turn now to the ways in which New Labour has enacted these economic beliefs in its policies.

Macro-economics

New Labour's macro-economic ideas link stability to low inflation and on to sustained growth and high levels of employment. They reject the Keynesian emphases on public works, fiscal policy, and government discretion for ones on the control of inflation, the manipulation of interest rates, and rules. New Labour's macro-economic policies aim first and foremost to create and sustain stablility. 'Government's first job is', we are told, 'to ensure a stable macro-economic environment.'[27] Ed Balls, an adviser to Brown, unpacks the principles that should inform government policy: 'stability through constrained discretion; credibility through sound, long-term policies; credibility through maximum transparency; the principle of trust through pre-commitment'.[28]

Brown's first significant act upon becoming Chancellor in 1997 was to give operational independence in the setting of interest rates to the Bank of England. In doing so, he clearly hoped to forestall the kind of run on the pound that often had followed the return of a Labour government. He also acted on New Labour's belief in macro-economic stability and low inflation as necessary contexts for supply-side regeneration. The Bank of England Act of 1998 established a Monetary Policy Committee of the Bank, chaired by the governor of the Bank, with a remit 'to maintain price stability, and subject to that, to support the economic policy of Her Majesty's Government, including its objectives for growth and employment'.[29] The Committee reaches its decisions about interest rates on the basis of majority voting. Its eight members consist of a roughly equal mix of Bank officials and economic experts who are appointed by the government but confirmed only after hearings in front of the Treasury Committee, which evaluates their competence and their independence from the government. It meets once a month, the individual voting records of its members are recorded, and its proceedings are published. The Committee also has to report to both the Treasury and Parliament. Interest rates will thus be fixed, New Labour tells us, in accord with long-term economic priorities as opposed to short-term political advantage. The concern with stability that informs the government's conception of long-term priorities appears here in the directions it has given to the Monetary Policy Committee. The Committee has responsibility for setting interest rates so as to meet the target for inflation, which the government has set at 2.5 per cent, and if inflation diverges from this target by more than 1 per cent, the governor of the Bank of England has to explain the discrepancy in an open letter to the Chancellor. The government also has made the currency operations of the Bank of England more visible in an attempt to foster greater confidence among the financial markets.

After Brown had relinquished control of monetary policy, he was left with fiscal policy, that is, with taxation and public expenditure. Mind you, of course, he has to conduct fiscal policy in a way that encourages the Bank to keep interest rates relatively low. New Labour's belief in rules and transparency was soon applied to fiscal policy. The Finance Act of 1998 gave a statutory basis to a Code for Fiscal Stability, which included both the 'golden rule' – the government will borrow over any economic cycle only to invest – and the 'sustainable investment rule' – the government will maintain public debt at a stable and prudent proportion of Gross Domestic Product over any economic cycle.[30] The Code requires the government publicly to state its fiscal objectives and regularly to report its progress in meeting them. It identifies five principles that will govern fiscal policy: transparency, stability, responsibility, fairness, and efficiency. More generally still, the government has replaced traditional annual spending plans with a three-year spending plan in an attempt to produce greater certainty about fiscal policy and thereby promote a long-term business culture that places a premium on planning and investment.

The government's quest for stability extends from the framework for policy to economic outcomes – sound public finances and low inflation. The Treasury obviously plays a vital role in New Labour's pursuit of such outcomes. Several early government initiatives increased its influence over other policy areas. Brown, 'the iron chancellor', was appointed Chair of the Cabinet's committee on economic affairs, when for over 30 years that post had been held by the Prime Minister. A Comprehensive Spending Review, conducted during New Labour's first year in office, redefined the institutional context for decisions about public expenditure. It sought to concentrate spending on the government's priorities, and to ensure greater stability, transparency, and control over public expenditure. Departments were encouraged to use techniques such as line-by-line analysis and zero budgeting to shift spending that might have been defined by inertia towards the specified priorities of employment, social justice, and public service. Stability was promoted by the shift to a three-year planning cycle. Transparency was promoted by a new system of 'contracts' in which Departments define detailed objectives and targets in consultation with the Treasury. Control over public expenditure was promoted through the continuous scrutiny by a Cabinet committee, again chaired by Brown, of the performance of the Departments in relation to these targets. All these initiatives have helped the government to keep tight control over public expenditure and thereby ensure stable outcomes. Brown stuck steadfastly to the Party's election pledges, refusing in particular to allow any significant increase in public expenditure until 2000, apart from boosts of £20 billion to health and £19 billion to education, both of which were funded largely by lottery money and a windfall tax on the utilities that had been privatised by the Conservatives. Public expenditure as a percentage of gross domestic product actually dropped from 41.2 per cent in 1997 to 37.75 in 2000. And although Brown proposed that public expenditure might rise by £43 billion over the period from 2000 to 2004, this rise would merely return the level of public expenditure to

40 per cent – the very level at which it stood when New Labour came to power in 1997.

While New Labour has maintained tight control of public expenditure, it has also tried to use fiscal policy to tackle some forms of poverty. Blair brought poverty onto the government's agenda in May 1999, when he announced, somewhat out of the blue, that he hoped to eliminate child poverty within a generation. The Treasury then adopted an aim of halving child poverty over ten years, while also specifying, in a public service agreement with the Department of Social Security, an interim target of reducing it by at least 25 per cent by 2004: these targets take 1998 as their baseline and define poverty in terms of those households that have an income of less than 60 per cent of the median.[31] At about the same time, the government announced an aspiration to address 'pensioner poverty' without adopting specific targets.[32] Although the government has not formulated plans to tackle poverty in general, it is worth noting that because a clear majority of the poor have a child or a pensioner in their household, the commitment to address child and pensioner poverty goes a long way towards being one to tackle poverty as such. Nonetheless, a particular focus on poverty among children and pensioners fits well with the communitarian themes that inform New Labour's policies. These themes suggest that work offers the best solution to poverty and social exclusion, so the primary role of the state is that of enabling and encouraging people to enter employment, but, as neither children nor pensioners can work, the state can tackle poverty among them only by other means.

Under New Labour, public expenditure has risen significantly on benefits that seek to tackle poverty among children and pensioners. The relevant policies here include several that tie in with the government's general focus on family life as discussed in the previous chapter; these include the Sure Start Maternity Grant, introduced in the 1999 Budget, which pays mothers £200 provided they contact a healthcare professional. The most dramatic rises have been to means-tested benefits, with, for example, the rates of income support to families with children or pensioners having been increased notably above the rate of inflation.[33] The government also has increased some benefits that are not means-tested, including child benefit and the annual winter fuel payments to pensioners. It has also introduced some new one-off payments, including free television licences for those over 75. Finally here the government has proposed various tax credits to improve the living standards of targeted groups: for example, the pension credit eliminates or reduces the rate of tax that pensioners pay on their savings thereby not only raising their living standard but also, the government hopes, increasing the incentives for people to save for their retirement.[34]

So, although New Labour's macro-economic policy emphasises stability and low inflation, we should not equate it entirely with that of the New Right, let alone with monetarism.[35] One difference appears in the redistributive effects of policies aimed at tackling child and pensioner poverty.

An equally important difference appears in Balls's invocation of a post-monetarist consensus that disavows not only the idea of a trade-off between inflation and unemployment, but also that of a 'natural' rate of unemployment unaffected by macro-economic policy.[36] This post-monetarist view has implications, in particular, for the way in which people conceive of the non-accelerating inflation rate of unemployment (NAIRU). The NAIRU appeared in the work of Milton Friedman, a monetarist, as an expression of his belief in a natural rate of unemployment that is in synch with the economy: the involuntarily unemployed act as a reserve army of labour who restrain wage bargaining, and any attempt to reduce the unemployment rate below a certain level removes this restraint thereby producing a fairly rapid build-up of inflationary pressures. New Labour appears to question Friedman's assumption that all members of the unemployed are effective in restraining wage bargaining. Richard Layard, who is an adviser in the Department of Education and Environment, has argued that the social exclusion of the long-term unemployed means that they should not be considered as effectively seeking work, and the same clearly could be said for groups such as lone parents and even young people who are, either in their own view or that of employers, not properly employable.[37] From this perspective, policies that tackle social exclusion can bring more people into the effective labour market and thereby restrain wage increases. Demand management that targets the socially excluded might lead, in other words, not only to higher rates of employment, higher tax returns, and lower expenditure on social security, but also a reduction of inflationary pressure. This receptiveness to some forms of demand management is a distinctive feature of New Labour's macro-economic thinking, and it probably provides part of the context in which the Treasury supports policies such as the New Deals.

A belief in globalisation leads to a greater stress on the importance of integrating all such macro-economic policies into regional and global processes. New Labour thus has sought to direct regional and global organisations in a way that corresponds to its account of globalisation. Because globalisation appears to be an irresistible process, the role of such organisations is, as Blair told the World Trade Organisation, to 'spread the benefits of globalisation' and maximise those of 'the electronic age and the borderless economy'.[38] On the one hand, then, New Labour supports the promotion of free markets, trade liberalisation, the deregulation of capital markets, and greater competition. Within the European Union (EU), for example, the government adopted the European Working Time Directive while negotiating for a range of exemptions within it. On the other hand, New Labour advocates measures to improve the supply-side in accord with its analysis of the new economy. Within the EU, for example, the government constantly argues for a range of measures – packaged as part of the 'Third Way' – that it believes would make Europe more competitive. At the Amsterdam Summit in 1997, Britain joined Germany in arguing successfully for deregulation to promote an adaptable workforce and to attract investment, and against the French proposal for extra investment to boost employment. The simultaneous promotion of liberalisation and supply-side reforms also provides the context in which New Labour approaches the social, developmental, and environmental issues that impinge upon regional and global economies. The government argues that social concerns are best addressed by raising prosperity through increases in the volume and value of global trade. Likewise, it implies that we can best help less developed states by facilitating their participation in a liberal, multilateral trading system. When it gets involved in bilateral aid, moreover, it seeks to do so by forming 'partnerships' with the recipients.[39] Finally here the government unpacks sustainable development in terms of a number of objectives that include prominently the 'maintenance of high and stable levels of economic growth and employment' based on skills and investment.[40]

The supply-side

Even in our times, Mandelson and Liddle tell us, 'governments can still take action to enhance skills, promote investment, and enlarge our economic capacity'.[41] If New Labour's macro-economic policies often draw on themes found in the proposals of the New Right, the same scarcely can be said of its interventionist stance towards the supply-side. Of course, macro-economic stability is itself a means by which New Labour seeks to attract investment in the supply-side of the economy. The government believes that supply-side measures are most likely to influence the decisions of companies if firms can expect prices to remain stable. More generally still, as Brown explains, 'because investment funds will only come to those countries that show they can pursue policies that achieve economic stability emphasis has to be placed on achieving monetary and fiscal stability'.[42]

To say that New Labour's supply-side strategy differs significantly from that of the New Right is not to deny that New Labour has occupied itself with both deregulation and tax reform. To the contrary, the government clearly hopes to assist business by reducing the burdens of regulation. It has established a Better Regulation Task Force to assess all legislative proposals in terms of their costs and benefits for business as well as their environmental impact; and it has sought to streamline the regulatory agencies that affect business by, for example, making the Contributions Agency a part of the Inland Revenue so that a single body deals with all matters relating to national insurance and taxation. Likewise, although the government has expanded the rights of Trade Unions, it has left intact much of the legislation on industrial relations passed during the 1980s, so much so, indeed, that Blair could reassure the Confederation of British Industry, 'Britain still has one of the most lightly regulated labour markets in the world – even compared to the US'.[43] The government also hopes to assist business through various tax reforms. It has committed itself, for instance, to reducing both corporation tax and capital gains tax. Interestingly, it has also introduced tax incentives to encourage business to invest in research and development. As these latter incentives suggests, New Labour places a distinct emphasis on supply-side intervention to develop the qualities new institutionalists proclaim as vital for competitiveness in our new times, namely, a skilled and flexible workforce, science and technology, small and medium-sized businesses, and partnerships and networks.

New Labour combines tax reform and deregulation with a commitment to active intervention by the state in the supply-side so as to promote skills and technology in a context of partnerships and networks. New Labour's supply-side socialism thus places great emphasis on the creation of a skilled, flexible, and entrepreneurial workforce. The attempts to promote such a workforce begin with education policy. Just as we located New Labour's welfare-to-work programmes alongside its efforts to provide people with the skills they need to get work and to prosper in work, so we might locate its industrial policy alongside its efforts to train people in the particular skills that business needs if it is to be competitive in the new global economy. The government promotes, in particular, the idea of 'lifelong learning' to emphasise the importance of education and training throughout people's working lives as a means of equipping them to deal with the rapidly changing technologies of our new times. When New Labour promotes lifelong learning, it seeks again to act as an enabler or catalyst for dynamic networks of individuals and organisations.[44] For example, a Young Enterprise Scheme provides support for students who want to run their own small company. Likewise, Individual Learning Accounts provide a setting in which the government provides a grant of £150 to individual citizens on the condition that they contribute a small initial sum and in the hope that employers too will contribute: citizens and employers get tax breaks on their contributions to these accounts, while citizens who have them are eligible for either a discount of 20 per cent on the cost of the training they eventually choose or a grant of £100 towards it.

While New Labour promotes lifelong learning, it recognises that the formation of human capital is concentrated in schools. Here the government has tried to improve the performance of schools by promoting partnerships and Zones. The Schools Standards and Frameworks Bill facilitated the creation of Education Action Zones in areas in which examination results are low and there are problems of social exclusion. The management boards of these Zones have the authority to restructure the school day and to modify the National Curriculum, typically to promote more vocational emphases. They are able to form innovative partnerships with local voluntary and private sector groups. The government even implied that the private sector might take over schools from democratic authorities if that was necessary to raise standards.[45] The idea of failing schools is one that draws attention to New Labour's regime of regulation with its threat of direct intervention when standards are not met: the government has established numeracy and literacy taskforces that prescribe what is to be taught; it relies on naming and shaming poor performers; and it has made arrangements for the centre to take over failing schools, or, in other words, to close them down and then reopen them with a 'fresh start' and a new head teacher.

New Labour also intervenes in the supply-side in order to promote technology. It seeks, in particular, to create the conditions and networks that it believes can enhance the ability of business to utilise technological developments. The DTI received a considerable increase in its science budget – even in the context of the tight reins being kept on public expenditure – with which to enhance science and foster links between businesses and universities. The government joined the Wellcome Trust in spending £1.4 billion over three years to improve the science and engineering base of British industry. In addition, it set up TradeUK as a public–private partnership between the DTI and two companies specialising in information technology – International Computers Limited and the Dialog Corporation. TradeUK assists small businesses to use information technology in order to compete more effectively in the world of electronic commerce by, for example, providing them with free space on the Internet and subsidised software. Finally, the government has introduced schemes to foster networks between research organisations and the businesses that develop the commercial potential of their research. A new fund facilitates collaboration between universities and businesses while the Research Careers Initiative does so between individual researchers and businesses. A special Enterprise Fund – itself a public–private partnership – provides funding for fledgling businesses in the high-technology sector if they otherwise have difficulties raising venture capital.

Supply-side intervention is necessary, in New Labour's view, to ensure a suitable level of investment and thus to improve factor inputs and so increase labour productivity. It is a means of overcoming the short-termism that flourished under the New Right. While such investment is most important for skills and technology, New Labour also has introduced broader schemes to promote capital investment generally. Just as many new institutionalists associate skills, technology, and innovation with small and medium-sized companies rather than the industrial giants of a bygone era, so New Labour focuses its attempts to promote investment on small businesses, arguing that they are both the engines of growth and the crucial source of new jobs. An expansion of the Small Firms Loan Guarantee Scheme provides additional finance for businesses that lack the collateral they need to attain it from the private sector. The Review of Banking Competition concentrated on ways of improving the finance available to small and medium-sized enterprises. Other legislation has enabled small businesses to charge interest in cases of late payment of commercial debt. Even broader attempts to promote investment include the creation of Regional Development Agencies and the introduction of further corporate tax allowances on research and development.

New Labour's supply-side socialism draws on the new institutionalism not only in its emphases on skills, technology, and small businesses, but also its faith in the benefits of partnerships and networks. The Labour Party has argued consistently that companies 'are interlinked and mutually dependent so their success depends on the strength of the networks between producers, suppliers, and investors'.[46] The government believes that 'to exploit our capabilities in people and technologies, businesses have to collaborate'; 'partnership is essential to competition'.[47] One expression of this belief is, of course, the broad shift from advocacy of public ownership and public provision to a greater reliance on the voluntary and private sectors. Partnerships between the public and private sector organisations now handle almost all major projects to improve the infrastructure. In addition, New Labour's supply-side interventionism includes active attempts to promote networks between and within businesses to make them more competitive. When Margaret Beckett took up office as Secretary of State for Industry in 1997, she wrote to the heads of various companies, telling them that the DTI wanted 'to build a real partnership with every part of industry, so that business can thrive and prosper'.[48] The government concentrates on two types of partnerships between companies – sectoral and geographic ones. The DTI provides special funds for companies in any area of business who want to form Industry Forums akin to the Society of Motor Manufacturers and Traders, which combines companies from all along the supply chain in the automotive industry. The new Regional Development Agencies facilitate the development of clusters, such as the Teeside Chemical Initiative, in which companies collaborate to attract new investment, improve local infrastructure, and share principles of best practice.[49] The government also promotes partnerships and networks within individual companies. It believes, 'a culture of flexibility, underpinned by principles of fairness and trust, creates the right conditions for a creative workforce and for business success'.[50] Hence it seeks to foster consultation within companies. It has made funds available, as part of its Fairness to Work strategy, for schemes that develop partnerships between managers and workers. The DTI has introduced a programme of 'knowledge management' that identifies and disseminates principles of best practice with respect to procedures for turning workers' ideas into workplace initiatives.

As we might expect, New Labour's use and promotion of partnerships and networks has raised concerns about central control in economic policy akin to those we saw it raised in social policy. The government relies once again on a mix of regulation, exhortation, and examples of best practice. So, for example, although the privatised utilities are not to be returned to the public sector, many are to be subject to enhanced regulation. Likewise, the Office of Fair Trading has been given increased powers with which to enforce the new rules of competition introduced by New Labour. While New Labour's regime of regulation provides means for reasserting central control, however, it is also supposed in economic matters to promote transparency and thus confidence and stability. So, for instance, when the Financial Services and Markets Bill of 1999 replaced a scheme of self-regulation with a Financial Services Authority, Brown told Parliament that the change would 'increase public confidence in the system' and 'ensure the future confidence of investors'.[51]

Evaluating New Labour

New Labour has a distinctive economic programme, which, like its welfare policies, is indebted to new institutionalism and communitarianism. Indeed, the new institutionalist and communitarian accounts of our times imply that welfare reform and economic policy are symbiotic means of developing the social qualities that are needed to be competitive in the new global economy. Blair speaks of giving 'absolute priority to education and skills as the means both of enhancing opportunity and creating an efficient economy'.[52] Education and training give individuals the means to avoid dependency and to make the best of their lives, and they provide the economy with the supply-side factors it needs in order to attract investment, add value, and generate growth and prosperity. A dynamic, competitive economy is, in turn, the way to create low levels of unemployment and greater social inclusion. Although the state can no longer promote social justice and prosperity by means of the Keynesian welfare state, it can do so through a Third Way that combines supply-side interventionism with welfare-to-work programmes to create a greater equality of skill-based assets and to render more equal the outcomes of the market economy.

How should we evaluate New Labour's economic policies? It is not surprising that evaluations here often mirror those passed on its welfare policies. One possibility is to examine once again how its policies measure up against the Party's values. Blair asks us to do just this: after becoming Prime Minister, he proclaimed his belief in 'equality', adding, 'if the next Labour Government has not raised the living standards of the poorest by the end of its time in office it will have failed'.[53] Much of the available evidence favours the government on this particular issue. Between 1997 and 2001, there was a slight fall in overall poverty and a larger proportionate fall in child poverty. What is more, models produced by the Microsimulation Unit at the University of Cambridge consistently suggest that the government's budgets have contributed to these reductions in levels of poverty.[54] Although these reductions are not thought to be sufficient to meet the government's own targets, Blair's governments could well have a greater impact on poverty than did most of their Labour predecessors in the twentieth century. Of course, the question would remain as to whether raising the living standards of the poorest is what social democrats have meant historically when they have called for equality. Equality requires, we might suggest, reduction in income disparities between the richest and the poorest members of society. However, the evidence is moderately favourable to New Labour even given this latter concept of equality. Although the government has not raised income tax even for the very wealthy, it has altered other taxes, notably abolishing mortgage tax relief, so that the Institute for Fiscal Studies estimates that, from 1997 to 2001, the income after tax of the poorest 10 per cent rose by 8.8 per cent while that of the top 30 per cent actually fell slightly.[55] Nonetheless, critics have pointed to several other disjunctures between New Labour's policies and social democratic values. They argue, for instance, that New Labour's supply-side measures serve to produce an efficient and competitive workforce rather than to provide individuals with resources for personal liberation or fulfilment.[56]

Another way to evaluate New Labour's economic policies is by reference to their effectiveness in meeting stated objectives. Here official statistics certainly suggest that the economy has done well under New Labour; inflation remains low, public expenditure is under control, the national debt has been reduced, and all with respectable rates of growth. Of course, there are debates as to whether this is due to government policies, the economic cycle, or fortuitous circumstances. Some critics suggest that New Labour has failed to address the structural problems that are responsible for the long-term decline of the economy.[57] There are also doubts over the ability of the government to sustain any benefits for which it might be responsible. Keynesian critics suggest that it will prove unable to sustain growth and to reduce unemployment in the absence of any attempts to manage demand. They argue, for example, that improved educational performance is of little value in the absence of a commitment to create the jobs for people then to take up. In addition, critics suggest that the good macro-economic news obscures the persistent concentration of unemployment and poverty in specific social groups and geographical areas: there is a suggestion here that the proliferation of Zones does not do enough to compensate for the ways in which policies benefit the dominant south-east of the country at the expense of other regions, and this suggestion would fit well alongside the general claim that New Labour has relied on neoliberal macro-economics when Britain would have been served better by regional industrial strategies.[58]

Other doubts concern the effectiveness of New Labour's supply-side measures. For a start, critics query the assumption that finance and industrial human capital are more mobile than human capital.[59] They point out that the mobility of new technologies depends on a range of factors that can be influenced by government policy. And they argue that highly skilled labour can move fairly easily across national boundaries after it has been trained. Furthermore, we might suggest that supply-side measures often require a certain macro-economic context rather than themselves being a cure for macro-economic ills. So, for example, the success of attempts to improve educational performance in regions characterised by high unemployment might depend on jobs being created in those regions in order to give greater point to educational achievement as well as to reduce poverty and the associated problems of truancy and illiteracy. Several critics argue, in more general terms, that the government's use of targets, tables, and competition serves only to shift blame on to schools and thereby increase educational inequalities and low performance.[60] Finally, although networks and partnerships are intended to promote initiative and flexibility at the local level, we have seen that they themselves can be arenas of conflict. While the state might decide such conflicts, critics argue that the top-down nature of such central intervention would merely exacerbate the obstacles to effective partnerships.[61] Political pressures for quick results certainly can undermine the policy innovation and long-term collaboration that are often said to be so important for disadvantaged regions. All of these complaints too would fit well alongside the general claim that New Labour has neglected regional industrial strategies based on a supply-side dirigisme designed so as to secure a dedicated supply of finance capital.[62]

While evaluations of New Labour's economic policies often mirror those passed on its welfare policies, we also might ask about the compatibility of the two. So, while the refusal to reverse the Conservative decision to index benefits to prices as opposed to earnings has contributed to New Labour's tight control over public expenditure, we might suppose that it hinders attempts to address inequality and overcome social exclusion. To some extent, the tensions between the government's broad economic and welfare policies have been masked by an expanding economy, which serves to keep public expenditure down and to provide the jobs that are said to be the best solution to poverty. In this case, however, awkward decisions are likely to be necessary following an economic downturn. Where will New Labour find the monies to improve public services, including health and education, if not from increased taxes? Perhaps New Labour might attempt to squeeze social security, but surely doing so would undermine the ambitions to tackle child and pensioner poverty. Or perhaps it might try to squeeze public sector pay, but then surely doing so would become increasingly difficult unless unemployment levels started to rise so as to act as a check on wages.

Critics have raised a wide range of objections to New Labour's welfare and economic policies in terms of both their fit with certain values and their effectiveness. Although I have considerable sympathy for many of these objections, I am struck by how often they are expressed in terms that replicate the same tropes of modernist empiricism that characterise the institutionalism and communitarianism on which New Labour has drawn to formulate its policies. Evaluations of New Labour typically proceed, I am suggesting, by means of atomisation, comparison, and classification, all of which serve to objectify aspects of social life so as to lend a dubious aura of expertise to the conclusions that are thus reached.

Commentaries on New Labour often rely on the modernist empiricist tropes of atomisation and analysis. The clearest examples are those collections of essays in which each author considers New Labour's record in a policy area in which he or she can claim expertise. The Department of Government at Manchester University has produced one such collection. 'It was agreed', the editors write, 'that individual members of staff would examine the policy areas of most interest to them guided by two simple questions: what did New Labour promise, and what have they delivered so far?'[63] 'We did not set out to come to a singular, collective judgement of the Blair Government's performance,' they add; rather, they 'left the individual contributors to draw their own conclusions and, not surprisingly, they are mixed'.[64] Of course, libraries are replete with collections of discordant essays. The crucial point about the Manchester collection is the division of the essays by policy area and the mode of evaluation that this implies is on offer. The collection clearly does not consist of a series of narratives of New Labour written from avowedly different theoretical positions. On the contrary, while there are one or two exceptions, the essays typically present themselves as theoretically innocent accounts of given empirical facts. New Labour gets atomised into a set of discreet promises made in distinct policy areas, and it is then evaluated by experts who assess its effectiveness in delivering these promises. The Manchester collection is meant to be, as its cover tells us, 'systematic', 'comprehensive', 'an audit'; it is not supposed to be perspectival, argumentive, or – at least in the sense I will soon describe – critical.

The analyses that inform evaluations of New Labour commonly rely, moreover, on comparison, classification, and, of course, objectification as the basis for claims to expertise. Most of the contributors to the Manchester collection evaluate New Labour, firstly, by comparing its policies with those of Conservative governments so as to classify it as a genuine Third Way or as neoliberalism in disguise. We are told, for example, that while New Labour's industrial and employment policy has a Third Way 'wrapper', it is 'remarkably similar' to that of John Major's government, and so not 'as novel as some of its proponents would have us believe'.[65] Similar modes of evaluation appear wherever New Labour is classified in relation to values or ideologies that are themselves adopted or condemned at least implicitly. For example, although Stephen Driver and Luke Martell classify New Labour as post-Thatcherite, rather than a capitulation to the New Right or an extension of Old Labour, they then constantly compare New Labour to Thatcherism in a manner that implies that its distance from the New Right carves out a distinctive Third Way.[66] Some contributors to the Manchester collection evaluate New Labour, secondly, by appealing to their insight into the inherent qualities or trajectories of social phenomena and thus divining whether or not New Labour's policies will be effective. It is suggested, for example, that New Labour's welfare reforms will not create a 'cohesive and secure' society because they encourage people to think of themselves as private beings concerned with their 'personal futures', rather than as citizens who by 'collective management' might direct wider 'forces' that 'they are powerless to control as individuals'.[67] Similar modes of evaluation appear wherever the effectiveness of policies is considered by reference to a political scientist's understanding of the world and that understanding of the world involves some form of objectification. For example, although Colin Hay argues for the constructed nature of New Labour's account of globalisation, he then goes on to condemn its policies for failing to address 'the persistent structural weaknesses of the British economy'.[68]

Objectification and claims to expertise are ubiquitous features of evaluations of New Labour. It is worth pausing to ask why this might be a matter of concern. Surely we should not condemn the very idea of evaluation? Besides, whenever we generalise or postulate an abstraction, we adopt a stance that resembles the sort of objectification that characterises evaluations of New Labour. The moral is not, then, that we should avoid generalisations and abstractions. It is, rather, that we should strive to ensure that the generalisations and abstractions we adopt are contingent and historicist rather than essentialist – a moral that echoes the one we drew when exploring the pitfalls of reified accounts of ideology. We might allow, moreover, that the contributors to the Manchester collection, Driver and Martell, and Hay all intended their evaluations of New Labour to be premised on just such contingent and historicist generalisations, or at least that they could rewrite them as such. Certainly I have been offering just such evaluations in locating New Labour in relation to various ideologies and in pointing to some difficulties that I believe affect its welfare reforms and economic policies. Let us be clear: the work of evaluation is an important part of political science.

Instead of quibbling over the contingent and historicist purity of evaluations of New Labour, we might ask about their limitations as a mode of critique. The reliance on atomisation, classification, and objectification often encourages, as in the Manchester collection, a concern to provide an audit, that is, a concern to identify the strengths and weaknesses of the government's policy with respect to specified values or outcomes. Although an audit can be a perfectly acceptable mode of evaluation – notably if it is aware of its own contingency and historicity – it still delimits critique to what we might describe as fault-finding. The critic identifies one or more faults, whether big or small, in the policies of the government: perhaps New Labour does not adopt the concept of equality that the critic favours; or perhaps it does not have policies in place to tackle what the critic takes to be the root causes of unemployment; or perhaps its current expenditure plans will not enable it to meet its targets for reducing poverty, or at least they will not according to the critic's models and projections. As with all critique, fault-finding becomes truly effective only when it is accompanied by recommendation of an alternative course of action but, even when it is, the mode of the critique remains that of fault-finding. It remains, in other words, a passing of judgement on the merits of a thing from a perspective that gestures at a given ethical or instrumental ideal from which the thing departs.

The limitations of fault-finding as a mode of critique will become clearer once we ask what follows from taking historicism and contingency seriously. To begin, we might examine the implications of the particularity of our own positions as critics of New Labour. Once we allow that our criticisms are not based on given facts, but rather infused with our own theoretical assumptions, we might well become somewhat hesitant to find fault; we might be wary of treating our particular theoretical perspective as a valid one from which to judge others. This hesitation might give rise to self-reflexive moments in our presentations of our evaluations of others, moments that suggest that our criticisms arise against the background of theoretical commitments and concepts that others might not share. It might lead us to be reflexive about the source of our authority, for while we cannot avoid taking a stance in a way that commits us to the epistemic authority of some set of beliefs, we might at least recognise that this authority is provisional and justified within a contingent set of concepts, and we might even recognise that we are offering a narrative that is just one among a field of possible narratives. In this way, we would move from fault-finding to critique. Instead of evaluating others in terms of apparently given concepts, values, or facts, we would find ourselves either juxtaposing rival narratives or asking what should follow from a set of concepts that we happen to share with those whom we are engaging.

Next we might examine the implications of the particularity of New Labour as the object of our critique. All too often political movements present themselves as based on given or neutral truths whether these are facts or values. Critique, as I am using the term, consists less of an evaluation of its object, than in the act of unmasking its object as contingent, partial, or both. It might unmask the contingency of its object by showing it to be just one among a field of possible narratives. And it might unmask the partiality of its object by showing how it arises against the background of an inherited tradition that is held by a particular group within society and perhaps even serves the interests of just that group. We might also add here that critique often has a clear evaluative import in that by unmasking the contingency and partiality of its object, it typically portrays its object, even if only tacitly, at best as being mistaken about its own nature and at worst as eliding its own nature in the interests of a group or class. Because critique thus privileges unmasking over evaluation, it tends to rely on philosophical or historical analysis. Critique deploys philosophical analysis to unpack the conceptual presuppositions of a movement or practice and often then to highlight elisions, contradictions, and gaps within these presuppositions. Critique deploys historical analysis to unpack the roots of these presuppositions and other related ideas in particular traditions, debates, or other contexts. We move from fault-finding to critique, in other words, when we shift our attention from the evaluation of a movement or practice in terms of a given set of criteria to the use of philosophical and historical analyses to bring into view the very theories or concepts that inform its nature and its own evaluations.

Conclusion

The preceding studies of New Labour's welfare and economic policies are intended to act as explanation and critique. We can explain the broad contours of New Labour's policies as a social democratic response to issues highlighted by the New Right, where this response draws not only on a social democratic tradition but also on new institutionalism and communitarianism. This explanation of New Labour concentrates on the beliefs of actors as they arise against the background of traditions and as they change in response to problems. It stands in contrast to those explanations that rapidly shift attention away from issues of meaning or belief. New Labour appears, in this view, as a contingent triumph of a particular web of beliefs, rather than as a product of a 'rational' politics of catch-up or a 'path dependent' development of social democracy in new times.

Because an interpretive approach explains New Labour in terms of a contingent historical process, it helps to shift our evaluation of its policies away from fault-finding and towards critique. Other approaches to political science often rely on objectification in order to atomise particular policies, values, or other areas of New Labour and then to assess them in the light of an alleged expertise in a given area. An interpretive approach prompts us, in contrast, to juxtapose New Labour's self-understanding with our narrative of it, where our narrative reveals the contingency and the partiality of New Labour's beliefs and the policies these inspire. The preceding explanation of New Labour also stands in contrast, then, to the self-image of a Third Way that has broken with the old ideological dogmatisms of state and market so as to adopt a pragmatic stance that focuses on the effectiveness of policy instruments in delivering ends.[69] This self-image presupposes that we can make a neutral, pragmatic judgement about effectiveness without presupposing theoretical biases. An interpretive approach suggests, on the contrary, that New Labour's professed pragmatism disguises a theoretical bias – what it stigmatises in others as an ideological dogmatism – taken from the new institutionalists in favour of networks as an alternative to hierarchies and markets.

6   Social democracy

Introduction

Interpretive approaches to political science are often charged with failing to allow for material or institutional reality and with lacking critical power. The preceding study of New Labour is in part an attempt to rebut these two charges. In the first place, because people act upon their beliefs, when interpretive studies reveal meanings, they exhibit the beliefs that explain people's actions and so the policies, institutions, and material reality generated by these actions. This study of New Labour has sought, then, to move from an elucidation of ideas to an explanation of welfare and economic policies in terms of these ideas. An interpretive approach does not lack an account of institutions; it just rethinks their nature; it disaggregates them, portraying them as products of contingent, and often competing actions that embody beliefs, which themselves arose against the background of particular traditions.

A disaggregated explanation of New Labour's welfare and economic policies acts, secondly, as a form of critique. New Labour often suggests that inexorable social forces compel us to stick to a limited range of modes of governance. It presents globalisation as an objective social process that requires states to adopt certain reforms, and it implies that its 'modernisation' of the Labour Party and British society are rational, or even inevitable, responses to these social processes, rather than the triumph of a particular ideological position. An interpretive approach suggests, on the contrary, that any narrative and so any mode of governance is contingent and contestable in that people from within other traditions might construct it differently and in that there are no inherent responses to dilemmas even within particular traditions. When we thus portray New Labour's beliefs and policies as contingent and contestable, we engage in critique. We challenge the self-understanding of those who expound these policies; we reveal to them the contingent, historical conditions of their beliefs, thereby undercutting their belief that these policies are necessary. What is more, we thereby open up the possibility of alternative narratives, policies, and practices. We unsettle the assumptions behind current modes of governance in a way that provides us with an opportunity to rethink how we might govern ourselves.

An interpretive approach explains New Labour's practice in terms of the ideas or beliefs that inform it. As such, it draws attention to the fact that New Labour's ideology is not just an attempt to comprehend the world but also the basis of a movement to remake the world. New Labour seeks to reform social democracy in terms largely set by the new institutionalism and communitarianism. An interpretive approach also denaturalises New Labour by portraying its ideology and practice as contingent and particular, not natural or rational. As such, it raises the possibility of our offering other proposals for the reform of social democracy. The awkward question is, of course: what proposals should we offer? We can glean some guidelines from what has been argued so far. For a start, we might locate our proposals to strands within the social democratic tradition. Because we inevitably reach the beliefs we do against the background of a social inheritance, it is perhaps best that we try to be self-conscious about the historicity of our proposals rather than having them masquerade as the product of neutral reason. In addition, we might indicate how our proposals cohere with an interpretive approach defined in contrast to the new institutionalism and communitarianism that we have found inform New Labour. It would be awkward, to say the least, if our alternative fell foul of the very failings that have led us to be critical of New Labour's reform of social democracy. We should try, in particular, to build a respect for contingency into our alternative so as to avoid the pitfalls of objectification as a basis of claims to expertise.

A history of socialism

Whereas New Labour often implies that the history of social democracy leads inexorably to its Third Way, as if its reforms represent the only possible future for social democracy in our new times, we might disaggregate the social democratic tradition in search of alternative visions based on different understandings of current circumstances. One way of disaggregating the social democratic tradition is in terms of the Marxism, Fabianism, and ethical socialism that emerged out of Victorian radicalism in the late nineteenth century.[1]

The Marxists of the Social Democratic Federation (SDF) and Socialist League started to describe themselves as social democrats because they thought social ills were integral to capitalism rather than consequences of a corrupt state. Early British Marxists adopted Marx's catastrophist vision of capitalist development. They argued that the market economy was leading not to happiness, wealth, and peace, but to crises of overproduction, the immiserisation of workers, and imperial rivalries. Capitalist competition led to the accumulation and concentration of capital, which then increased productive capacity, but, because this increased production

soon outstripped demand, capitalists were forced into ever-harsher competition, which led to a crisis characterised by bankruptcies, cutbacks, and
unemployment. The growth of fixed capital, the pressure to reduce costs,
and unemployment all forced wages down; in doing so, they led to the
immiserisation of the workers and the further accumulation of capital.
The intensity of competition prompted capitalists to use the state to secure
markets through imperialism and to seek refuge in trusts and cartels that
further concentrated capital. Before long, the further accumulation and
concentration of capital resulted in an even worse economic crisis.
Capitalism was, they concluded, self-destructive.

Many British Marxists believed that the failings of capitalism made state
intervention in civil society essential. H. M. Hyndman appealed to a
'principle of State management' in 1881 just after reading Marx.[2] Soon
afterwards, at the founding meeting of the SDF, he issued a pamphlet
with the significant title *The Text Book of Democracy*. The pamphlet
argued, 'the time is coming when all will be able to recognise that its [the
state's] friendly influence is needed to prevent serious trouble, and lead
the way to a happier period'.[3] The Marxists believed not only that the
state had to intervene in civil society to secure a just and stable society
but also that freedom had to be secured by a democratic political system.
Hyndman insisted, 'a great democratic English Republic has ever been the
dream of the noblest of our race', and 'to bring about such a Republic
is the cause for which we Socialists agitate to-day'.[4] The programme of
the SDF called not only for a parliament based on universal suffrage but
also for popular control of this parliament to be reinforced through measures such as annual elections, referenda, a principle of delegation, abolition
of the House of Lords, and an elected civil service.

Although Marxists often accepted the need for a more interventionist
state, their economic theory did not compel them so to do. Because they
believed that the evils of capitalism arose from private ownership of the
means of production, some argued that a civil society without such ownership would be harmonious and self-regulating. While members of the SDF
generally believed that a democratic state could act as a suitable vehicle
for common ownership, other Marxists were notably more hostile to the
state. William Morris defended a form of anarcho-communism, arguing
that the absence of private property would remove almost all cause for
disagreement so that civil society could become a self-regulating sphere
from which politics would be more or less absent.[5] Other Marxists, notably
Tom Mann, favoured a form of syndicalism; they located democratic rule
in industrial units composed of producers rather than geographical units
composed of citizens.

The SDF appealed almost exclusively to popular and Tory radicals.
Liberal radical converts to social democracy tended to join the Fabian
Society in the context of the collapse of classical economics. During the
1870s and 1880s, economists such as W. S. Jevons and Alfred Marshall

developed various versions of marginalist economics. Fabians such as George Bernard Shaw and Sidney Webb then drew on marginalism to construct theories of rent as exploitation. Shaw argued that capitalists exploited workers in part by the exercise of their monopoly of the means of production and in part because as landlords they appropriated the rents that arose from natural advantages of fertility. Webb argued that interest was strictly analogous to land rent since it derived from an advantageous industrial situation. Both Shaw and Webb believed that any economy necessarily produced rent understood as a social surplus. Rent was unearned in their view because it reflected natural or social variations of fertility or industrial situation, and it did not contribute to the maintenance of the supply of land or capital necessary to the efficient functioning of the economy but rather arose from permanent or temporary quasi-monopolies. As Webb explained, 'an additional product determined by the relative differences in the productive efficiency of the different sites, soils, capitals and forms of skill above the margin has gone to those exercising control over those valuable but scarce productive forces'.[6] Many Fabians believed, in addition, that rent promoted economic inefficiencies. According to Sidney and Beatrice Webb, child labour, variable local rates, and so forth all generated forms of rent or 'bounties' that enabled inefficient companies to flourish.[7] The free market led, in their view, to an uncoordinated industrial system that was composed of numerous fragmented centres of management that knew little about each other's activities. This lack of coordination resulted in duplication, temporary blockages, and other unnecessary forms of waste. Capitalism was, the Fabians concluded, unjust and inefficient.

Fabian economic theories, unlike those of the Marxists, virtually compelled their adherents to call for a more interventionist state since rent arose not just under capitalism but within any economy. For Marxists, surplus value arose from the buying and selling of labour in a capitalist economy, so collective ownership of the means of production would eliminate it irrespective of the particular role given to the state. For Fabians, rent arose from the variable productivity of different lands, and arguably capitals, so the only viable solution appeared to be for the state to appropriate it.[8] As Shaw wrote, 'economic rent, arising as it does from variations of fertility or advantages of situation, must always be held as common or social wealth, and used, as the revenues raised by taxation are now used, for public purposes'.[9] Although the Fabians did not believe that an extended role for the state had to bring greater bureaucracy, they acknowledged that socialism would make the integrity and efficiency of the state absolutely vital. They hoped to ensure such integrity by means of democracy; they wanted 'to gather the whole people into the State, so that the State may be trusted with the rent of the country'.[10] However, because they generally drew on the liberalism of Jeremy Bentham and J. S. Mill, not the republicanism that fed into the SDF, they defined democracy as representative government almost to the exclusion of other forms of popular control over the executive.

The third strand to make up British socialism was an ethical one based on a moral critique of capitalism. Ethical socialists denounced the free market and competition in favour of a moral economy and cooperation. They argued that even if capitalism brought material benefits, these were outweighed by its social costs – poverty, urban squalor, immorality, and social dislocation. Besides, they added, the commodities produced in a market economy often met artificial wants, not genuine needs, since production in it responded primarily to the changing whims and fashions of the wealthy. But the worst facet of capitalism was, in their view, the support it lent by way of individualism and competition to people's mean and selfish instincts. Edward Carpenter complained of self-consciousness being 'almost a disease, when the desire of acquiring and grasping objects, or of enslaving men and animals, in order to administer to the self, becomes one of the main motives of life'.[11]

Ethical socialists rarely appealed to sophisticated economic theories to reveal the unjust or inefficient nature of capitalism. Indeed, Carpenter dismissed the debate over the nature of value as akin to disputes among medieval scholastics.[12] The important thing was, he argued, not to provide a formal theory of abstract economic processes, but to examine the actual results of these processes and then to assess their moral acceptability. Ethical socialists wanted everyone to acknowledge, in Wilfrid Richmond's words, that 'economies are within the sphere of conscience'.[13] This idea of a moral economy had perilously little to say about the role of the state in social democracy. Ethical socialists typically defined socialism as the enactment of a spirit of democracy, fellowship, or brotherhood. Carpenter spoke of realising the 'instinct of loving Union which lies at the root of every human Soul'.[14] The Christian Social Union promoted, more concretely, 'white lists' of producers and retailers who met specified criteria with respect to fair wages, decent working conditions, and so forth. The ethical socialists believed mainly in a personal democracy in which relationships were based on equality and love. They thought that the particular role played by the state was of little importance compared to a personal transformation and a consequent revolution in civil society. On the one hand, they implied that if economic interactions were governed by suitable moral values, there would be little need for the state to intervene: Carpenter advocated a nongovernmental society based on cooperative units of production.[15] On the other, they argued that debates about the economic role to be played by the state should not be allowed to detract from the vital need for a moral revolution within civil society: Carpenter believed that all forms of socialism and anarchism embodied the same ideal, and the key thing was to spread the ideal without worrying about the material form it might take.

A significant fault-line divided the early socialists. Some, notably the Fabians and many Marxists, argued that the state had to take on new functions and play a more active role in civil society. They called for an extension of democracy to ensure that an active state remained trust-worthy. Others, notably the ethical socialists and syndicalists, argued that civil society needed to be purged of all those abuses they associated with competitive individualism and capitalism. They called for the democrati-sation of civil society itself. For the ethical socialists, civil society needed to embody the democratic spirit of true fellowship. For Marxists attracted to syndicalism, the associations in civil society needed to be made thor-oughly democratic.[16] One of the main debates among socialists thus concerned the relative roles to be played under socialism by a democratic state and democratic associations within civil society. To simplify, we might say that the view that came to dominate the Labour Party fused ethical socialism with Fabian economics to emphasise the role of the state, but that this view was always challenged by socialists influenced by syndi-calist themes in Marxism or non-governmental ones in ethical socialism

The leading figures in the early Labour Party – Keir Hardie, Philip Snowden, and Ramsay MacDonald – condemned capitalism in much the same terms as had the ethical socialists. Snowden condemned the compet-itive market for bringing out our 'animal instincts' not our moral ones; 'it makes men hard, cruel, selfish, acquisitive economic machines'.[17] MacDonald defended the idea of 'buying in the best market', where the idea of 'the best' had to include the welfare of producers, not just cheap-ness.[18] These Labour politicians turned to the Fabians for an economic analysis of capitalism that buttressed their moral views. Snowden followed Webb's theory of interest as analogous to land rent, arguing that 'just as the landlord gets an unearned income from the increase in the value of land, so the capitalist gets an unearned increment from improvements in productive methods and in other ways not the result of his own efforts or abilities'.[19] MacDonald followed the Webbs's denunciation of the uncoordinated nature of the market, arguing that whereas capitalism relied on a haphazard and chaotic clash of individual interests, socialism would eliminate waste by organising economic life on a scientific basis.[20]

The Labour Party's reliance on Fabian economics led it to emphasise various forms of state intervention at the expense of attempts to democ-ratise civil society. For a start, the existence of an unearned increment present in all economies suggested that the state should be in charge of collecting this surplus and using it for the benefit of the community. The Labour Party's mock budget of 1907 advocated, for example, 'taxation' so as to collect 'unearned ... increments of wealth' and then use them 'for communal benefit'.[21] Hardie, MacDonald, and Snowden advocated a range of measures to deal with the social surplus in the economy. To secure the surplus, they wanted taxation, legislative restrictions on property rights, and eventually public ownership of the means of pro-duction. To deploy the surplus for communal benefit, they wanted a considerable extension of social welfare legislation. They also advocated various degrees of public ownership of the means of production in order to end the anarchic nature of capitalist production. When Labour politicians thus turned to the state to correct the failings that they believed were inherent in the market economy, they countered fears about a too powerful state by stressing the ethical nature of a truly democratic state. MacDonald explained, 'the democratic State is an organisation of the people, democratic government is self-government, democratic law is an expression of the will of the people who have to obey the law'.[22] Here Labour politicians defined democracy in terms taken again from the ethical socialists and the Fabians; they equated democracy with a spirit of fellowship and representative institutions, rarely showing enthusiasm for other forms of popular control.

While the dominant outlook in the Labour Party drew on Fabian economics, opposition to this outlook often drew on forms of Marxism drifting towards syndicalism and forms of ethical socialism incorporating a non-governmental ideal.[23] The leading British syndicalists, including Mann and James Connolly, were Marxists who had belonged to the SDF. They argued, first, that to overcome the ills of capitalism required a transformation of industry and society with no, or almost no, role being played by the state. Because Marxist economics did not demand a greater role for the state, they could envisage a harmonious civil society in which the capitalist system of private property had been replaced by one based on worker-owned industrial units. They argued, second, that any leadership soon became a self-serving bureaucracy unless it were subject to strong democratic control, so even worker-owned industrial units had to be subject to popular control through measures such as a principle of delegation. The syndicalists and many other Marxists opposed the Labour Party's restricted view of democracy as requiring little more than representative government. They proposed instead an extension of popular control through devices such as the initiative and referenda.

Ethical socialism often incorporated a romantic medievalism in which craftsmen conjoined in guilds were seen as an approximation to the ideal of fellowship. A. J. Penty developed such medievalism in his *The Restoration of the Gild System*, which in its preface acknowledged a debt to John Ruskin and Carpenter, and which inspired the other begetters of guild socialism, A. R. Orage and S. G. Hobson.[24] The early guild socialists drew on themes from the ethical socialist tradition. They argued, first, that the ideal of fellowship consisted of a social spirit of democracy: individuals should exercise full control over their own daily activities in a cooperative and decentralised society, so, as Penty explained, 'it is necessary to transfer the control of industry from the hands of the financier into those of the craftsman'.[25] They argued, second, that the cure for capitalism lay in this moral ideal of fellowship, an ideal to which the political realm was largely irrelevant and perhaps even detrimental. Because the moral economy did not require state intervention – indeed because state-owned industries were capable of retaining the commercial ethic of private companies – social democrats should focus not on parliamentary politics but on promoting an ideal of fellowship. The guild socialists defined democracy to go beyond representative government so as to include local control of institutions in civil society where these institutions were to be largely autonomous from the state.

By the end of the First World War, the Labour Party had accepted social democratic ideas that committed it to an extended role for the state. This commitment gained additional strength from the many liberals who found their way into the Labour Party as it became the leading alternative to the Conservatives. Liberals often had reflected on the dilemmas posed by economic cycles, marginalism, and a moral disquiet at the effects of the market, and they had thus come to adopt ideas that resembled those of the social democrats. J. A. Hobson explained cycles in the economy as products of a form of underconsumption endemic to the free market, while Marshall introduced the concepts of producers' and consumers' surpluses into neoclassical economics.[26] Liberals too began to challenge the idea that the market constituted a harmonious, self-regulating system. They too turned to the state to put right the failings of the market, and to democracy to ensure the state could be trusted to play this role. They thereby provided a bridgehead for the introduction of Keynesian ideas into the Party. At the same time, however, opposition in the Party continued to draw on themes from Marxism and ethical socialism that opposed its statism and its restricted concept of democracy. Not long after the First World War, for instance, pluralists such as G. D. H. Cole and Harold Laski fused guild socialism with syndicalism, and also aspects of Fabian thought, in an attempt to revitalise democratic impulses within the Party.[27]

We can explain contemporary proposals for the reform of social democracy, at least to some extent, by situating them in relation to this history. New Labour emerged as a response to dilemmas such as inflation, welfare dependency, and the changing nature of the working class, against the background of the dominant tradition within the Labour Party, with its roots in Fabianism, ethical socialism, and liberalism. Various themes that characterise this tradition remain prominent in New Labour's thought and practice. New Labour remains wedded, for example, to concepts of community and the state that ultimately are monolithic or unitary ones as opposed to the pluralism associated with syndicalism and non-governmental socialism. Even when New Labour appeals to networks to deliver services, it still tends, as we have seen, to be preoccupied with techniques by which the centre can try to impose itself in order to define patterns of behaviour and eventual outcomes. New Labour appears to remain wedded, similarly, to policy-making processes that privilege expertise in the context of representative democracy as opposed to the forms of dialogue that have been evoked by some Marxists and ethical socialists.

It has turned to networks, for example, because experts – the new institutionalists and policy-wonks influenced by them – maintain they are an effective form of service delivery, rather than because of a commitment to extend participation. Indeed, participation itself is invoked as a means to efficiency and effectiveness more than as an extension of democracy.

Just as New Labour as a whole replicates the statism and the restricted conception of democracy that characterise the dominant tradition in the Party, so we could go on to disaggregate it in terms of the strands that fed into this dominant tradition. Tony Blair, Gordon Brown, and Peter Mandelson might act respectively here as exemplars of ethical socialist, Fabian or social democratic, and liberal socialist strands within New Labour. Blair emphasises the value of community, relates this to his own Christian faith, and places a heavy emphasis on moral exhortation. Brown appears to be more concerned to relate New Labour's ideas and especially its policies to values such as equality. Mandelson is perhaps the most committed to liberal themes such as choice and markets, which he suggests are not only pragmatically useful but also morally superior to equality and state intervention.

For our purposes, however, the point to reiterate is that other traditions of social democracy provide resources with which to develop alternative visions. Of course, we could disaggregate these traditions too. Marxism includes both a strand that believes in the state and expertise, as did many in the SDF, and a strand that looks askance at such beliefs, as did Morris and many of the syndicalists. Related strands of Marxism appear in contemporary responses to New Labour. There are, first, the more orthodox Marxists who believe in the state and expertise. When they evaluate New Labour, they often begin or end with fault-finding in relation to their own supposed expertise on the true nature of contemporary capitalism and its political and ideological effects.[28] New Labour itself is, as we have seen, profoundly indebted to an orthodox Marxist version of the new times thesis; post-Fordism, the global economy, information technology, or risk society are given facts or objectified processes that generate or require certain responses if social democracy is to prosper or even survive.[29] Then there are, second, more critical Marxists who are sceptical of the state and expertise. These Marxists take up the heritage of the Chartists, William Morris, E. P. Thompson, George Orwell, Raymond Williams, and the Gramscian twist added by Stuart Hall, in order to query representation and knowledge, often on behalf of democracy.[30] When these Marxists evaluate New Labour, they typically go beyond fault-finding to engage in critique.[31] They shift attention from the managerial issue of how we can best cope with objectified new times to the political one of how we can remake our world. Critique is, then, one of the alternatives that we can draw out from the history of social democracy. If we want to ally such critique to substantive visions of how we might remake our world, we can also draw out themes of participation, pluralism, and dialogue that have long resided in oppositional movements within the Labour Party.

The open community

While critique opens up alternatives, it can be properly effective only when it is conjoined with the defence of substantive proposals. We have to act in the world, so we cannot renounce our current mode of life, no matter how much we may come to doubt it, unless we conceive of an alternative as preferable. Even if critique might lead people to question their current actions and practices, they would have no reason to modify their activities unless that critique also suggested, explicitly or implicitly, that a substantive alternative was preferable. Unfortunately the dependence of critique upon the defence of an alternative is not always made clear. Rather, interpretive accounts of critique often replay the tension between structuralist and humanist analyses of meaning.[32] On the one hand, the structuralist legacy in post-structuralism sometimes appears to preclude all appeals to agency, freedom, or the good, and so to leave interpretivists offering only critique. In this view, people are not situated agents who can choose how to be or how to act, so all talk of freedom is an illusion, and interpretivism is merely the critical practice of revealing the illusory nature of such talk. On the other hand, interpretivists often are willing to defend situated agency, although not autonomy, and so to offer substantive accounts of the self, freedom, and inclusion that can act as part of an alternative ethic.[33] There is, then, a tension within the critical strand of Marxism between post-structuralist appeals to signifiers and discourses, which often seem to deny situated agency, and the more humanist legacy of Thompson, Williams, and Hall, which remains committed to situated agency, freedom, and at times emancipation. Interpretivists oscillate between a critique of all substantive ethics and invoking their own alternative. At times they appear to want to straddle these surely incompatible positions by appealing to critique as a pathway to new thinking and yet not advocating any path. They contest governance in the hope that doing so 'might require us to think about how we are asked to constitute ourselves today and how we might think differently about that request', but they do not propose that we think differently in any particular way.[34] At other times they seem to ignore the gap between a meta-ethical recognition of the partiality of all actions and the ethical or political question of how we should act. They seem to confuse recognition of the ubiquity of hegemony with an argument for democratic hegemony, when what is clearly needed for the latter is an account of why we should prefer democratic hegemony to any other form of hegemony.[35] Today interpretivists are muddled over whether or not they have epistemic grounds for advocating ethical and policy positions, let alone over the specific positions they should advocate.

It seems implausible no doubt that any set of philosophical or theoretical commitments ever could lead unquestionably to one ethic. Interpretive approaches, like all others, can support a wide variety of moral principles. Nonetheless, it is worth noting that the contrast between situated agency and autonomy provides us with the theoretical resources we need not only to sustain critique but also to develop alternatives in the way we have to if our critiques are to bite. Provided we are willing to grant that the capacity for situated agency has moral value, we can begin to defend a substantive vision. This vision might begin by restating social democratic values such as community, welfare, and empowerment. Then it might go on to allow for the ways in which a recognition of contingency prompts us to open up such values. Whereas New Labour adopts a rather closed vision, ours might open out to a pluralist democracy and dialogic public policy.

Interpretive approaches often draw, as we have seen, on the argument that individuals necessarily construe their experiences and engage in their reasoning in the context of the prior sets of theories they inherit as traditions. In this view, individuals cannot reach beliefs through their experiences and their reasoning except in the context of such an inheritance. No doubt they reach the beliefs they do through their experiences and their reasoning, but they can neither have experiences nor exercise their reason apart from within a theoretical context. They depend on tradition or community to give them initial sets of theories against the background of which they then can exercise their agency so as to modify their inheritance. Our very concept of an individual is, therefore, one of an individual embedded within community. We can properly make sense of the idea of an individual only as a socially embedded self. No matter how far we push our concepts back, whether historically or logically, we cannot reach a state of nature, a realm of pure reason, an existential freedom, or a place behind a veil of ignorance; we cannot reach a temporal or conceptual place where people exist outside of tradition and community and unaffected by them. Interpretivism might support a social democratic ethic of fellowship precisely because its analysis of the self leads to recognition of human interdependence. The life of each individual is necessarily a common one lived in the context of relations with others. When interpretivists talk ethics, therefore, they should accept that freedom, the good life, or whatever other end they might invoke, can be realised only in relation to others within community. Because each individual necessarily pursues the good together with others, we are bound to others in fellowship. As fellows, we provide each other with the context in which each of us has our individual life.

Once we begin talking ethics, the community of fellows represents the ethical corollary of human interdependence. It is different in kind from a specific organisation based on combination. Organisations arise when people combine to pursue particular purposes, albeit that these purposes often differ and at times conflict with one another. Although people sometimes find themselves members of organisations by virtue of their birth, combination is typically a voluntary activity; individuals join an organisation because they believe it will facilitate their pursuit of some purpose. Hence the structure of an organisation typically derives at least in part from the overlapping purposes of its members, and likewise the place of each member within an organisation typically derives at least in part from the role that she plays in the pursuit of those purposes. By contrast, fellowship exists in community conceived as an ethical expression of human interdependence. We just do constitute the community in that our individuality arises out of our relations with others. The community of fellows is not an organisation established for specific purposes by acts of will. It is the inextricable background against which individuals can establish organisations to pursue purposes. Although fellowship can go with combination – the community can establish organisations, perhaps with the purpose of expressing its communal identity – the two need not go together. If they did go together, moreover, the relevant organisation would still be expressive of community, not constitutive of it. The characteristic error of liberal individualism is, then, to conceive of social life solely in terms of combination to the exclusion of fellowship. Individualists mistakenly regard people as autonomous beings who stand outside of all social contexts and choose whether or not to associate with others. Really, people exist only in relations of fellowship with others, and the community they thus form constitutes the ineluctable background against which they choose whether or not to join with others in organisations for specific purposes. Community is conceptually prior to all organisation.

People can form all sorts of organisations exhibiting a wide variety of contingent characteristics against the background of community. Typically the characteristics of an organisation will reflect the diverse purposes and values in accord with which it is created and maintained. At times these purposes and these values exhibit little self-conscious recognition of the ethical connotations of fellowship, as is surely the case with slave societies, radical patriarchies, and racial apartheids. On other occasions the relevant purposes and values might exhibit a much greater awareness of the ethical connotations of fellowship. The question to be answered now is: what values should we adopt once we recognise our fellowship within community?

Our relation of fellowship to others should make us concerned with their welfare. One reason for being concerned with their welfare is simply that as our fellows they are people about whom we should care. Our lives are entwined with theirs in such a way that their well-being should be a thing of importance to us. We are social beings whose self is constituted in part by our relations to others, so properly to care for our self is to care for these relations, and, because these relations depend in part on the welfare of others, properly to care for our self is to care for the welfare of others. It is also possible to couch the reasons why we care about our fellows in terms that appeal to self-interest. We might say that our freedom or our good depends on others having a certain standard of welfare. Because the good life – whatever it may be – can be pursued, let alone realised, only in the context of community, the good of any individual depends on that of others. Because we can pursue our good only if the other members of the community provide us with a suitable context in which so to do, our good depends on our fellows having a level of material comfort, education, and the like such that they can provide a suitable context for our activities.

Our relation of fellowship to others also should make us concerned with their empowerment. Whereas organisations can ascribe people different positions in order to enable them to fulfil different functions in pursuit of specific purposes, the community is composed of moral equals. Of course, the fact of fellowship does not imply that people have equal capacities or that they are equally capable of fulfilling a particular function within an organisation; it implies only that we all occupy equivalent positions within the community. Because fellowship entails moral equality, the members of the community should take each other, as they do themselves, to be individuals who have ends they wish to pursue. Besides, when we say that the community denotes the social context within which individuals pursue specific purposes, we obviously imply that individuals have a capacity to pursue their own ends. As fellows, then, we should seek to enhance the choices and opportunities available to one another. We might do so in part by promoting their welfare so as to ensure that they have a certain level of education, health, and income. And we might do so in part by giving them a platform from which to speak and by involving them in decision-making processes.

An interpretive approach is quite compatible with social democratic values such as community, welfare, and empowerment. Yet these values are highly abstract ones that can be given very different content. Earlier we saw how New Labour gives them content by reworking social democracy in the light of communitarianism. Interpretivism can inspire alternatives to New Labour by giving them a different content. In particular, the interpretivist emphasis on contingency can correct the explicit or implicit assumption that community embodies a fixed identity. Both New Labour and the communitarians often depict communities as based on an ideal of consensus, that is, on fixed identities or shared values. Amitai Etzioni defines a community as a group of people among whom we find both a crisscrossing web of affect-laden relationships and 'a measure of commitment to a set of shared values, norms, and meanings'; he does so, incidentally, fully aware of the corollary – 'there are no communities that do not draw a line between members and outsiders'.[36] New Labour believes, likewise, that we all share, or at least that we all should share, the strong values that define our rights and responsibilities.[37] It imagines British society to be characterised by common values and interests rather than difference and conflict. Blair appeals to 'a popular politics reconciling themes which in the past have wrongly been regarded as antagonistic'.[38] We might ask, however, if all these oppositions can be reconciled quite so easily. The government is willing to speak out and legislate in ways that draw the line, at the very least, so as to exclude groups such as the young unemployed, single mothers, and the homeless. While the content of the government's social policies has thus led some critics to accuse it of social conservatism, the more general issue here is the validity of postulating a consensus irrespective of the content one gives to it.

Why do communitarians postulate shared values? In Etzioni's words:

> the reasons communities need shared moral cultures [are] ... that without shared values, communities are unable to withstand centrifugal forces (a neofunctional argument) and that if one studies those entities that are commonly viewed as communities, they tend to have a core of such shared values (an empirical argument).[39]

Let us begin by examining the empirical argument. It is a mistake all too characteristic of modernist empiricism to imagine that this could be an empirical argument untainted by theory. While we indeed can identify common meanings held by almost any group of people, this does not reflect an empirical truth about communities, but rather our ability to define such meanings at a suitably abstract level. What is at issue here, then, is not an empirical argument, but a theoretical one about how we should conceive of the relationship between individuals and communities. Should we say, as I do, that observers can define values so abstractly that they are common to all the members of a group, or should we say, as Etzioni implies, that a community is constituted by shared values from which its members cannot deviate? If individuals were constituted by a communal identity from which they could not deviate, as Etzioni's position seems to require, then we would be able to deduce the core of their beliefs from knowledge of the nature of the community to which they belong. But, of course, we cannot do so. People can come to reject any belief no matter how sacrosanct it seemed to their predecessors. What is more, because every aspect of the community is thus open to rejection, the idea of the community cannot possibly include within it that of a fixed identity. Communitarians might object that if people rejected a belief that their predecessors held sacrosanct, they would no longer belong to that community. But this reply is entirely bogus. It reduces what was supposed to be an empirical claim to the fiat of a definition of communities in terms of allegedly fixed values, where, moreover, this definition relies on the mistaken trope of objectification, when, as we have seen, the fact of agency implies that tradition or community is the contingent product of the ways in which individuals have adopted and modified their social inheritance, not a fixed entity in which we locate individuals because they exhibit its core features.

Let us turn now to the neofunctional argument, an argument that Blair echoes when he claims, 'social order' depends on 'strong values, socially shared'.[40] This argument hides a preference for a particular type of community under the guise of an apparently neutral claim about social order. If the community is, as I have been suggesting, an ineluctable expression of our interdependence, then it cannot be destroyed by centrifugal forces. Rather, these forces can lead only to the rise of one organisational expression of community rather than another. Hence the neofunctional argument merely expresses a preference for the type of organisation that arises in the absence of such forces; it implies only that if we want such organisations, we should promote shared values. Besides, even if we equated community with such organisations, as Etzioni seems to do, the neofunctional argument still would imply only that we should promote these organisations if we prefer them to the alternatives without giving us any reason to prefer them to the alternatives. Communitarians might reply that we should prefer these organisations because the alternative is social disorder. But why should we equate the alternatives with social disorder? The only arguments on offer here are the empirical one, which we have found to fail, and the neofunctional one, which would then become circular and vacuous. Etzioni's neofunctional argument is not an argument at all; it simply voices the moral prejudice it purports to justify.

Ironically, when communitarians define communities by reference to shared values, they mimic liberal individualism in confusing fellowship with combination and community with organization. They reduce the community, which is actually the ethical expression of our interdependence, to organisations, which are formed to promote particular purposes or ways of life. This conflation of community with organisation typically inspires the idea that we should be governed by fixed principles of the right or the good, for these principles are allegedly constitutive of our purposes or ways of life. Liberal individualists characteristically postulate neutral or even universal principles of the right, which all reasonable people will accept. Communitarians deny the neutrality of liberal theories only then to postulate fixed concepts of the good as being constitutive of particular communities. In contrast, interpretivism might prompt us to oppose all such fixed principles as reductions of difference to sameness. It might suggest, contrary to Etzioni's empirical argument, that the communitarian invocation of consensus relies on objectification so as to imply that norms and values are present from the outset and so constitutive of community, when really they are constantly being produced, challenged, and transformed by our situated agency. It also might suggest, contrary to Etzioni's neofunctional argument, that the communitarian preference for relatively closed communities based on consensus is one that we can challenge in the name of more open communities that actively delight in such challenges and transformations. Although individuals exist only in the context of community, they are nonetheless situated agents who can reject the attachments and moral claims given to them by community. If we value this capacity for situated agency, we might promote an open community that encourages the expression of diversity through pluralism and dialogue.

Pluralism against objectification

New Labour draws on both individualist and communitarian beliefs in fixed principles. Following the dominant tradition in the Party, it remains loyal to the liberal account of democracy as representative government; it makes comparatively few references to other forms of popular control over the executive and organisations in civil society. Democracy is, in this view, largely a matter of constitutional protections for fixed principles of the right or a universal and natural freedom; it consists principally of the rule of law and popular sovereignty, which have normative value because they treat individuals as free and equal. Within the context of representative democracy, New Labour follows communitarianism in invoking shared values as the grounds of many of its welfare policies.

Interpretivists reject the idea of a universal or natural freedom as being tied to that of autonomy. Instead they can defend an ideal of freedom couched in terms of situated agency. What difference might this alternative concept of freedom make to our analysis of democracy? One difference seems to be that we might think of freedom as inherently embedded in particular practices.[41] Many of our democratic norms arose as attempts to protect an illusionary autonomy that supposedly exists outside of social practices. A focus on agency suggests, in contrast, that we might be more concerned with the ways in which people actively make their own freedom through their participation in self-governing practices. Following oppositional traditions in the Labour Party, we might seek to promote participation by means of pluralism and dialogue rather than incorporation and consultation.

An open community would treat its members as situated agents capable of rejecting any prescribed set of values as they participate in practices constituted by their activity. Because people always exist against a social background, we cannot isolate their reasoning from social pressures. The crucial question is, rather, that of the nature of these pressures: are they examples of violence or deliberation? Violence arises, in this contrast, whenever an individual or group denies the situated agency of another. The powerful issue laws or commands, and any failure to comply with them can result in punishment. The subject of the law or command is treated as an object to be compelled to act in a certain way by the threat of force. Deliberation appears, in contrast, when we treat others as situated agents who we might convince of the rightness of acting in a certain way so that they choose so to do. Not all forms of communication constitute deliberation since bribes, threats, and the like do not attempt to convince others through an appeal to reason. Equally, deliberation need not presuppose a prior commitment to reasonableness or to seeking a consensus since we can treat others as situated agents even in the absence of such commitments. Deliberation takes the form of continuous persuasion and debate. The process of debate induces people to reflect on their beliefs and preferences, possibly altering them in the light of what others say and thereby exercising their situated agency and their capacity for local reasoning so as to consider what ideals and policies they are willing to endorse. What matters is, we might say, less the gaining of consent by the state than the capacity of citizens to step back, consider, and voice differing perspectives in debate. Although a participatory democracy surely would include some violence, we might attempt to strengthen deliberation in place of the violence that currently lurks in the coercive power of the state and the financial power of the market.

An emphasis on deliberation as opposed to violence points towards a similar emphasis on ethical conduct rather than prescriptive rules. Rules are, in this contrast, proclamations that purport to define how others should or should not act; they are typically both external to the actor and given prior to the action. Ethical conduct arises when the actor interprets, modifies, or even challenges a looser, flexible, more open-ended set of norms. Whereas moral rules seek to impose requirements and restrictions upon people, an ethic constitutes a practice in which people negotiate their own relationship to just such requirements and restrictions. No doubt a participatory democracy will have to include some moral rules, including those that set out, at least provisionally, a constitutional framework for deliberation. Even so, a participatory democracy might seek to ensure that these rules remain flexible enough to leave plenty of room for individuals to devise new forms of ethical conduct and even to bring the rules themselves into question at regular intervals.

A participatory ideal raises suspicions about the suspension of democratic decision that so often accompanies theoretical constructions of ideal constitutions or theories of justice. It is worth inquiring, however, what a participatory democracy that foregrounds deliberation and conduct might look like. Few interpretivists want to repudiate liberal rights and liberties as opposed to supplementing them. In their view, freedom is not only abstract rights and liberties under the rule of law; it is, at least as importantly, concrete practices in particular circumstances. To begin, though, we might endorse many of the features of liberal democracy. Democracy relies on rights to protect deliberation and conduct; it requires rights of privacy, free speech, and association as well as the right to vote. These rights do not just protect individual difference; they also safeguard public and private spaces for deliberation and conduct. To such rights, we might add other principles that also facilitate these things, including a free press, open government, and independent courts of law. Democracy relies similarly, of course, on devices to bring deliberation and conduct to bear on our processes of collective decision-making, and some of these mechanisms are widespread in liberal democracies, including elected legislatures, public hearings, and procedures for appeal and redress. While interpretivists might endorse all of these aspects of liberal democracy, they would do so as part of an account of a practice of freedom. This practice then might depart from other aspects of liberal democracy. A suitable practice of freedom requires, we might argue, that citizens can debate and remake even these liberal rights and mechanisms; it requires that we adopt other rights and devices so as to extend democracy to other areas of our community; and it requires that we decentre the state, perhaps handing over aspects of governance to other associations.

To begin, we might seek to locate liberal rights and mechanisms in a democratic practice. Democracy does not stand, in this view, as a universally rational order based on a neutral reason or the allegedly given fact of individual autonomy. It is a historical and mutable construct that we can defend and debate only by using our particular, contingent set of concepts. Even the rights and devices of liberal democracy are thus legitimate targets for evaluation and critique. When we elucidate or enact a vision of democracy, we are not laying down given maxims so much as interpreting and developing a historical set of inter-subjective concepts and practices.

Once we take democracy to be historically contingent in this way, we open up the possibility of adding to the rights and devices of liberal democracy others that have a more socio-economic focus. A historically contingent account of democracy implies that rights are social not natural: because we cannot make sense of the idea of an individual coming before the community, we also cannot make sense of the idea of natural or pre-social rights; because individuals exist only within social contexts, they can bear rights only against a social background, so all rights are social in that a society grants them to individuals because it holds the relevant liberties and powers to be essential to human flourishing – we postulate rights to protect what we regard as the vital interests of our fellows, say, their freedom from certain restraints or their access to a minimum level of welfare. Hence we need not defend a right to private property let alone a full-blown one. Any right people have to property must be one that the community gives them, so it can not be sacrosanct. Hence, also, we can place rights associated with social justice on an equal footing with those to political liberties and powers. Because rights are designed to promote human flourishing, our view of which rights are most important will depend on our view of flourishing, which might lead us to pay as much attention to the economy as to the state. Here social democrats have championed various rights and devices that seek to bring democracy to bear on the socio-economic sphere. The dominant tradition in the Labour Party has favoured devices that rely on state intervention to control industry in the interests of social rights; the state has relied on taxation and welfare benefits to ensure rights to education, housing, and a minimum income, and it has relied on various forms of intervention to subject economic groups to the will of representative government. Equally, oppositional traditions in the Labour Party have proposed that we supplement or even supplant these devices and rights with others. They have proposed popular control of the state and organisations in civil society, with worker ownership and participation, consumer organisations, and local bodies all providing ways of extending our democratic practices to economic groups.

If we were to promote a participatory democracy that emphasised deliberation and conduct, we might seek to devolve various aspects of governance to various associations within civil society. These associations could provide policy-makers with information, voice the concerns of their members, and play an active role in devising and implementing a range of policies. A pluralist democracy of this sort might appeal as a way of improving the effectiveness of public policy. It seems likely, for example, that involving diverse groups and individuals in the process of policy-making would bring more relevant information to bear on the policies, and also give those affected by policies a greater stake in making them work. A pluralist democracy also might appeal, however, as a way of fostering opportunities for participation, deliberation, and conduct. If we devolved aspects of governance to various groups in civil society, we would increase the number and range of organisations through which citizens could enter into democratic processes. Citizens could get involved through a diverse cluster of identities and concerns, perhaps as members of a religion or race, as people living in a city or region, as people engaged in some occupation, as consumers, and so on. Associations might act, then, as sites for the development of a civic consciousness that fostered deliberation on policy and participation in its formulation and enactment. What is more, because these associations could be self-governing, they need not be bound tightly by rules laid down by the state. Rather, their members could interpret, develop, and even modify our democratic norms through their own conduct. Associations might act as sites for citizens to enact and remake democratic practices.

The involvement of groups in the policy process raises the risk of a self-serving factionalism in tension with popular sovereignty and political equality, as many critics have pointed out. To lessen this risk, we might invoke norms in relation to which groups and their members should conduct themselves. No doubt the most important norm would be that individuals should be free to join and leave groups as they wish. Even groups that conceive of themselves as being based on objectified identities should have to open themselves up to those who fell outside of the criteria by which they sought to define themselves. More generally, groups would pose less of a threat to political equality if they were organised democratically. They should be neither highly centralised nor too reliant on market mechanisms. Groups should provide many and varied opportunities for participation, and they should have strong lines of accountability based on indirect and direct representation and even on outright ownership. If the state made such norms compulsory, or if it specified too many of their details, it would undermine much of the value of groups as sites of deliberation and conduct. Nonetheless, even when the state foregoes legislation – and there might be times when legislation is appropriate – it still could deploy administrative codes, taxes, and subsidies to encourage democratic and open groups.

A pluralist democracy also runs the risk that the most wealthy and powerful groups might exercise a disproportionate influence upon public policy. Although this risk seems to be just as present in all other democratic systems, we still might reduce it by invoking norms in relation to which the state should conduct its relations with other groups. No doubt the most important norms here would be general ones of importance in all democracies, including norms that sustain open and accountable government. In addition, however, the state again might deploy a range of administrative controls, tax incentives, subsidies, and even legislation in order to equalise somewhat the resources and influence of comparable groups.

We can draw on oppositional traditions within the Labour Party to unpack social democracy so as to ascribe a role in governance to a wide range of democratic groups in civil society. Because we are dealing with fuzzy boundaries rather than sharp dichotomies, we should not be surprised that this vision finds echoes in New Labour's liberal and communitarian democracy, notably in its devolution programme and in its advocacy of partnerships between the public sector and voluntary and private sector organisations. As well as these echoes, however, we find important contrasts. In general, New Labour appears to remain wedded to a liberal ideal of democracy as an ideal constitution derived from given principles of reason albeit that these principles have not yet been fully implemented. A pluralist democracy attempts, in contrast, to develop and extend a contingent democratic practice to associations of producers, consumers, and others. So, whereas New Labour has adopted a liberal agenda of constitutional reform, composed of devolution to national parliaments and of doses of electoral reform, a pluralist vision encourages us to invent and establish new fora in which citizens can deliberate, formulate policies, and connect with the state. Whereas New Labour typically relies on indirect representation within the institutions of the state, our pluralist democracy seeks to assign aspects of governance to democratic associations other than the state. Whereas New Labour promotes partnerships in which the state plays an active role, even seeking to regulate and control outcomes, a pluralist democracy would hand aspects of governance over to associations other than the state. Whereas New Labour's partnerships aim to deliver services more effectively with little concern for the inner workings of the organisations with which the state cooperates, a pluralist democracy is committed to extending democratic principles to businesses, unions, and other groups within civil society.

A pluralist democracy also differs from the communitarianism with which New Labour fills out its liberal agenda. Here our account of pluralist democracy opposes the communitarian tendency to reify communities or groups as if they were based on given identities or values. New Labour appears to believe that there is – or at least that there ought to be – consensus on the ethical content of citizenship such that the state should enforce the civic responsibilities associated with communitarian accounts of the good society. A pluralist democracy attempts, in contrast, to embrace that ethical pluralism which it postulates as perfectly legitimate. It allows various groups to establish different clusters of responsibilities. It appeals to deliberation and compromise, not an ideal consensus, as the means of addressing any tensions between the responsibilities established by different groups. So, whereas New Labour emphasises the importance of people acting virtuously, democratic pluralism concentrates on giving them opportunities to remake their collective practices without requiring them to do so in any given way, and without even suggesting that they have a responsibility to take up the opportunities made available to them. Whereas New Labour implies that people act virtuously when they fulfil their obligations and thereby contribute to the common good, democratic pluralism focuses on processes of decision-making without postulating a substantive concept of the common good against which outcomes might be measured, for even the content of the values associated with the open community, such as welfare and empowerment, are to be determined through democratic processes. Whereas New Labour implies that individuals must act virtuously if we are to have an integrated society, democratic pluralism relies on deliberation and compromise to resolve differences among individuals and groups and so to establish a more decentred social order. All these contrasts between New Labour and democratic pluralism reflect that between communitarianism and the open community. Communitarians typically invoke substantive concepts of virtue and the common good. But these concepts tend to be exclusionary, and, we might add, they can preclude the type of compromises that make democracy effective. Hence the open community seeks instead to allow people to make their own practices, virtues, and inter-subjective goods through a range of democratic processes.

Dialogue against expertise

We have seen that interpretivism can inspire a vision of an open community in which freedom consists of situated agency within particular practices and so is associated with the possibilities of participation, deliberation, and conduct rather than with the protection of a spurious autonomy.

We have also seen that some strands of social democracy can inspire us to promote these possibilities by means of a pluralism in which aspects of governance are transferred from the state to other democratic associations. Even if we decentred the state by giving such a role to other groups, however, we would do well to ask: what space do the state and these other groups offer for participation, deliberation, and conduct? When we address this question, we might draw once again on oppositional traditions of socialism to construct alternative visions to that which New Labour offers us. New Labour follows the dominant tradition in the Party in that it adheres to a liberal democracy in which the people vote for their representatives who then pass legislation which is implemented by professional civil servants: the rule of law and popular sovereignty help to protect an apparently natural freedom, while legislation and implementation are left to the expertise of, respectively, politicians and civil servants. Within the context of this liberal democracy, New Labour follows the new institutionalism in suggesting that expertise reveals networks generally to be the most effective structures for delivering policies. Because interpretivists reject the type of expertise to which this liberal and institutionalist model of democracy appeals, they might promote different ways of formulating and implementing public policy.

To begin, we again might endorse many of the features of liberal democracy. Here, too, liberal rights and devices safeguard private and public spaces for deliberation and conduct. They also help to bring deliberation and conduct to bear on our processes of collective decision-making. Democracy benefits from rights to free speech and to the vote, and from devices such as elected legislatures and the rule of law. In particular, we might endorse here the emphasis on elected legislatures acting as vehicles of popular sovereignty to direct and oversee administrative agencies, although, if we are pluralists, we will favour a wide diversity of such legislative fora. No matter how much we invoke deliberation and conduct, there will be moments when decisions have to be made, and at those moments majority rule through a legislature would seem to be an appropriate way of closing discussion and making a collective judgement. Similarly, no matter how many avenues for participation we establish in administrative agencies, complex modern societies appear to require a division of labour between the legislative fora that make laws and the agencies that implement them. Any such division of labour seems to require, in turn, that the legislatures constrain and oversee the agencies: democracy would be a sham if administrative acts were not accountable to the legislative bodies that authorise them. Even when we envisage rights and devices that extend deliberation and conduct in the formulation and implementation of public policy, so we should bear in mind, then, that they are supposed to support, not supplant, existing opportunities for legislative oversight and judicial review.

The importance of liberal rights and mechanisms does not imply that they are sufficient. On the contrary, a focus on democracy as a practice suggests that they pay insufficient attention to participation, deliberation, and conduct in the stages of collective decision-making that come before and after the legislative act. Whereas liberal constitutions often treat people as autonomous beings with incorrigible preferences that need merely to be represented adequately at the moment of legislative decision, a concern with democratic practice conceives of people as agents who construct and modify their preferences and beliefs through deliberation and conduct with others. Whereas liberal constitutions often distinguish sharply between policy issues and managerial ones, with the latter being left to administrative agencies, a concern with democratic practice acknowledges that our reasoning typically involves a reflexivity in which we further specify our ends when we choose the means by which to realise them.

Our democratic practice consists of stages of public debate, legislative decision, and implementation. Proposed laws and policies emerge out of public debate before then being drafted by legislators who also decide whether to enact them. If enacted, they are then implemented by agencies, which, in the process, typically specify their content still further. The stages of legislation and implementation are subject to various modes of feedback and oversight to keep them subject to popular will as expressed in debate. Each of these stages can be opened up to greater participation, deliberation, and conduct through a variety of rights and devices. So, although elected legislatures are arguably the organisations most open to influence by the public, and although we thus might ascribe primacy to them, a concern with democracy as a practice might encourage us to devise additional rights and devices to bring democratic values to bear on public debate and policy implementation. When we devise such rights and mechanisms, they will not be fixed principles derived from a pure reason, but rather contingent, invented possibilities. Our democratic practices should be the sites in which we decide which inventions we do and do not adopt.

Once we renounce ideal constitutions designed to protect an alleged autonomy in favour of practices of situated agency, we free ourselves to invent, modify, and reject rights and devices in the stages of public debate, legislative decision, and administrative implementation. We might propose for the stage of public debate modes of deliberation and conduct such as public hearings and deliberative polls. We might suggest for the stage of legislative decision modes of deliberation and conduct such as the citizens' initiative and referendum. We even might propose that decisions sometimes be made by citizens' juries or deliberative polls, with all citizens having an equal right or opportunity to participate, or to be selected for participation, in such decision-making bodies. In general, we might advocate more face-to-face modes of debate leading to more direct modes of decision-making.

While we might propose a range of democratic devices for the stages of debate and decision, our focus should fall perhaps on the stage of implementation. Many liberal devices cover the stages of debate and decision whereas that of implementation is left by and large to the expertise of an unelected civil service. Besides, a disaggregated account of the state highlights the democratic deficit in the agencies – departments, commissions, public–private partnerships, and others – that are involved in the implementation of public policy. For these reasons, our focus should fall on the promotion of a dialogic public policy. As we have seen, democratic principles suggest that agencies should operate in a liberal framework that includes the rule of law and fidelity to legislative decisions. Within this framework, however, we can promote processes of dialogue that seek to increase citizen participation within agencies. In doing so, we might divide the stage of implementation itself into sub-stages such as those of publicity, decision, and review. In the sub-stage of publicity, agencies might not only make known the rules and decisions on the basis of which they intend to act, but also invite comments on them from citizens, and even commission surveys, deliberative polls, and the like to garner opinion on them. During the stage of decision, agencies might involve citizens through all sorts of rarely used mechanisms; they might create committees as sites for face-to-face negotiations between agency representatives and various citizens, and they might provide stakeholders with places on the drafting committees that define their operating rules and procedures. Citizens thereby might help to make decisions and draft rules at all administrative levels from the central civil service to local benefit offices. In the stage of review, the agencies might be accountable not only to the legislature but also directly to citizens; such direct accountability could be enhanced by means such as the requirement to report to committees of citizens or even by the direct election of agency officials.

Dialogic modes of public policy are said by critics to allow particular groups to dominate or capture agencies. In response, we might argue that this risk is equally present in all other administrative systems. We also might propose that we lessen the risk of capture by appealing to various norms in relation to which agencies should conduct themselves. No doubt the most important norms would be those associated with publicity and accountability since they enable citizens to monitor and challenge the conduct of agencies. In addition, a norm of openness might preclude agencies from restricting the participants in negotiating and drafting committees to a given list of stakeholders, requiring them instead to involve all citizens who make a case that they have an interest in any given issue, or maybe even to involve all citizens who express such an interest. Perhaps a diffuse public voice could be added to such committees by introducing a norm of service akin to that which currently operates with respect to juries. Likewise, a norm of fairness might require agencies to offer financial or technical support to groups or individuals who want to be involved in negotiating or drafting committees but who would be at a disadvantage due to their lack of these resources. Here too, of course, if the state made such norms compulsory or if it specified their content in too much detail, it would undermine much of the value of agencies as possible sites of conduct. What matters is that we have a range of administrative codes, procedures, and subsidies that ensure that a dialogic public policy remains open and democratic.

We can draw on oppositional traditions within the Labour Party to unpack social democracy so as to promote a dialogic public policy instead of a reliance on allegedly neutral experts. While this vision finds echoes in the liberal and institutionalist themes that characterise New Labour's policies, notably in its belief that networks should involve the relevant stakeholders, there are also important differences here. Whereas New Labour appears to be wedded almost exclusively to a liberal democracy in which public policy is implemented by a managerial elite who are subject to direction and supervision by a political elite who in turn are accountable to the popular will through elections, a dialogic approach would promote deliberation and conduct throughout the policy-making process including the stage of implementation. Whereas liberal models typically deduce ideal democratic constitutions from principles that are given by an allegedly pure reason, a dialogic approach makes the constitution of democracy itself a matter to be decided within our democratic practice. Whereas liberal models typically rely on the assumption that administration can be a purely neutral or technical matter of implementing the will of the legislature, a dialogic approach allows for popular involvement in the processes by which administrative agencies actively interpret and define the will of the legislature.

A dialogic approach to public policy offers a contrast to the way in which New Labour, with its debt to an institutionalist approach to networks, often brushes aside democratic values such as participation, deliberation, and conduct in a rush to promote efficiency, effectiveness, and best value. Institutionalists who acknowledge that networks have their own typical problems often try to improve the capacity of the state to manage networks by devising appropriate tools.[42] New Labour too adopts a technical stance towards the management of networks, even adopting many of the tools advocated by institutionalists. It assumes that the centre can devise and impose devices that foster integration within networks and thereby realise its own objectives. Policies such as Action Zones have a centralising thrust in that they attempt to coordinate departments and local authorities by imposing a new style of management on agencies; agencies are to operate and be evaluated by criteria that are defined by the centre. The government openly says that while it does 'not want to run local services from the centre', it 'is not afraid to take action where standards slip'.[43]

Interpretivism undercuts the idea of a set of tools for managing networks. If networks are constructed differently, contingently, and continuously, we cannot have a tool kit for managing them. Interpretivism encourages us to forsake alleged techniques of management for a practice of learning by telling stories and listening to them. Although statistics, models, and comparison can have a place in such stories, we should not become too preoccupied with them. We should recognise that they too are narratives about how people have acted or will react given their beliefs and their desires. No matter what rigour we bring to bear, we can only tell stories about how people have acted in the past and then judge how they might act in the future. Because the fate of policies depends on the diverse ways in which civil servants and citizens understand them and respond to them from within various traditions, we are most likely to judge their fate adequately if we enter a dialogue with these others so as to learn about their worldviews and how they think they might react to different possible policies. Interpretivism suggests, then, that policies typically will be more effective as well as more democratic if they are based on engagement and negotiation with the concrete activities and struggles of governance in the field.

Conclusion: within Labour

New Labour is a prominent example of the future for social democracy in Britain and beyond. It represents its Third Way as the necessary product of a refashioning of social democracy to meet the demands of new times. In contrast, I have interpreted the Third Way as a contingent refashioning of one strand of social democracy; it reworks the dominant tradition within the Labour Party by drawing on new institutionalism and communitarianism to respond to issues raised by the New Right. New Labour follows the dominant tradition within the Party in privileging representative democracy as the context within which experts then can formulate and implement policies to solve social problems. It follows the new institutionalism in promoting networks and partnerships as the primary means of delivering services. It follows communitarianism in attempting to reform the welfare state so as to foreground personal responsibility within the settings of family and work. The broad contours of New Labour's policies often derive from these beliefs in liberal democracy, new institutionalism, and communitarianism. Its welfare reforms have tried to transform the role of the state into that of an enabling partner concerned to promote responsibility as well as to guarantee rights; they have encouraged a broad shift towards joined-up governance and networks as modes of service delivery. Likewise, its economic policies have combined a focus on macro-economic stability with efforts to revitalise the supply-side of the economy through government involvement in training and networks.

When we interpret the Third Way as a contingent refashioning of one strand of social democracy, we open up a space for imagining other futures for social democracy. These alternatives might emerge from other traditions within the Labour Party or without, and they might respond to the issues raised by the New Right in novel ways or they might simply deny the pertinence of these issues. One alternative arises from a commitment to an interpretive approach to political science that rejects the objectifications and the claims to scientific expertise that characterise the new institutionalism and communitarianism. The new institutionalism and communitarianism objectify types of organisation and even types of society so as to claim expertise about how they operate and how governments can manage them and improve their operation. New Labour adopts the conclusions offered by such expertise when it seeks to promote and steer networks and when it seeks to promote individual responsibility and social order through welfare-to-work schemes. In contrast, an interpretive approach to political science highlights situated agency and contingency in ways that undermine such expertise. It concentrates on the ways in which citizens actively make their social and political practices through their situated agency. If we then attach moral value to such situated agency, we can draw on oppositional traditions within the Labour Party to devise alternatives to the Third Way such as those associated with a pluralist democracy and a dialogic public policy.

While interpretivism can prompt an alternative vision to that of New Labour, this vision leaves important questions to be answered. It implies that, if we are to talk ethics, we should do so in terms of human interdependence, and so using concepts such as community, welfare, and empowerment, but it does not thereby tell us much about the substantive content that we should give to these concepts. How much welfare do we owe one another? What measures are needed to empower disadvantaged people? Questions about the substantive content of our ethical concepts are, I have been arguing, best left open in that they should be decided not by an allegedly pure reason or spurious expertise but by means of participation, deliberation, and conduct within a pluralist democracy and a dialogic public policy. However, there also remains the crucial question of the agent by which we should hope to realise our alternative visions. For over a century, the Labour Party has been the leading vehicle of hopes for social change in Britain. Throughout that time there have been Jeremiahs who lament the Party's failures and prophesy doom for those who place their hopes in it. To conclude, I want to argue that the preceding interpretation of New Labour undercuts such counsels of despair.

Social democrats surely need an organised political party in which to debate their ideals and policies and through which to seek to implement these policies in legislation. The alternative appears to be to withdraw from politics by placing one's hope in social movements, cultural practices, or – most emptily of all – a voluntaristic commitment to messianic eschatology.[44] Although such withdrawal can bring moral or critical purity, it risks self-righteousness, and it confronts vast practical and ethical problems. In practice, it faces the problem of ensuring that social democratic ideals and practices dominate the relevant social movements or cultural practices. The Labour Party has the advantage here of being an overtly social democratic group, for, while social and cultural movements can have an appropriate organisational form, they characteristically have specific purposes – say, pleasure or the promotion of the interests of a particular group – that marginalise or even conflict with those of social democracy. Besides, even if purists ensured that social democratic ideals dominated the relevant movements, they still would face the practical problem of bringing these ideals to bear on society as a whole: presumably they cannot deploy the relevant movements to promote legislation since doing so would involve their admitting, at least tacitly, to the need for an organised political party to enact legislation. In ethical terms, such purism faces the problem of how to give democratic legitimacy to ideals and policies without their being debated and voted upon in any legislative forum based on popular sovereignty. Why should other members of society acquiesce in ideals and policies that dominate a social movement but have received no kind of mandate from the population as a whole?

Because social democrats need an organised political party, the only plausible arguments for ceasing to place our hope in Labour are those that suggest that it is not an appropriate party. The more theoretical Jeremiahs argue here that we should not place our hopes in Labour because it is rotten at core; parliamentary socialism is doomed to disappoint us because of the essential properties of the state within a capitalist system.[45] This argument for despair relies on the by now familiar process of objectification so as to ascribe essential or core characteristics to institutions based on allegedly objective social facts. Hence an interpretive approach undercuts the theoretical basis of despair simply by drawing attention to the contingency of social life. The Labour Party does not have a given nature, or fixed limits, such that it is bound to disappoint us. On the contrary, it is a contingent and changeable product of a struggle over what it should be. No doubt some of those engaged in this struggle believe in organisational patterns and public policies with which we – whoever 'we' might be here – disagree profoundly. Equally, however, others do not, and there is no given social or political logic making necessary the triumph of the former over the latter.

The more empirical Jeremiahs might counsel despair on the grounds that New Labour is deeply committed to ideals and policies that differ considerably from those of social democracy.[46] Although there is room for considerable debate about both New Labour and the ideals and policies that social democrats should promote, the form of this argument relies on too monolithic an account of Labour; it neglects the diverse views that continue to inspire Labour's parliamentarians, Party activists, and Party members, let alone those who are broadly sympathetic to the Party. Hence, an interpretive approach undercuts the empirical basis of despair by disaggregating the Labour Party and thereby drawing our attention to the diversity of voices that can be found within it. Even if the dominant voices in New Labour appear to be wedded to things such as liberal democracy, communitarian values, and an institutionalist approach to networks, there are voices in the Party advocating alternative ideals and policies. What is more, several of these voices bear a resemblance to the alternative described above, but then that should not surprise us both because that alternative has drawn on oppositional traditions within the Party, and because these oppositional traditions – with their roots in Marxism and ethical socialism – always have overlapped with themes in the dominant outlook within the Party. New Labour might not be what we want, but that is no reason to despair of the Party; it is a reason, rather, to work through democratic processes to promote our alternative visions within the Party as well as the wider society of which it is a part.

Notes

1 Political science

1 Accounts of the transformation include S. Driver and L. Martell, *New Labour: Politics after Thatcherism* (Cambridge: Polity, 1998), pp. 6–31; R. Heffernan, *New Labour and Thatcherism: Political Change in Britain* (Basingstoke: Macmillan, 2000), pp. 65–84; T. Jones, *Remaking the Labour Party: From Gaitskell to Blair* (London: Routledge, 1996); S. Ludlam, 'The Making of New Labour', in S. Ludlam and M. Smith, eds, *New Labour in Government* (Basingstoke: Macmillan, 2001), pp. 1–31; E. Shaw, *The Labour Party since 1979: Crisis and Transformation* (London: Routledge, 1994); M. Smith and J. Spear, eds, *The Changing Labour Party* (London: Routledge, 1992); and G. Taylor, *Labour's Renewal? The Policy Review and Beyond* (Basingstoke: Macmillan, 1997). For reminiscences by some of those involved, see P. Gould, *The Unfinished Revolution: How the Modernisers Saved the Labour Party* (London: Little Brown, 1998); and N. Kinnock, 'Reforming the Labour Party', *Contemporary Record* 8 (1994), 535–54.
2 Blair told other European leaders that they had to 'modernise or die' in T. Blair, Speech to the Party of European Socialists Congress, Malmo, Sweden, 6 June 1997.
3 P. Arestis and M. Sawyer, eds, *The Economics of the Third Way: Experiences from around the World* (Cheltenham: Edward Elgar, 2001); G. Kelly, ed., *The New European Left* (London: Fabian Society, 1999); L. Martell, C. van der Anker, M. Brownes, S. Hooper, P. Larkin, C. Lees, F. McCowan, and N. Stammers, *Social Democracy: Global and National Perspectives* (Basingstoke: Palgrave, 2001); and S. White, ed., *New Labour: The Progressive Future?* (Basingstoke: Palgrave, 2001).
4 R. Reich, 'We Are All Third Wayers Now', *American Prospect* 43 (1999), 46–51.
5 Cm. 4310, *Modernising Government* (London: Stationery Office, 1999).
6 The case of Mrs T derives from collaboration with Rod Rhodes. I am grateful to him for allowing me to use it. The social workers involved have read and agreed to a longer version of what is repeated here.
7 J. Burrow, *Whigs and Liberals: Continuity and Change in English Political Thought* (Oxford: Oxford University Press, 1988); S. Collini, D. Winch, and J. Burrow, *That Noble Science of Politics: A Study in Nineteenth-Century Intellectual History* (Cambridge: Cambridge University Press, 1983); and M. Francis and J. Morrow, *A History of English Political Thought in the Nineteenth Century* (London: Duckworth, 1994), pp. 96–8.
8 S. Collini, *Liberalism and Sociology: L. T. Hobhouse and Political Argument in Britain, 1880–1914* (Cambridge: Cambridge University Press, 1979); and

S. Den Otter, *British Idealism and Social Explanation* (Oxford: Clarendon Press, 1996).

9 W. Everdell, *The First Moderns* (Chicago: University of Chicago Press, 1997); M. Schabas, *A World Ruled by Number: William Stanley Jevons and the Rise of Mathematical Economics* (Princeton: Princeton University Press, 1990); and H. Stuart Hughes, *Consciousness and Society: The Reorientation of European Social Thought 1890–1930* (New York: Vintage Books, 1961).

10 J. Bryce, *Modern Democracies*, 2 vols (London: Macmillan, 1921); and, for comment, Collini *et al.*, *Noble Science*, pp. 236–46.

11 H. Finer, *Foreign Governments at Work* (New York: Oxford University Press, 1921); and H. Finer, *Theory and Practice of Modern Government* (Westport, CT: Greenwood Press, 1970).

12 J. Hayward, 'British Approaches to Politics: The Dawn of a Self-Deprecating Discipline', in J. Hayward, B. Barry, and A. Brown, eds, *The British Study of Politics in the Twentieth Century* (Oxford: Oxford University Press, 1999), p. 6.

13 Collini *et al.*, *Noble Science*, pp. 368–77; J. Harris, 'Political Thought and the Welfare State 1870–1914: An Intellectual Framework for British Social Policy', *Past and Present* 135 (1992), 116–41; and J. Stapleton, *Englishness and the Study of Politics: The Social and Political Thought of Ernest Barker* (Cambridge: Cambridge University Press, 1994).

14 M. Bevir and D. O'Brien, 'From Idealism to Communitarianism: The Inheritance and Legacy of John Macmurray', *History of Political Thought* 24 (2003), 305–29.

15 See C. Hood, 'British Public Administration: Dodo, Phoenix, or Chameleon?', in Hayward *et al.*, eds, *British Study*, p. 309; and W. Mackenzie, *Politics and Social Science* (Harmondsworth: Penguin, 1967), p. 64, as cited approvingly in Hayward, 'British Approaches', p. 33.

16 D. Englander and R. O'Day, eds, *Retrieved Riches: Social Investigation in Britain 1880–1914* (Aldershot: Scholar Press, 1995).

17 W. Mackenzie, 'Pressure Groups in British Government', *British Journal of Sociology* 6 (1955), 284–96; and also R. Rhodes, *Beyond Westminster and Whitehall* (London: Unwin Hyman, 1988); J. Richardson and G. Jordan, *Governing Under Pressure: The Policy Process in a Post-Parliamentary Democracy* (Oxford: Martin Robertson, 1979); and R. Rose, *Do Parties Make a Difference?* (London: Macmillan, 1980).

18 D. Marsh and R. Rhodes, eds, *Policy Networks in British Government* (Oxford: Clarendon Press, 1992); D. Marsh, *Comparing Policy Networks* (Buckingham: Open University Press, 1998); and Richardson and Jordan, *Governing Under Pressure*.

19 J. Douglas, 'The Overloaded Crown', *British Journal of Political Science* 6 (1976), 483–505; and A. King, 'Overload: Problems of Governing in the UK in the 1970s', *Political Studies* 38 (1975), 284–96.

20 R. Rhodes, *Understanding Governance: Policy Networks, Governance, Reflexivity, and Accountability* (Buckingham: Open University Press, 1997), chapter 3; and G. Stoker, ed., *The New Management of British Local Government* (London: Macmillan, 1999).

21 J. March and J. Olsen, 'The New Institutionalism: Organisational Factors in Political Life', *American Political Science Review* 78 (1984), 738.

22 P. Hall, *Governing the Economy* (New York: Oxford University Press, 1986), p. 20.

23 N. Johnson, 'The Place of Institutions in the Study of Politics', *Political Studies* 23 (1975), 271–83.

24 D. Saunders, 'Behavioural Analysis', in D. Marsh and G. Stoker, eds, *Theories and Methods in Political Science* (Basingstoke: Palgrave, 2002), pp. 45–89.

25 Whether or not behaviouralists are willing to unpack their explanation in such terms depends on how strictly they adhere to positivist concerns about avoiding appeals to unobservable entities and on how much they owe to Hume's concept of causation.

26 Compare C. Taylor, 'Interpretation and the Sciences of Man', *Review of Metaphysics* 25 (1971–2), 3–51.

27 Early exponents of rational choice theory often privileged self-interest in this way. See A. Downs, *An Economic Theory of Democracy* (New York: Harper and Row, 1957), pp. 27–8.

28 See respectively J. Elster, *Ulysses and the Sirens* (Cambridge: Cambridge University Press, 1984); and J. Elster, *Sour Grapes: Studies in the Subversion of Rationality* (Cambridge: Cambridge University Press, 1983), p. 1.

29 P. Schoemaker, 'The Expected Utility Model: Its Variants, Purposes, Evidence and Limitations', *Journal of Economic Literature* 20 (1982), 529–63.

30 D. Chong, 'Rational Choice Theory's Mysterious Rivals', in J. Friedman, ed., *The Rational Choice Controversy* (New Haven: Yale University Press, 1996). Other examples include M. Hinich and M. Munger, 'Political Ideology, Communication, and Community', in W. Barnett, M. Hinich, and N. Schofield, eds, *Political Economy: Institutions, Competition, and Representation* (Cambridge: Cambridge University Press, 1993); W. Mitchell, 'The Shape of Public Choice to Come: Some Predictions and Advice', *Public Choice* 77 (1993), 133–44; D. North, 'Toward a Theory of Institutional Change', in Barnett *et al.*, eds, *Political Economy*; and C. Vicchaeri, *Rationality and Co-ordination* (Cambridge: Cambridge University Press, 1993), partic. pp. 221–4.

31 They say that the causal efficacy of norms derives from 'the strong emotions their violations can trigger'. See J. Elster, *The Cement of Society* (Cambridge: Cambridge University Press, 1989), p. 100.

32 They allow for an individual acting on norms simply by putting 'community values into his or her utility function'. See T. Brennan, 'A Methodological Assessment of Multiple Utility Frameworks', *Economics and Philosophy* 5 (1989), 189–208.

33 R. Bernstein, *The Restructuring of Social and Political Theory* (Philadelphia: University of Pennsylvania Press, 1976); and B. Fay, *Contemporary Philosophy of Social Science* (Oxford: Blackwell Publishers, 1996). In so far as political scientists remain wedded to a lukewarm positivism, perhaps they are ignorant of this literature or perhaps they believe the need to reconcile their idea of political science with philosophical insights is less important than the need to retain the vestiges of scientific expertise and predictive power.

34 For an attempt to distinguish a discursive or constructivist institutionalism, see J. Campbell and O. Pedersen, eds, *The Rise of Neoliberalism and Institutional Analysis* (Princeton: Princeton University Press, 2001).

35 M. Foucault, *The Archaeology of Knowledge*, trans. A. Sheridan-Smith (London: Tavistock, 1972); and M. Foucault, *Power/Knowledge: Selected Interviews and Other Writings, 1972–77*, ed. C. Gordon (Brighton: Harvester, 1980).

36 Q. Skinner, 'Motives, Intentions, and the Interpretation of Texts', in J. Tully, ed., *Meaning and Context: Quentin Skinner and his Critics* (Cambridge: Polity Press, 1988), pp. 68–78.

37 M. Dean, 'Culture Governance and Individualisation', in H. Bang, ed., *Governance as Social and Political Communication* (Manchester: Manchester University Press, 2003), p. 123.

38 For example, although Gordon tells us that techniques of power do not dominate people but rather operate through their freedom, the studies that follow his introduction include virtually no examples of agents applying norms in

creative ways that transform power. See C. Gordon, 'Governmental Rationality: An Introduction', in G. Burchell, C. Gordon, and P. Miller, eds, *The Foucault Effect: Studies in Governmentality* (London: Harvester Wheatsheaf, 1991), p. 5.

39 Dean rightly complains, 'the problem with contemporary sociological accounts is that they are pitched at too general a level and propose mysterious, even occult, relations between general processes and events (e.g. globalization, de-traditionalisation) and features of self and identity'. But he remains apparently unaware of the extent to which his narrative appears to rely on the equally mysterious, even occult, impact of an overarching 'individualizing power' upon the practices and activities it allegedly generates. See Dean, 'Culture Governance', p. 126.

40 For a full account of these concepts and their role in the human sciences, see M. Bevir, *The Logic of the History of Ideas* (Cambridge: Cambridge University Press, 1999).

2 Institutionalism

1 See P. Self, *Government by the Market: The Politics of Public Choice* (London: Macmillan, 1993); and, for the role of think-tanks, R. Cockett, *Thinking the Unthinkable: Think-Tanks and the Economic Counter Revolution* (London: HarperCollins, 1995).

2 M. Granovetter, 'The Strength of Weak Ties', *American Journal of Sociology* 78 (1973), 1360–80; M. Granovetter, 'Economic Action and Social Structure: The Problem of Embeddedness', *American Journal of Sociology* 91 (1985), 481–510; P. DiMaggio and W. Powell, 'The Iron Cage Revisited: Institutional Isomorphism and Collective Rationality in Organizational Fields', in W. Powell and P. DiMaggio, eds, *The New Institutionalism in Organizational Analysis* (Chicago: Chicago University Press, 1991); W. Powell, 'Neither Market nor Hierarchy: Network Forms of Organization', *Research in Organizational Behaviour* 12 (1990), 295–336; R. Rhodes, *Understanding Governance: Policy Networks, Governance, Reflexivity, and Accountability* (Buckingham: Open University Press, 1997), chaps. 2 and 4; and G. Stoker, 'Urban Political Science and the Challenge of Urban Governance', in J. Pierre, ed., *Debating Governance* (Oxford: Oxford University Press, 2000), p. 93.

3 Biographies include D. MacIntyre, *Mandelson: The Biography* (London: HarperCollins, 1999); J. Rentoul, *Tony Blair* (London: Little Brown, 1995); P. Routledge, *Gordon Brown: The Biography* (London: Simon and Schuster, 1998); P. Routledge, *Mandy* (London: Simon and Schuster, 1999); and J. Sopel, *Tony Blair: The Moderniser* (London: Bantam Books, 1995).

4 Cm. 4176, *Our Competitive Future: Building the Knowledge Driven Economy* (London: Stationery Office, 1998).

5 T. Blair, *New Britain: My Vision of a Young Country* (London: Fourth Estate, 1996), pp. 291–6.

6 General studies include P. Hall and R. Taylor, 'Political Science and the Three Institutionalisms', *Political Studies* 44 (1996), 936–57; J. Kato, 'Institutions and Rationality in Politics: Three Varieties of Neo-Institutionalists', *British Journal of Political Science* 26 (1996), 553–82; V. Lowndes, 'Varieties of New Institutionalism: A Critical Appraisal', *Public Administration* 74 (1996), 181–97; and K. Thelen, 'Historical Institutionalism in Comparative Politics', *Annual Review of Political Science* 2 (1999), 369–404.

7 Although I believe the persistence of the Westminster model plays a significant and baneful role in British institutionalism and in New Labour, I devote

little space to it here because of its prominence in M. Bevir and R. Rhodes, *Interpreting British Governance* (London: Routledge, 2003).

8 R. Adcock, 'The Emergence of Political Science as a Discipline: History and the Study of Politics in America 1875–1910', *History of Political Thought* 24 (2003).

9 For examples of the new techniques and systematic theory, see respectively A. Campbell, P. Converse, W. Miller, and D. Stokes, *The American Voter* (New York: Wiley, 1960); and D. Easton, *The Political System: An Inquiry into the State of Political Science* (New York: Knopf, 1953).

10 P. Hall, *Governing the Economy: The Politics of State Intervention in Britain and France* (New York: Oxford University Press, 1986), partic. pp. 17–20; and J. March and J. Olsen, 'The New Institutionalism: Organizational Factors in Political Life', *American Political Science Review* 78 (1984), 734–49.

11 As Peter Hall, a leading new institutionalist, explains, 'whereas the earlier institutionalism militated cross-national comparisons, this approach utilizes them to identify the most salient institutional determinants of policy'. Hall, *Governing the Economy*, p. 20.

12 C. Friedrich, 'Comments on the Seminar Report', *American Political Science Review* 48 (1953), 658–61; and S. Beer, 'Political Science and History', in M. Richter, ed., *Essays in Theory and History* (Cambridge, MA: Harvard University Press, 1970), pp. 41–73.

13 T. Skocpol, *States and Social Revolutions* (Cambridge: Cambridge University Press, 1979).

14 T. Skocpol, 'Theory Tackles History', *Social Science History* 24 (2000), 675–6.

15 M. Taylor, 'Structure, Culture and Action in the Explanation of Social Change', *Politics and Society* 17 (1989), 115–62.

16 March and Olsen, 'New Institutionalism', 747.

17 M. Blyth, 'Institutions and Ideas', in D. Marsh and G. Stoker, eds, *Theory and Methods in Political Science* (Basingstoke: Palgrave, 2002), pp. 292–310. At times the dismissal of theory as hostile to big substantive issues works by an implicit assimilation of all theory to the universal pretensions of behaviouralism as in T. Skocpol, 'Emerging Agendas and Recurrent Strategies in Historical Sociology', in *Vision and Method in Historical Sociology* (Cambridge: Cambridge University Press, 1984), pp. 356–91.

18 The problem of collective action was highlighted by K. Arrow, *Social Choice and Individual Values* (New York: Wiley, 1951). Rational-choice institutionalists respond along lines suggested by O. Williamson, 'Transaction-Cost Economics: The Governance of Contractual Relations', *Journal of Law and Economics* 22 (1979), 223–61.

19 For critical elections and junctures, see W. Burnham, *Critical Elections and the Mainsprings of American Politics* (New York: W. W. Norton, 1970); and R. Collier and D. Collier, *Shaping the Political Arena: Critical Junctures, the Labor Movement, and Regime Dynamics in Latin America* (Princeton: Princeton University Press, 1991). For the assimilation of such concepts by British political scientists, see G. Evans and P. Norris, eds, *Critical Elections: Voters and Parties in Long-Term Perspective* (London: Sage, 1999); and D. Richards and M. Smith, 'How Departments Change: Windows of Opportunity and Critical Junctures in Three Departments', *Public Policy and Administration* 12 (1997), 62–79.

20 P. Pierson, 'Increasing Returns, Path Dependence, and the Study of Politics', *American Political Science Review* 92 (2000), 251–67; and J. Mahoney, 'Path Dependence in Historical Sociology', *Theory and Society* 29 (2000), 507–48.

21 Rhodes, *Understanding Governance*, p. 79.

22 P. Evans and J. Stephens, 'Studying Development since the Sixties: The Emergence of a New Comparative Political Economy', *Theory and Society* 17 (1988), 734.

23 D. Osborne and T. Gaebler, *Reinventing Government: How the Entrepreneurial Spirit is Transforming the Public Sector* (Reading, MA: Addison-Wesley, 1992); K. Ohmae, *The End of the Nation State* (New York: Free Press, 1996); and W. Reinecke, *Global Public Policy: Governing without Government?* (Washington, DC: Brookings Institution Press, 1994).

24 Rhodes, *Understanding Governance*, partic. chaps 1 and 3; and G. Stoker, 'Introduction: The Unintended Costs and Benefits of New Management Reform for British Local Governance', in G. Stoker, ed., *The New Management of British Local Governance* (London: Macmillan, 1999), pp. 1–21.

25 Stoker, ed., *New Management*; G. Stoker, ed., *The New Politics of British Local Governance* (London: Macmillan, 2000); and R. Rhodes, ed., *Transforming British Government*, 2 vols (London: Macmillan, 2000).

26 M. Granovetter, 'Business Groups', in N. Smelser and R. Swedberg, eds, *Handbook of Economic Sociology* (Princeton: Princeton University Press, 1994), pp. 453–75; and Powell, 'Neither Market nor Hierarchy'.

27 Granovetter, 'Economic Action'; and Powell and DiMaggio, *New Institutionalism*.

28 Institutionalists, more generally, fuse 'good', in the sense of promoting solidarity or community, with 'good', in terms of a quasi-Darwinian notion of viability or success. Perri 6, for example, says, 'a "good" institution ... is a more viable one than others that might, in a given social setting, emerge, be created ... [it] is one that promotes organic rather than mechanical solidarities'. Perri 6, 'Neo-Durkheimian Institutional Theory', Paper to Conference on Institutional Theory in Political Science, Loch Lomond, 1999.

29 P. Evans, *Embedded Autonomy: States and Industrial Transformation* (Princeton: Princeton University Press, 1995); Granovetter, 'Business Groups'; W. Powell, K. Koput, and L. Smith-Doerr, 'Interorganizational Collaboration and the Locus of Innovation: Networks of Learning in Biotechnology', *Administrative Science Quarterly* 41 (1996), 116–45; and R. Putnam, *Making Democracy Work: Civic Traditions in Modern Italy* (Princeton: Princeton University Press, 1993), partic. p. 160.

30 R. Rhodes, *Beyond Westminster and Whitehall* (London: Unwin-Hyman, 1988), pp. 77–8; D. Marsh and R. Rhodes, eds, *Policy Networks in British Government* (Oxford: Clarendon Press, 1992), p. 251; and S. Wilks and M. Wright, 'Conclusion: Comparing Government–Industry Relations: States, Sectors, and Networks', in S. Wilks and M. Wright, eds, *Comparative Government Industry Relations* (Oxford: Clarendon Press, 1987), p. 300.

31 Powell and DiMaggio, eds, *New Institutionalism*; and Marsh and Rhodes, *Policy Networks*, p. 261.

32 T. Blair, *The Third Way: New Politics for a New Century*, Fabian Pamphlet no. 588 (London: Fabian Society, 1998); and A. Giddens, *The Third Way: The Renewal of Social Democracy* (Cambridge: Polity Press, 1998).

33 Blair, *Third Way*, p. 1.

34 T. Blair, 'Why Modernisation Matters', *Renewal* 1 (1993), 4–11.

35 Commission on Social Justice, *Social Justice: Strategies for National Renewal* (London: Vintage, 1994), p. 77.

36 Labour Party, *A New Economic Policy for Britain: Economic and Employment Opportunities for All* (London: Labour Party, 1995).

37 A. Giddens, *The Third Way and Its Critics* (London: Polity Press, 2000), p. 24. For other discussions of American influences and parallels, see A. Deacon, 'Learning from the US?', *Policy and Politics* 28 (2000), 5–18; C. Hay, 'New

Labour and "Third Way" Political Economy: Paving the European Road to Washington', in M. Bevir and F. Trentmann, eds, *Critiques of Capital in Modern Britain and America: Transatlantic Exchanges 1800 to the Present Day* (Basingstoke: Palgrave, 2002), pp. 195–219; D. Jänicke, 'New Labour and the Clinton Presidency', in D. Coates and P. Lawler, eds, *New Labour in Power* (Manchester: Manchester University Press, 2001), pp. 34–48; D. King and M. Wickham-Jones, 'Bridging the Atlantic: The Democratic (Party) Origins of Welfare to Work', in M. Powell, ed., *New Labour, New Welfare State? The 'Third Way' in British Social Policy* (Bristol: Policy Press, 1999), pp. 257–80; and R. Walker, 'The Americanization of British Welfare', *International Journal of Health Services* 29 (1999), 679–97. Other countries – notably Australia – also provided inspiration for New Labour. See B. Frankel, 'Beyond Labourism and Socialism: How the Australian Labor Party Developed the Model of New Labour', *New Left Review* 221 (1997), 3–33; C. Pierson and F. Castles, 'Australian Antecedents of the Third Way', *Political Studies* 50 (2002), 683–702; and A. Scott, *Running on Empty: 'Modernizing' the British and Australian Labour Parties* (Sydney: Pluto Press, 2000).

38 On competing versions of the Third Way – albeit with common features – see S. Driver and L. Martell, *Blair's Britain* (Cambridge: Polity, 2002), pp. 91–4; and S. White, 'The Ambiguities of the Third Way', in S. White, ed., *New Labour: The Progressive Future?* (Basingstoke: Palgrave, 2001), pp. 3–17.

39 Blair, *New Britain*, p. 300.

40 Compare Granovetter, 'Economic Action'; Perri 6, 'Neo-Durkheimian'; and Blair, *New Britain*.

41 Perri 6, *Escaping Poverty: From Safety Nets to Networks of Opportunity* (London: Demos, 1997). Also see M. Granovetter, *Getting a Job: A Study of Contracts and Careers* (Cambridge, MA: Harvard University Press, 1974).

42 D. Clark, speech, 'The Civil Service and the New Government', London, 17 June 1997.

43 C. Leadbeater, *Living on Thin Air* (Harmondsworth: Penguin, 1999).

44 G. Mulgan, *Connexity* (London: Jonathan Cape, 1997).

45 Cm. 4011, *Modern Public Services for Britain: Investing in Reform* (London: Stationery Office, 1998).

46 Blair, *New Britain*, p. 302.

47 Cm. 3805, *New Ambitions for Our Country: A New Contract for Welfare* (London: Stationery Office, 1997), p. v.

48 Blair, *New Britain*, p. 292.

49 Leadbeater, *Living on Thin Air*.

50 Cited in J. Heastfield, 'Brand New Britain', *LM Magazine*, November 1997. Also see M. Leonard, *Britain: Renewing Our Identity* (London: Demos, 1997).

51 C. Leadbeater and G. Mulgan, *Mistakeholding: Whatever Happened to Labour's Big Idea?* (London: Demos, 1996); and G. Stoker, 'The Three Projects of New Labour', *Renewal* 8 (2000), 7–15.

52 *Observer*, 31 May 1998.

53 Perri 6, *Holistic Government* (London: Demos, 1997); and Perri 6, D. Leat, K. Seltzer, and G. Stoker, *Governing in the Round: Strategies for Holistic Government* (London: Demos, 1999).

54 J. Pierre and G. Stoker, 'Towards Multi-Level Governance', in P. Dunleavy, A. Gamble, and I. Holliday, eds, *Developments in British Politics* no. 6 (Basingstoke: Macmillan, 2000).

55 Rhodes, *Understanding Governance*, pp. 17–19.

56 P. Hennessey, 'The Blair Style of Government', *Government and Opposition* 33 (1998), 3–20.

57 Cm. 4310, *Modernising Government* (London: Stationery Office, 1999), pp. 56 and 6.

58 Cm. 4045, *Bringing Britain Together: A National Strategy for Neighbourhood Renewal* (London: Stationery Office, 1998).

59 W. Kickert, E.-H. Klijn, and J. Koppenjan, 'Managing Networks in the Public Sector: Findings and Reflections', in W. Kickert, E.-H. Klijn, and J. Koppenjan, eds, *Managing Complex Networks: Strategies for the Public Sector* (London: Sage, 1998).

60 Stoker, 'Urban Political Science', pp. 98–104.

61 G. Mulgan and Perri 6, 'The Local is Coming Home: Decentralisation by Degrees', *Demos Quarterly* 9 (1996), 3–7.

62 V. Lowndes, 'Rebuilding Trust in Central/Local Relations: Policy or Passion?', in L. Pratchett, ed., *Renewing Local Democracy* (London: Frank Cass, 2000).

63 Department of Health, *The New NHS, Modern and Dependable: A National Framework for Assessing Performance* (London: Stationery Office, 1998); and Department of Health, *A First Class Service: Quality in the New NHS* (London: Stationery Office, 1999).

64 Compare Perri 6, *Holistic Government*.

65 Compare C. Leadbeater, *The Rise of the Social Entrepreneur* (London: Demos, 1997); and C. Leadbeater and S. Goss, *Civic Entrepreneurship* (London: Demos, 1998).

66 Perri 6 *et al.*, *Governing in the Round*.

67 Perri 6, *Holistic Government*.

3 Communitarianism

1 T. Blair, *Let us Face the Future*, Fabian Pamphlet no. 571 (London: Fabian Society, 1995), p. 12. On New Labour's peculiar construction of the Party's past, see E. Shaw, *The Labour Party since 1945* (Oxford: Blackwell, 1996), pp. 206–29.

2 The surveys referred to are respectively W. Stead, 'The Labour Party and the Books that Helped Make it', *Review of Reviews* 33 (1906), 568–82; *New Society*, 13 December 1962; *New Society*, 2 December 1975; and *New Statesman and Society*, 30 September 1994.

3 G. Brown and T. Wright, 'Introduction', to *Values, Visions and Voices: An Anthology of Socialism* (Edinburgh: Mainstream Publishing, 1995), pp. 13 and 29. Also see S. Driver and L. Martell, *New Labour: Politics after Thatcherism* (Cambridge: Polity, 1998), pp. 179–81.

4 M. Beer, *A History of British Socialism*, 2 vols (London: George Allen and Unwin, 1953); and A. Benn, *A Future for Socialism* (London: Fount, 1991).

5 A. Heywood, *Political Ideologies* (London: Macmillan, 1992), p. 11.

6 A. Vincent, *Modern Political Ideologies* (Oxford: Blackwell, 1992).

7 A. Vincent, 'New Ideologies for Old?', *Political Quarterly* 69 (1998), 57. Although Vincent does not show this, Blair occasionally evokes new liberals, albeit less often than he does ethical socialists. See, for instance, T. Blair, *New Britain: My Vision of a Young Country* (London: Fourth Estate, 1996), pp. 14–15.

8 Vincent, 'New Ideologies', 55.

9 M. Freeden, *Ideologies and Political Theory: A Conceptual Approach* (Oxford: Clarendon Press, 1996).

10 M. Freeden, 'The Ideology of New Labour', *Political Quarterly* 70 (1999), 45.

11 Freeden, 'New Labour', 44.

12 D. Marquand, 'The Blair Paradox', *Prospect*, May 1998. Also see C. Russell, 'New Labour: Old Tory Writ Large?', *New Left Review* 219 (1996), 78–88.

13 M. Seliger, *Ideology and Politics* (London: Allen and Unwin, 1976).

14 E. Shaw, *The Labour Party since 1979: Crisis and Transformation* (London: Routledge, 1994); and I. Budge, 'Party Policy and Ideology: Reversing the 1950s?', in G. Evans and P. Norris, eds, *Critical Elections: Voters and Parties in Long-Term Perspective* (London: Sage, 1999), pp. 1–22.

15 P. Mandelson and R. Liddle, *The Blair Revolution: Can New Labour Deliver?* (London: Faber and Faber, 1996), p. 4.

16 S. Pierson, *Marxism and the Origins of English Socialism* (Ithaca: Cornell University Press, 1973); and S. Pierson, *British Socialism: The Journey from Fantasy to Politics* (Cambridge, MA: Harvard University Press, 1979).

17 T. Wright, *Tawney* (Manchester: Manchester University Press, 1987), p. 19.

18 W. Temple, *Christianity and Social Order* (London: Shepherd-Walwyn, 1976), p. 97.

19 E. Carpenter, *Towards Democracy* (London: Gay Men's Press, 1985), p. 410.

20 Contrast T. Bale, 'The Logic of No Alternative? Political Scientists, Historians and the Politics of Labour's Past', *British Journal of Politics and International Relations* 1 (1999), 192–204.

21 The Labour Party, *Made in Britain: A New Economic Policy for the 1990s* (London: Labour Party, 1991); and The Labour Party, *Rebuilding the Economy* (London: Labour Party, 1994).

22 Mandelson and Liddle, *Blair Revolution*, pp. 27 and 151.

23 C. Gore, *The Social Doctrine of the Sermon on the Mount* (London: Percival, 1892), pp. 10–12.

24 T. Blair, Speech to the Party of European Socialists' Congress, Malmo, 6 June 1997.

25 Mandelson and Liddle, *Blair Revolution*, p. 22.

26 Mandelson and Liddle, *Blair Revolution*, p. 155.

27 T. Bale, 'Managing the Party and the Trade Unions', in B. Brivati and T. Bale, eds, *New Labour in Power: Precedents and Prospects* (London: Routledge, 1997); P. Dorey, 'The Blairite Betrayal: New Labour and the Unions', in G. Taylor, ed., *The Impact of New Labour* (Basingstoke: Macmillan, 1999), pp. 190–207; and S. Ludlam, 'New Labour and the Unions: The End of the Contentious Alliance', in S. Ludlam and M. Smith, eds, *New Labour in Government* (Basingstoke: Macmillan, 2001), pp. 111–29.

28 G. Brown, The Anthony Crosland Memorial Lecture, London, 13 February 1997.

29 Department for Education and Employment, Employability at the Heart of British Presidency Agenda, Press Release, 4 February 1998.

30 B. Gould, *Socialism and Freedom* (London: Macmillan, 1985), p. 65.

31 Mandelson and Liddle, *Blair Revolution*, pp. 72–3.

32 T. Blair, Reforming Welfare – Building on Beveridge, Speech to the Southampton Institute, 13 July 1994.

33 Department for Education and Employment, New Year, New Deal, New Hope, Press Release, 5 January 1998.

34 T. Blair, Speech to Women's Institute, 7 June 2000.

35 The Commission on Social Justice, *Social Justice: Strategies for National Renewal* (London: Vintage, 1994).

36 Blair, *New Britain*, p. 298.

37 T. Blair, Speech to the Labour Party Conference, 30 September 1997; Blair, *New Britain*, p. 238.

38 T. Blair, Values and the Power of Community, Speech to Global Ethics Foundation, Tübingen University, 30 June 2000.

39 Department for Education and Employment, New Year. Even before the formulation of the New Deal the Labour Party had declared: 'there will be no ... option of remaining permanently on full benefit. Where there is a suitable offer, people will be expected to take this up. We believe this is fair – rights and responsibilities must go together.' See The Labour Party, *New Life for Britain* (London: Labour Party, 1996).

40 W. Morris, *The Collected Works of William Morris* (London: Longmans, 1910–15), vol. 16: *News from Nowhere*, p. 230.

41 E. Hobsbawm *et al.*, *The Forward March of Labour Halted* (London: New Left Books, 1981). Also see, for behaviouralist analyses, A. Heath, R. Jowell, J. Curtice, and B. Taylor, eds, *Labour's Last Chance? The 1992 Election and Beyond* (Aldershot: Dartmouth, 1994). For a behaviouralist attempt to reconsider such analyses following the electoral triumph of New Labour, see A. Heath, R. Jowell, and J. Curtice, *The Rise of New Labour: Party Policies and Voter Choices* (Oxford: Oxford University Press, 2001). Although New Labour responded to an issue highlighted by behaviouralists as well as Marxists, it conceived and responded to this issue in ways noticeably differently from the former, as is indicated by P. Gould, 'Why Labour Won', in I. Crewe, B. Gosschalk, and J. Bartle, eds, *Political Communications: Why Labour Won the General Election of 1997* (London: Frank Cass, 1998), p. 3. For the presence of such issues within the Labour Party, see, for example, T. Blair, *Socialism*, Fabian Pamphlet no. 565 (London: Fabian Society, 1992); G. Radice, *Southern Discomfort*, Fabian Pamphlet no. 555 (London: Fabian Society, 1992); and G. Radice and S. Pollard, *More Southern Discomfort: Year On – Taxing and Spending*, Fabian Pamphlet no. 560 (London: Fabian Society, 1993).

42 Although the Labour Party initially opposed the sale of council houses, New Labour has almost tried to make the policy its own with Mandelson and Liddle emphasising that a Labour Policy Unit had advocated such a policy in the 1970s only to find their proposal blocked by entrenched interests within the Party. See Mandelson and Liddle, *Blair Revolution*, pp. 12 and 225. Gould also makes clear the importance of the policy for the Party's development. See Gould, *Socialism*, pp. 19–20.

43 Mandelson and Liddle, *Blair Revolution*, pp. 105–8.

44 F. Field, with commentaries by P. Alcock, A. Deacon, D. Green, and M. Phillips, *Stakeholder Welfare* (London: Institute of Economic Affairs, 1996), p. 26.

45 Blair, *New Britain*, pp. 299–300.

46 Mandelson and Liddle, *Blair Revolution*, p. 33. Also see C. Bryant, *Possible Dreams: A Personal History of British Christian Socialists* (London: Hodder and Stoughton, 1996), pp. 293–5; and A. Wilkinson, 'New Labour and Christian Socialism', in G. Taylor, ed., *The Impact of New Labour* (Basingstoke: Macmillan, 1999), partic. pp. 47–49.

47 T. Wright, *Who Wins Dares: New Labour – New Politics*, Fabian Pamphlet no. 579 (London: Fabian Society, 1997), p. 6.

48 *Independent*, 12 April 1997.

49 F. Field, *An Agenda for Britain* (London: Fount, 1993), p. 20.

50 F. Field, *Making Welfare Work: Reconstructing Welfare for the Millennium* (London: Institute for Community Studies, 1995), p. 3.

51 Blair, *New Britain*, pp. 291–6.

52 T. Blair, Speech to the IPPR, 14 January 1999.

53 Active Community Unit, *Giving Time, Getting Involved* (London: Cabinet Office, 1999), p. 9.

54 Blair, *New Britain*, p. 58.

55 Blair, *New Britain*, p. 215.

56 Philosophical communitarianism emerged from social humanism, not functionalism and modernist empiricism. See M. Bevir and D. O'Brien, 'From Idealism to Communitarianism: The Inheritance and Legacy of John Macmurray', *History of Political Thought* 24 (2003), 305–29.

57 J. Sopel, *Tony Blair: The Moderniser* (London: Bantam Books, 1995), p. 145; A. Etzioni, *The Third Way to a Good Society* (London: Demos, 2000).

58 A. Etzioni, *The New Golden Rule: Community and Morality in a Democratic Society* (London: Profile Books, 1997), p. 61.

59 A. Etzioni, ed., *The Essential Communitarian Reader* (Oxford: Rowman and Butterfield, 1998), p. x.

60 'Lonely in America: An Interview with Robert Putnam', *Atlantic Unbound*, 21 September 2000.

61 H. Tam, *Communitarianism: A New Agenda for Politics and Citizenship* (New York: New York University Press, 1998), p. 8.

62 W. Galston, *Liberal Purposes: Goods, Virtues and Diversity in the Liberal State* (Cambridge: Cambridge University Press, 1991).

63 Galston, *Liberal Purposes*, p. 284.

64 Etzioni, *Spirit of Community*, p. 4.

65 Blair, *New Britain*, p. 236; and Blair, *Third Way*, p. 3.

66 Mandelson and Liddle, *Blair Revolution*, pp. 47–8; and G. Brown, Speech to the News International Conference, Sun Valley, Idaho, 17 July 1998.

67 Of course there are differences between institutionalism, communitarianism, and other outgrowths of modernist empiricism such as socio-economics. It is just that the similarities are of greater relevance in explaining their common location within New Labour. For an account of the differences between communitarianism and socio-economics – an account that tellingly relies on the modernist empiricist trope of classification rather than a historical narrative – see R. Coughlin, 'Whose Morality? Which Community? What Interests? Socio-economic and Communitarian Perspectives', *Journal of Socio-Economics* 25 (1996), 135–56.

68 For a discussion of political science, see M. Landau, 'The Myth of Hyperfactualism in the Study of American Politics', *Political Science Quarterly* 83 (1968), 378–99. Landau himself was inspired by the broad functionalism and systems theory I describe below, and, as such, he wanted to defend work inspired by such modernist empiricism against the behaviouralist, or structural-functionalist, charge of 'hyperfactualism'.

69 J. Burrow, *Evolution and Society: A Study in Victorian Social Theory* (Cambridge: Cambridge University Press, 1966); G. Stocking, *Victorian Anthropology* (New York: Free Press, 1987); and G. Stocking, *After Taylor: British Social Anthropology, 1888–1951* (Madison: University of Wisconsin Press, 1995).

70 A. Radcliffe-Brown, 'The Mother's Brother in South Africa', *South African Journal of Science* 21 (1924), 542–55.

71 On the Harvard group, see W. Scott, *Chester I. Barnard and the Guardians of the Managerial State* (Lawrence: University of Kansas Press, 1992); and on the human relations group, see R. Gillespie, *Manufacturing Knowledge: A History of the Hawthorne Experiments* (New York: Cambridge University Press, 1993).

72 P. Selznick, 'Foundations of the Theory of Organization' *American Sociology Review* 13 (1948), 25–35; P. Selznick, *TVA and the Grass Roots* (Berkeley: University of California Press, 1953), chap. 2; and P. Selznick, *Leadership in Administration: A Sociological Interpretation* (Berkeley: University of California Press, 1957). Selznick later contributed to the communitarian movement. See P. Selznick, *The Moral Commonwealth: Social Theory and the Promise of Community* (Berkeley: University of California Press, 1994).

73 A. Etzioni, *The Organizational Structure of the Kibbutz* (New York: Arno Press, 1980); A. Etzioni, *A Comparative Analysis of Complex Organizations: On Power, Involvement, and their Correlates* (New York: Free Press, 1961); and A. Etzioni, 'Toward a Theory of Societal Guidance', in E. Etzioni-Halevy and A. Etzioni, eds, *Social Change: Sources, Patterns, and Consequences* (New York: Basic Books, 1973).

74 Etzioni, *New Golden Rule*, p. 13.

75 A. Etzioni, 'Encapsulated Competition', *Journal of Post-Keynesian Economics* 7 (1985), 287–302.

76 M. Cohen, J. March, and J. Olsen, 'A Garbage Can Model of Organization Choice', *Administrative Science Quarterly* 17 (1972), 1–25; J. March and J. Olsen, 'The New Institutionalism: Organizational Factors in Political Life', *American Political Science Review* 78 (1984), 734–49; and J. March and J. Olsen, *Rediscovering Institutions* (New York: Free Press, 1989).

77 J. March and J. Olsen, *Democratic Governance* (New York: Free Press, 1995).

78 Skocpol appears to be denouncing universal theory, rather than functional explanation, in, for example, T. Skocpol, 'Uses of Comparative History in Macrosocial Inquiry', *Comparative Studies in Society and History* 22 (1980), 174–96. Her own work often exhibits a functionalist hue as when she appears to explain the rise of the welfare state by reference to its role in maintaining the state or social order especially in a time of war. See T. Skocpol, *Protecting Soldiers and Mothers: The Political Origins of Social Policy in the United States* (Cambridge, MA: Harvard University Press, 1992).

79 R. Putnam, *The Beliefs of Politicians: Ideology, Conflict, and Democracy in Britain and Italy* (New Haven: Yale University Press, 1973).

80 R. Putnam, *Bowling Alone: The Collapse and Revival of American Community* (New York: Simon and Schuster, 2000), p. 19.

81 J. Straw, *Policy and Ideology* (Blackburn: Blackburn Labour Party, 1993), p. 29.

4 The welfare state

1 For a fuller analysis, see M. Bevir, *The Logic of the History of Ideas* (Cambridge: Cambridge University Press, 1999), pp. 265–308. For an account of New Labour in such terms, see C. Hay, 'New Labour and "Third Way" Political Economy: Paving the European Road to Washington?', in M. Bevir and F. Trentmann, eds, *Critiques of Capital in Modern Britain and America: Transatlantic Exchanges 1800 to the Present Day* (Basingstoke: Palgrave Macmillan, 2002), pp. 195–219.

2 Likewise, when people present their policies in one particular way, they do so because of their beliefs; it is just that the relevant beliefs are those they hold about proper and effective media management. On New Labour and the media, see B. Frankel, 'The Hand of History: New Labour, News Management and Governance', in S. Ludlam and M. Smith, eds, *New Labour in Government* (Basingstoke: Macmillan, 2001), pp. 130–44; R. Heffernan, 'Media Management: Labour's Political Communication Strategy', in G. Taylor, ed., *The Impact of New Labour* (Basingstoke: Macmillan, 1999), pp. 50–67; N. Jones, *Sultans of Spin: The Media and the New Labour Government* (London: Weidenfeld and Nicholson, 1999); and N. Jones, *The Control Freaks: How New Labour Gets Its Own Way* (London: Politico's, 2001).

3 T. Blair, *New Britain: My Vision of a Young Country* (London: Fourth Estate, 1996), pp. 290–321. Although constitutional reform is arguably another key strand in New Labour's agenda – see T. Blair, Modernising Central Government, Speech to the First Senior Civil Service Conference, 13 October 1998;

and S. Driver and L. Martell, *New Labour: Politics after Thatcherism* (Cambridge: Polity, 1998) – I do not consider it here partly because it is not of equal importance for alternative accounts of New Labour and partly because the Westminster model is a major concern of M. Bevir and R. Rhodes, *Interpreting British Governance* (London: Routledge, 2003).

4 Of particular note here is the earlier disaggregated account of New Labour by M. Kenny and M. Smith, 'Interpreting New Labour: Constraints, Dilemmas and Political Agency', in Ludlam and Smith, eds, *New Labour*, pp. 234–55.

5 See C. Hay, 'Labour's Thatcherite Revisionism: Playing the Politics of Catch-up', *Political Studies* 42 (1994), 700–7; R. Heffernan, *New Labour and Thatcherism: Political Change in Britain* (Basingstoke: Macmillan, 2000); and, for welfare policy, P. Ainley, 'New Labour and the End of the Welfare State? The Case of Lifelong Learning', in G. Taylor, ed., *The Impact of New Labour* (Basingstoke: Macmillan, 1999), pp. 93–105. Hay later revised the 'catch-up' thesis in a way that reflects the impact of an ideational turn. See C. Hay, *The Political Economy of New Labour: Labouring under False Pretences* (Manchester: Manchester University Press, 1999), chap. 3. The position closest to mine describes New Labour as post-Thatcherite – Driver and Martell, *New Labour* – although that raises questions about why New Labour has responded to Thatcherism as it has.

6 General institutionalist studies include H. Kitschelt, *The Transformation of European Social Democracy* (Cambridge: Cambridge University Press, 1994). Institutionalism often informs, more particularly, those accounts of New Labour as a continuation of earlier revisionism within the Party: see M. Kenny and M. Smith, 'Discourses of Modernisation: Comparing Gaitskell, Blair, and the Reform of Clause IV', in C. Pattie *et al.*, eds, *British Elections and Parties* (London: Frank Cass, 1997), pp. 110–26; and D. Leonard, ed., *Crosland and New Labour* (Basingstoke: Macmillan, 1999). The position closest to mine describes New Labour as a recasting of social democracy – M. Wickham-Jones, 'Recasting Social Democracy: A Comment on Hay and Smith', *Political Studies* 43 (1995), 698–702 – although that raises questions about whether this recasting was a response to constraints or dilemmas and of what explains its particular content.

7 See not only T. Blair, *The Third Way: New Politics for a New Century*, Fabian Pamphlet no. 588 (London: Fabian Society, 1998); and A. Giddens, *The Third Way: The Renewal of Social Democracy* (Cambridge: Polity Press, 1998); but also B. Brivati, 'Earthquake or Watershed? Conclusions on New Labour in Power', in B. Brivati and T. Bale, eds, *New Labour in Power: Precedents and Prospects* (London: Routledge, 1997), pp. 183–99; and M. Temple, 'New Labour's Third Way: Pragmatism and Governance', *British Journal of Politics and International Relations* 2 (2000), 302–25.

8 Bevir and Trentmann, eds, *Critiques of Capital*; and M. Bevir and F. Trentmann, eds, *Markets in Contexts: Ideas and Politics in the Modern World* (Cambridge: Cambridge University Press, 2004).

9 *The Independent*, 6 July 1995.

10 P. Mandelson and R. Liddle, *The Blair Revolution: Can New Labour Deliver?* (London: Faber and Faber, 1996), p. 143.

11 Mandelson and Liddle, *Blair Revolution*, p. 153; P. Mandelson, Coordinating Government Policy, Speech to Conference on Modernising the Policy Process, London, 16 September 1997.

12 Cm. 3805, *New Ambitions for Our Country: A New Contract for Welfare* (London: Stationery Office, 1997), p. 9.

13 Blair, *New Britain*, p. 302.

14 Cm. 3805, *New Ambitions*, p. v.
15 Cm. 3805, *New Ambitions*, p. 80.
16 T. Blair, The Will to Win, Speech, Aylesbury Estate, 2 June 1997.
17 G. Brown, Speech Launching the New Deal, Dundee, 5 January 1998.
18 Cm. 3805, *New Ambitions*.
19 Cm. 4103, *A New Contract for Welfare: Support for Disabled People* (London: Stationery Office, 1998).
20 Cm. 4101, *A New Contract for Welfare: Principles into Practice* (London: Stationery Office, 1998); and Cm. 4102 *A New Contract for Welfare: The Gateway to Work* (London: Stationery Office, 1998). For the broad Jobcenter Plus scheme, see Cm. 5084, *Towards Full Employment in a Modern Society* (London: Stationery Office, 2001).
21 Cm. 4102, *A New Contract for Welfare*, p. 9.
22 Cm. 4076, *Pre-Budget Report: Steering a Stable Course for Lasting Prosperity* (London: Stationery Office, 1998), p. 61.
23 Blair, *New Britain*, p. 247.
24 Contrast J. Peck, 'New Labourers? Making a New Deal for the "Workless Class", *Environment and Planning C: Government and Policy* 17 (1999), 345–72; and J. Peck and N. Theodore, ' "Work First": Workfare and the Regulation of Contingent Labour Markets', *Cambridge Journal of Economics* 24 (2000), 119–38.
25 Cm. 4179, *A New Contract for Welfare: Partnership in Pensions* (London: Stationery Office, 1998), p. iii.
26 F. Field, *How to Pay for the Future: Building a Stakeholder's Welfare* (London: Institute of Community Studies, 1996); F. Field, *Stakeholder Welfare* (London: Institute of Economic Affairs, 1996); F. Field, *Reflections on Welfare Reform* (London: Social Markets Foundation, 1998); and Mandelson and Liddle, *Blair Revolution*, p. 145. The government presented its policy in Cm. 4179, *Partnership in Pensions*.
27 Field, *How to Pay*, p. 64.
28 Field, *How to Pay*, p. 66.
29 F. Field, *Reforming Welfare* (London: Social Market Foundation, 1997), p. 27.
30 Cm. 4310, *Modernising Government* (London: Stationery Office, 1999), pp. 35 and 41.
31 Cm. 4014, *Modern Local Government: In Touch with the People* (London: Stationery Office, 1998), pp. 64–78; and Local Government Association, *Best Value: A Statement of Objectives* (London: Local Government Association, 1998). For an attempt to disaggregate the practice of Best Value, see M. Geddes and S. Martin, 'The Policy and Politics of Best Value: Currents, Crosscurrents, and Undercurrents in the New Regime', *Policy and Politics* 28 (2000), 379–95.
32 Cm. 4310, *Modernising Government*, p. 41.
33 Cm. 4011, *Modern Public Services for Britain: Investing in Reform* (London: Stationery Office, 1998), p. 33.
34 Cm. 3807, *The New National Health Service: Modern, Dependable* (London: Stationery Office, 1997), p. 13.
35 Cm. 3807, *New National Health*, p. 14.
36 Cm. 4169, *Modernising Social Services: Promoting Independence, Improving Protection, Raising Standards* (London: Stationery Office, 1998), p. 31; Cm. 3807, *New National Health*, p. 10.
37 Cm. 3889, *Next Steps Report 1997* (London: Stationery Office, 1998); and Cm. 4273, *Next Steps Report 1998* (London: Stationery Office, 1999).
38 Cm. 3889, *Next Steps 1997*, pp. 4–11; and Cm. 4273, *Next Steps 1998*, pp. 9–15.

39 Cm. 3889, *Next Steps 1997*, pp. 12–13; Cm. 4273, *Next Steps 1998*, pp. 16–17.
40 Cm. 4310, *Modernising Government*, p. 30.
41 Compare M. Burch and I. Holliday, 'New Labour and the Machinery of Government', in D. Coates and P. Lawler, eds, *New Labour in Power* (Manchester: Manchester University Press, 2000), pp. 65–79.
42 *New Statesman*, 1 August 1997
43 Cm. 4169, *Modernising Social Services*, p. 31.
44 Cm. 4310, *Modernising Government*, p. 32.
45 Cm. 4310, *Modernising Government*, p. 23.
46 Cm. 4014, *Modern Local Government*, p. 2. Also see H. Atkinson, 'New Labour, New Local Government?', in Taylor, ed., *Impact of New Labour*, pp. 133–46.
47 Cm. 3807, *New National Health*, p. 45.
48 P. Toynbee and D. Walker, *Did Things Get Better? An Audit of Labour's Successes and Failures* (Harmondsworth: Penguin, 2001), p. 105.
49 Cm. 4310, *Modernising Government*, p. 16.
50 Cm. 4310, *Modernising Government*, p. 57.
51 Cm. 4181, *Public Services for the Future: Modernisation, Reform, Accountability* (London: Stationery Office, 1998).
52 Cm. 4181, *Public Services*, p. 5.
53 Cm. 4169, *Modernising Social Services*, p. 8; Cm. 4181, *Public Services*, p. 3.
54 Blair, *New Britain*, p. 292.
55 Cm. 4169, *Modernising Social Services*, p. 65.
56 Cm. 4169, *Modernising Social Services*, pp. 67–83.
57 Cm. 4169, *Modernising Social Services*, pp. 85–95.
58 Department of Health, *The New NHS, Modern and Dependable: A National Framework for Assessing Performance* (London: Crown Copyright, Stationery Office, 1998), p. 2.
59 NHS Executive, Department of Health, *A First Class Service: Quality in the New NHS* (Crown Copyright, Stationery Office, 1999), paras 2.8–2.31.
60 NHS Executive, *First Class Service*, paras 4.46–4.56.
61 NHS Executive, *First Class Service*, paras 2.32–2.43.
62 NHS Executive, *First Class Service*, paras 4.3–4.45.
63 NHS Executive, *First Class Service*, paras 4.57–4.63.
64 See Roy Hattersley's comments in *The Independent*, 30 July 1997.
65 B. Jordan, *The New Politics of Welfare: Social Justice in a Global Context* (London: Sage, 1998); and R. Levitas, *The Inclusive Society? Social Exclusion and New Labour* (Basingstoke: Macmillan, 1998).
66 S. Crine, *Reforming Welfare: American Lessons*, Fabian Pamphlet no. 567 (London: Fabian Society, 1994).
67 G. Boyne, 'Processes, Performance and Best Value in Local Government', *Local Government Studies* 25 (1999), 1–15; P. Vincent-Jones, 'Competition and Contracting in the Transition from CCT to Best Value: Towards a More Reflexive Regulation', *Public Administration* 77 (1999), 273–91; and J. Wilson, 'From CCT to Best Value: Some Evidence and Observations', *Local Government Studies* 25 (1999), 38–52.
68 C. Paton, 'New Labour's Health Policy: The New Healthcare State', in M. Powell, ed., *New Labour: New Welfare State? The 'Third Way' in British Social Policy* (Bristol: Policy Press, 1999), pp. 51–76.
69 Boyne, 'Processes'; and E. Clarence and C. Painter, 'Public Services under New Labour: Collaborative Discourses and Local Networking', *Public Policy and Administration Review* 13 (1998), 15.

70 S. Cope and J. Goodship, 'Regulating Collaborative Government: Towards Joined-Up Government', *Public Policy and Administration Review* 14 (1999), 10.

71 J. Rouse and G. Smith, 'Accountability', in Powell, ed., *New Labour*, pp. 235–56; and M. Rowe, 'Joined-Up Accountability: Bringing the Citizen Back In', *Public Policy and Administration Review* 14 (1999), 91–102.

72 T. Blair, Progress through Modernisation, Speech to the Socialist International Conference, Paris, 8 November 1999.

5 The economy

1 67 H.C.Deb. ser. 6 col. 473 (1984); 125 H.C.Deb. ser. 6 col. 537 (1988). As late as 1994, Blair spoke of using 'demand-management techniques to stimulate the market' in 'a traditional Keynesian way'. See *New Statesman and Society*, 15 July 1994.

2 P. Mandelson and R. Liddle, *The Blair Revolution: Can New Labour Deliver?* (London: Faber and Faber, 1996), p. 6.

3 G. Brown, Mansion House Speech, London, 11 June 1998.

4 T. Blair, A Modern Britain in a Modern Europe, Speech at the Annual Friends of Nieuwspoort Dinner, The Hague, 20 January 1998.

5 T. Blair, *New Britain: My Vision of a Young Country* (London: Fourth Estate, 1996), p. 118.

6 Mandelson and Liddle, *Blair Revolution*, p. 74; G. Brown, Mansion House Speech, London, 11 June 1998.

7 Cm. 3978, *Stability and Investment for the Long Term* (London: Stationery Office, 1998), p. 7.

8 Blair, *New Britain*, p. 84.

9 G. Brown, Mansion House Speech, London, 12 June 1997.

10 Blair, *New Britain*, p. 86; G. Brown, Preparing Britain for the Future, Speech, 4 September 1996.

11 G. Brown, Mansion House Speech, London, 12 June 1997.

12 Blair, *New Britain*, p. 81; Mandelson and Liddle, *Blair Revolution*, pp. 74–5.

13 Brown, Mansion House Speech, London, 11 June 1998.

14 *Financial Times*, 16 March 2000.

15 Labour Party, *A New Economic Future for Britain* (London: Labour Party, 1995).

16 94 H.C.Deb. ser. 6 col. 502 (1986).

17 G. Brown, *Where There is Greed: Margaret Thatcher and the Betrayal of Britain's Future* (Edinburgh: Mainstream, 1989), p. 19.

18 T. Blair, Speech, Guildhall, London, 16 November 1998.

19 G. Brown, *Fair is Efficient*, Fabian Pamphlet no. 563 (London: Fabian Society, 1994), p. 21.

20 Mandelson and Liddle, *Blair Revolution*, p. 89; and Cm. 4176, *Our Competitive Future: Building the Knowledge Driven Economy* (London: Stationery Office, 1998), p. 6.

21 Compare N. Thompson, *Political Economy and the Labour Party* (London: UCL Press, 1996), pp. 267–85.

22 Blair, *New Britain*, p. 110.

23 Blair, *New Britain*, p. 109; Brown, *Where There is Greed*, p. 10; and G. Brown, 'Foreword', in C. Crouch and D. Marquand, *Re-inventing Collective Action* (Oxford: Blackwell, 1995), p. 4.

24 Cm. 4176, *Our Competitive Future*, p. 7.

25 Cm. 4176, *Our Competitive Future*, p. 39.

26 T. Blair, 'Foreword', to Cm 4176, *Our Competitive Future*.

27 Cm. 4176, *Our Competitive Future*, p. 12.
28 E. Balls, 'New Principles for Government', *CentrePiece* 3 (1998), 20.
29 Bank of England Act, 1998, Section 15.1.
30 Cm. 3978, *Stability and Investment*, p. 5.
31 Cm. 4808, *Spending Review 2000: Public Service Agreements 2001–2004* (London: Stationery Office, 2000).
32 Cm. 4900, *The Pension Credit: A Consultation Paper* (London: Stationery Office, 2000).
33 For recent expenditure plans, see Cm. 5424, *Departmental Report: The Government's Expenditure Plans 2002–3 to 2003–4* (London: Stationery Office, 2002).
34 Cm. 4900, *Pension Credit*.
35 Contrast P. Arestis and M. Sawyer, 'The Macroeconomics of New Labour', *Economic Issues* 4 (1999), 39–58.
36 E. Balls, 'Open Macroeconomics in an Open Economy', *Scottish Journal of Political Economy* 45 (1998), 113–32.
37 R. Layard, 'Preventing Long-term Unemployment', in D. Snowes and G. de la Dehasa, eds, *Unemployment Policy* (Cambridge: Cambridge University Press, 1997).
38 T. Blair, Speech to the Second Ministerial Meeting of the World Trade Organisation, Geneva, 19 May 1998.
39 R. Young, 'New Labour and International Development', in D. Coates and P. Lawler, eds, *New Labour in Power* (Manchester: Manchester University Press, 2001), pp. 254–67.
40 Cm. 4345, *A Better Quality of Life: A Strategy for Sustainable Development in the UK* (London: Stationery Office, 1999), p. 3.
41 Mandelson and Liddle, *Blair Revolution*, p. 6.
42 G. Brown, Speech to TUC Conference on Economic and Monetary Union, 13 May 1999.
43 T. Blair, Speech to the Confederation of Business Annual Dinner, 16 May 2000. Also see Cm. 3968, *Fairness at Work* (London: Stationery Office, 1998).
44 The contrast here is with the more corporatist approach developed by the Party in the late 1980s. See D. King and M. Wickham Jones, 'Training Without the State? New Labour and the Labour Markets', *Policy and Politics* 26 (1998), 439–55.
45 Department for Education and the Employment, Invitation to Help Invent the Educational Future, Press Release, 6 January 1998.
46 Labour Party, *Winning for Britain: Strategy for Industrial Success* (London: Labour Party, 1993), p. 4.
47 Cm. 4176, *Our Competitive Future*, p. 38.
48 Margaret Beckett, Letter to Business Large and Small, Business Support Organisations, and to Trade Unions, 3 May 1997.
49 Cm. 4176, *Our Competitive Future*, p. 46.
50 Cm. 4176, *Our Competitive Future*, p. 47.
51 294 H.C.Deb. ser. 6 col. 510 (1999).
52 T. Blair, *Socialism*, Fabian Pamphlet no. 565 (London: Fabian Society, 1992), p. 6.
53 *The Guardian*, 16 December 1998.
54 The most recent study is D. Piachaud and H. Sutherland, 'Changing Poverty Post-1997', CASE paper no. 63 (London: Centre for the Analysis of Social Exclusion, 2002). Also see H. Immervoll, L. Mitton, C. O'Donoghue, and H. Sutherland, 'Budgeting for Fairness: The Distributional Effects of Three Labour Budgets', Microsimulation Unit Research Note no. 32, March 1999;

H. Sutherland and R. Taylor, 'The 2000 Budget: The Impact on the Distribution of Household Incomes', Microsimulation Unit Research Note no. 35, March 2000; and H. Sutherland, 'Five Labour Budgets: Impacts on the Distribution of Household Incomes and on Child Poverty', Microsimulation Unit Research Note no. 41, May 2001.

55 T. Clark, M. Myck, and Z. Smith, *Fiscal Reforms Affecting Households, 1997–2001* (London: Institute for Fiscal Studies, 2001).

56 Thompson, *Political Economy*, pp. 280–2.

57 C. Hay, *The Political Economy of New Labour: Labouring under False Pretences?* (Manchester: Manchester University Press, 1999), partic. pp. 181–208.

58 R. Dickens, P. Gregg, and J. Wadsworth, 'New Labour and the Labour Market', *Oxford Review of Economic Policy* 16 (2000), 95–113; and Hay, *Political Economy*, partic. pp. 181–208. For an examination of the extent to which New Labour has addressed concerns about uneven development, see J. Goddard and P. Chatterton, 'Regional Development Agencies and the Knowledge Economy: Harnessing the Potential of Universities', *Environment and Planning C: Government and Policy* 17 (1999), 685–99.

59 Thompson, *Political Economy*, p. 273.

60 A. Gibson and S. Asthana, 'Local Markets and the Polarization of Public-Sector Schools in England and Wales', *Transactions of the Institute of British Geographers* 25 (2000), 303–19; and G. Vulliamy and R. Webb, 'Stemming the Tide of Rising School Exclusion: Problems and Possibilities', *British Journal of Educational Studies* 48 (2000), 119–33.

61 C. Painter and E. Clarence, 'UK Local Action Zones and Changing Urban Governance', *Urban Studies* 38 (2001), 1215–32.

62 Hay, *Political Economy*, partic. pp. 181–208.

63 D. Coates and P. Lawler, 'Preface' to Coates and Lawler, eds, *New Labour in Power* (Manchester: Manchester University Press, 2000), p. ix.

64 Coates and Lawler, 'Preface', p. x.

65 D. Coates, 'New Labour's Industrial and Employment Policy', in Coates and Lawler, eds, *New Labour in Power*, pp. 133–4.

66 S. Driver and L. Martell, *Blair's Britain* (Cambridge: Polity Press, 2002).

67 B. Wood, 'New Labour and Welfare Reform', in Coates and Lawler, eds, *New Labour in Power*, p. 194.

68 Hay, *Political Economy*, p. 165.

69 Some commentators more or less accept this self-image of New Labour. See Driver and Martell, *Blair's Britain*, partic. pp. 79–82; and M. Temple, 'New Labour's Third Way: Pragmatism and Governance', *British Journal of Politics and International Relations* 2 (2000), 302–25.

6 Social democracy

1 Compare S. Pierson, *Marxism and the Origins of British Socialism* (Ithaca: Cornell University Press, 1973).

2 H. Hyndman, 'The Dawn of a Revolutionary Epoch', *Nineteenth Century* 9 (1881), 17.

3 H. Hyndman, *The Text Book of Democracy: England for All* (London: E. Allen, 1881), p. 31.

4 *Justice*, 14 June 1884.

5 W. Morris, *The Collected Works of William Morris*, intro. M. Morris (London: Longmans, 1910–15), vol. 16: *News from Nowhere*.

6 S. Webb, *English Progress towards Social Democracy*, Fabian Tract no. 15 (London: Fabian Society, 1892), p. 5.

7 S. and B. Webb, *Industrial Democracy* (London: Longmans, 1902), partic. pp. 863–72.

8 Initially Webb advocated the moralisation of the capitalist – S. Webb, 'The Economics of a Positivist Community', *Practical Socialist* 1 (1886), 37–9 – but he quickly rejected this solution on the grounds that it would not address the inefficiencies of capitalism – S. Webb, 'Rome: A Sermon in Sociology', *Our Corner* 12 (1888), 53–60 and 79–89.

9 G. Shaw, 'The Economic', in G. Shaw, ed., *Fabian Essays in Socialism*, (London: Walter Scott, 1890), p. 27.

10 G. Shaw, 'The Transition to Social Democracy', in Shaw, ed., *Fabian Essays*, p. 182.

11 E. Carpenter, *The Art of Creation* (London: G. Allen, 1904), p. 50.

12 E. Carpenter, 'The Value of the Value Theory', *To-day* 11 (1889), 22–30.

13 W. Richmond, *Christian Economics* (London: Rivingtons, 1888), p. 25.

14 E. Carpenter, *Angel's Wings* (London: Swan Sonnenschein, 1898), p. 226.

15 E. Carpenter, 'Transitions to Freedom', in E. Carpenter, ed., *Forecasts of the Coming Century* (Manchester: Labour Press, 1897), pp. 174–92.

16 The divisions were, of course, not as clear-cut as this suggests: for example, Sydney Olivier, a Fabian, held views remarkably close to those described as ethical socialism – see S. Olivier, *Sydney Olivier: Letters and Selected Writings*, ed. M. Olivier (London: G. Allen and Unwin, 1948). Moreover, many of the early socialists changed their beliefs somewhat, often under one another's influence: for example, the Webbs briefly showed signs of being influenced by syndicalism – see S. and B. Webb, *A Constitution for the Socialist Commonwealth of Great Britain* (London: Longmans, 1920).

17 P. Snowden, *Socialism and Syndicalism* (London: Collins, 1913), p. 84.

18 R. MacDonald, *The Zollverein and British Industry* (London: Grant Richards, 1903), p. 163.

19 Snowden, *Socialism and Syndicalism*, p. 117.

20 R. MacDonald, 'Socialism', in *Ramsay MacDonald's Political Writings*, ed. B. Barker (London: Allen Lane, 1972), pp. 99–162.

21 P. Snowden, 'The Socialist Budget 1907', in J. Hardie, ed., *From Socialism to Serfdom* (Hassocks: Harvester, 1974), p. 7.

22 R. MacDonald, *Socialism and Society* (London: Independent Labour Party, 1905), p. 70.

23 On socialist debates about the nature and role of democracy, see L. Barrow and I. Bullock, *Democratic Ideas and the British Labour Movement, 1880–1914* (Cambridge: Cambridge University Press, 1996).

24 A. J. Penty, *The Restoration of the Gild System* (London: Swan Sonnenschein, 1906).

25 Penty, *Restoration*, p. 57.

26 J. Hobson and A. Mummery, *The Physiology of Industry* (London: John Murray, 1889); and A. Marshall, *Principles of Economics*, ed. C. Guillebaud (London: Macmillan, 1961).

27 P. Hirst, ed., *The Pluralist Theory of the State: Selected Writings of G. D. H. Cole, J. N. Figgis, and H. J. Laski* (London: Routledge, 1989).

28 See, respectively, C. Hay, *The Political Economy of New Labour: Labouring under False Pretences?* (Manchester: Manchester University Press, 1999); and L. Panitch and C. Leys, *The End of Parliamentary Socialism: From New Left to New Labour* (London: Verso, 1997). Even when these more orthodox Marxists denounce the naturalising and depoliticising nature of New Labour, they typically do so not by critique, but by appealing to their expertise in revealing an ideological effect of contemporary capitalism. See P. Burnham, 'New Labour and the Politics of Depoliticisation', *British Journal of Politics and International Relations* 3 (2001), 127–49.

29 On orthodox and critical strands in Third Way theory and New Labour, see A. Finlayson, 'Third Way Theory', *Political Quarterly* 70 (1999), 271–9; and M. Kenny and M. Smith, 'Interpreting New Labour: Constraints, Dilemmas and Political Agency', in S. Ludlam and M. Smith, eds, *New Labour in Government* (Basingstoke: Macmillan, 2001), p. 235.

30 Compare M. Kenny, *The First New Left: British Intellectuals after Stalin* (London: Lawrence and Wishart, 1995); and D. Lloyd and P. Thomas, *Culture and the State* (London: Routledge, 1998).

31 See Finlayson, 'Third Way'; and many of the essays in A. Coddington and M. Perryman, eds, *The Moderniser's Dilemma: Radical Politics in the Age of Blair* (London: Lawrence and Wishart, 1998); and T. Bewes and J. Gilbert, eds, *Cultural Capitalism: Politics after New Labour* (London: Lawrence and Wishart, 2000).

32 Contrasting readings of Foucault here include, respectively, W. Brown, 'Genealogical Politics', in J. Moss, ed., *The Later Foucault: Politics and Philosophy* (London: Sage, 1998), pp. 33–49; and P. Dews, 'The Return of the Subject in Late Foucault', *Radical Philosophy* 51 (1989), 37–41.

33 Without a concept of agency, of course, we would have no reason to conceive of people as having ends of their own, so we would have no grounds for advocating principles of inclusion; we would come to see principles of participation, deliberation, and conduct as lacking even the potential to inspire anything more than further strategic techniques of power.

34 M. Dean, 'Culture Governance and Individualisation', in H. Bang, ed., *Governance as Social and Political Communication* (Manchester: Manchester University Press, 2003), p. 135.

35 Compare S. Critchley, 'Ethics, Politics, and Radical Democracy – The History of a Disagreement', in S. Critchley and O. Marchant, eds, *Laclau: A Critical Reader* (London: Routledge, 2004).

36 A. Etzioni, 'Is Bowling Together Sociologically Lite?', *Contemporary Sociology* 30 (2001), 223–4.

37 Vigorous assertions of the cultural unity of the United Kingdom as a community accompanied even the promotion of devolution. See T. Blair, Speech on Scottish Parliament, Strathclyde University, 12 November 1998.

38 T. Blair, *The Third Way: New Politics for a New Century*, Fabian Pamphlet no. 588 (London: Fabian Society, 1998), p. 1.

39 Etzioni, 'Bowling Together', 224.

40 T. Blair, *New Britain: My Vision of a Young Country* (London: Fourth Estate, 1996), p. 80.

41 Compare J. Tully, 'Wittgenstein and Political Philosophy: Understanding Practices of Critical Reflection', *Political Theory* 17 (1989), 172–204; and J. Tully, 'Political Philosophy as a Critical Activity', *Political Theory* 30 (2002), 533–55.

42 See, for example, W. Kickert, E.-H. Klijn, and J. Koppenjan, eds, *Managing Complex Networks: Strategies for the Public Sector* (London: Sage, 1998).

43 Cm. 4310, *Modernising Government* (London: Stationery Office, 1999), p. 55.

44 For appeals to social movements and cultural practices, see J. Gilbert, 'Beyond the Hegemony of New Labour', in Bewes and Gilbert, eds, *Cultural Capitalism*, pp. 223–44; and for one to messianic eschatology, see J. Derrida, *Specters of Marx: The State of the Debt, the Work of Mourning, and the New International*, trans. P. Kamuf (London: Routledge, 1994).

45 See Panitch and Leys, *End of Parliamentary Socialism*; and, for the background theory, R. Miliband, *Parliamentary Socialism: A Study in the Politics*

of Labour (London: Merlin, 1961); and R. Miliband, *The State in Capitalist Society* (New York: Basic Books, 1969).

46 This argument would echo those, considered in the chapter on communitarianism, which see New Labour as having broken with a tradition of social democracy that they thus implicitly reify.

Bibliography

Newspapers

Atlantic Unbound
Financial Times
Guardian
Independent
Justice
LM Magazine
New Society
New Statesman
New Statesman and Society
Observer
Prospect

Government documents

Active Community Unit. *Giving Time, Getting Involved*. London: Cabinet Office, 1999.

Bank of England Act, 1998.

Cm. 3805. Department of Social Security. *New Ambitions for Our Country: A New Contract for Welfare*. London: Stationery Office, 1997.

Cm. 3807. Department of Health. *The New National Health Service: Modern, Dependable*. London: Stationery Office, 1997.

Cm. 3889. Chancellor of the Duchy of Lancaster. *Next Steps Report 1997*. London: Stationery Office, 1998.

Cm. 3968. Department of Trade and Industry. *Fairness at Work*. London: Stationery Office, 1998.

Cm. 3978. Chancellor of the Exchequer. *Stability and Investment for the Long Term*. London: Stationery Office, 1998.

Cm. 4011. Chancellor of the Exchequer. *Modern Public Services for Britain: Investing in Reform*. London: Stationery Office, 1998.

Cm. 4014. Department of the Environment, Transport and Regions. *Modern Local Government: In Touch with the People*. London: Stationery Office, 1998.

Cm. 4045. Social Exclusion Unit. *Bringing Britain Together: A National Strategy for Neighbourhood Renewal*. London: Stationery Office, 1998.

Cm. 4076. HM Treasury. *Pre-Budget Report: Steering a Stable Course for Lasting Prosperity*. London: Stationery Office, 1998.

Cm. 4101. Department of Social Security. *A New Contract for Welfare: Principles into Practice*. London: Stationery Office, 1998.

Cm. 4102. Department of Social Security. *A New Contract for Welfare: The Gateway to Work*. London: Stationery Office, 1998.

Cm. 4103. Department of Social Security. *A New Contract for Welfare: Support for Disabled People*. London: Stationery Office, 1998.

Cm. 4169. Department of Health. *Modernising Social Services: Promoting Independence, Improving Protection, Raising Standards*. London: Stationery Office, 1998.

Cm. 4176. Department of Trade and Industry. *Our Competitive Future: Building the Knowledge Driven Economy*. London: Stationery Office, 1998.

Cm. 4179. Department of Social Security. *A New Contract for Welfare: Partnership in Pensions*. London: Stationery Office, 1998.

Cm. 4181. Chief Secretary to the Treasury. *Public Services for the Future: Modernisation, Reform, Accountability*. London: Stationery Office, 1998.

Cm. 4273. Minister for the Cabinet Office. *Next Steps Report 1998*. London: Stationery Office, 1999.

Cm. 4310. Prime Minister and Minister for the Cabinet Office. *Modernising Government*. London: Stationery Office, 1999.

Cm. 4345. Department of the Environment, Transport and Regions. *A Better Quality of Life: A Strategy for Sustainable Development for the UK*. London: Stationery Office, 1999.

Cm. 4808. Prime Minister and Minister for the Cabinet Office. *Spending Review 2000: Public Service Agreements 2001–2004*. London: Stationery Office, 2000.

Cm. 4900. Department of Social Security. *The Pension Credit: A Consultation Paper*. London: Stationery Office, 2000.

Cm. 5084. Department of Education and Employment. *Towards Full Employment in a Modern Society*. London: Stationery Office, 2001.

Cm. 5424. Department for Work and Pensions. *Departmental Report: The Government's Expenditure Plans 2002–3 to 2003–4*. London: Stationery Office, 2002.

Department for Education and Employment. 'New Year, New Deal, New Hope'. Press Release. 5 January 1998.

Department for Education and Employment. 'Invitation to Help Invent the Educational Future'. Press Release. 6 January 1998.

Department for Education and Employment. 'Employability at the Heart of British Presidency Agenda'. Press Release. 4 February 1998.

Department of Health. *The New NHS, Modern and Dependable: A National Framework for Assessing Performance*. London: Stationery Office, 1998.

Department of Health. *A First Class Service: Quality in the New NHS*. London: Stationery Office, 1999.

Parliamentary Debates, Commons, 6th Series.

Books and articles

Adcock, R. 'The Emergence of Political Science as a Discipline: History and the Study of Politics in America 1875–1910', *History of Political Thought* 24 (2003), 481–508.

Ainley, P. 'New Labour and the End of the Welfare State? The Case of Life-long Learning'. In *The Impact of New Labour*, (ed.) G. Taylor. Basingstoke: Macmillan, 1999.

Arestis, P. and Sawyer, M. 'The Macroeconomics of New Labour', *Economic Issues* 4 (1999), 39–58.

—— and —— (eds) *The Economics of the Third Way: Experiences from around the World*. Cheltenham: Edward Elgar, 2001.

Arrow, K. *Social Choice and Individual Values*. New York: Wiley, 1951.

Atkinson, H. 'New Labour, New Local Government?' In *Impact of New Labour*, (ed.) G. Taylor. Basingstoke: Macmillan, 1999.

Bale, T. 'Managing the Party and the Trade Unions'. In *New Labour in Power: Precedents and Prospects*, (eds) B. Brivati and T. Bale. London: Routledge, 1997.

—— 'The Logic of No Alternative? Political Scientists, Historians and the Politics of Labour's Past', *British Journal of Politics and International Relations* 1 (1999), 192–204.

Balls, E. 'New Principles for Government', *CentrePiece* 3 (1998) 20–2.

—— 'Open Macroeconomics in an Open Economy', *Scottish Journal of Political Economy* 45 (1998), 113–32.

Bang, H. (ed.) *Governance as Social and Political Communication*. Manchester: Manchester University Press, 2003.

Barnett, W., Hinich, M. and Schofield, N. (eds) *Political Economy: Institutions, Competition, and Representation*. Cambridge: Cambridge University Press, 1993.

Barrow, L. and Bullock, I. *Democratic Ideas and the British Labour Movement, 1880–1914*. Cambridge: Cambridge University Press, 1996.

Beckett, M. 'Letter to Business Large and Small, Business Support Organisations, and to Trade Unions'. 3 May 1997.

Beer, M. *A History of British Socialism*, 2 vols. London: George Allen and Unwin, 1953.

Beer, S. 'Political Science and History'. In *Essays in Theory and History*, (ed.) M. Richter. Cambridge, MA: Harvard University Press, 1970.

Benn, A. *A Future for Socialism*. London: Fount, 1991.

Bernstein, R. *The Restructuring of Social and Political Theory*. Philadelphia: University of Pennsylvania Press, 1976.

Bevir, M. *The Logic of the History of Ideas*. Cambridge: Cambridge University Press, 1999.

—— and O'Brien, D. 'From Idealism to Communitarianism: The Inheritance and Legacy of John Macmurray', *History of Political Thought* 24 (2003), 305–29.

—— and Rhodes, R. *Interpreting British Governance*. London: Routledge, 2003.

—— and Trentmann, F. (eds) *Critiques of Capital in Modern Britain and America: Transatlantic Exchanges 1800 to the Present Day*. Basingstoke: Palgrave Macmillan, 2002.

—— and —— (eds) *Markets in Historical Contexts: Ideas and Politics in the Modern World*. Cambridge: Cambridge University Press, 2004.

Bewes, T. and Gilbert, J. (eds) *Cultural Capitalism: Politics after New Labour*. London: Lawrence and Wishart, 2000.

Blair, T. *Socialism*. Fabian Pamphlet no. 565. London: Fabian Society, 1992.

—— 'Why Modernisation Matters'. *Renewal* 1 (1993), 4–11.

—— 'Reforming Welfare – Building on Beveridge'. Speech to the Southampton Institute. 13 July 1994.

—— *Let us Face the Future*. Fabian Pamphlet no. 571. London: Fabian Society, 1995.

—— *New Britain: My Vision of a Young Country*. London: Fourth Estate, 1996.

—— 'The Will to Win'. Speech, Aylesbury Estate. 2 June 1997.

—— Speech to the Party of European Socialists Congress, Malmo, Sweden. 6 June 1997.

—— Speech to the Labour Party Conference. 30 September 1997.

—— *The Third Way: New Politics for a New Century*. Fabian Pamphlet no. 588. London: Fabian Society, 1998.

—— 'A Modern Britain in a Modern Europe'. Speech at the Annual Friends of Nieuwspoort Dinner, The Hague. 20 January 1998.

—— Speech to the Second Ministerial Meeting of the World Trade Organisation, Geneva. 19 May 1998.

—— 'Modernising Central Government'. Speech to the First Senior Civil Service Conference. 13 October 1998.

—— Speech on Scottish Parliament, Strathclyde University. 12 November 1998.

—— Speech. Guildhall, London. 16 November 1998.

—— Speech to the IPPR. 14 January 1999.

—— 'Progress through Modernisation'. Speech to the Socialist International Conference, Paris. 8 November 1999.

—— Speech to the Confederation of Business Annual Dinner. 16 May 2000.

—— Speech to the Women's Institute. 7 June 2000.

—— 'Values and the Power of Community'. Speech to Global Ethics Foundation, Tübingen University. 30 June 2000.

Blyth, M. 'Institutions and Ideas'. In *Theory and Methods in Political Science*, (eds) D. Marsh and G. Stoker. Basingstoke: Palgrave, 2002.

Boyne, G. 'Processes, Performance and Best Value in Local Government', *Local Government Studies* 25 (1999), 1–15.

Brennan, T. 'A Methodological Assessment of Multiple Utility Frameworks', *Economics and Philosophy* 5 (1989), 189–208.

Brivati, B. 'Earthquake or Watershed? Conclusions on New Labour in Power'. In *New Labour in Power: Precedents and Prospects*, (eds) B. Brivati and T. Bale. London: Routledge, 1997.

—— and Bale, T. (eds) *New Labour in Power: Precedents and Prospects*. London: Routledge, 1997.

Brown, G. *Where There is Greed: Margaret Thatcher and the Betrayal of Britain's Future*. Edinburgh: Mainstream, 1989.

—— *Fair is Efficient*. Fabian Pamphlet no. 563. London: Fabian Society, 1994.

—— Foreword to *Re-inventing Collective Action*, by C. Crouch and D. Marquand. Oxford: Blackwell, 1995.

—— 'Preparing Britain for the Future'. Speech. 4 September 1996.

—— The Anthony Crosland Memorial Lecture, London. 13 February 1997.

—— Mansion House Speech, London. 12 June 1997.

—— Speech Launching the New Deal, Dundee. 5 January 1998.

—— Mansion House Speech, London. 11 June 1998.

—— Speech to the News International Conference, Sun Valley, Idaho. 17 July 1998.

—— Speech to TUC Conference on Economic and Monetary Union. 13 May 1999.

—— and Wright, T. (eds) *Values, Visions and Voices: An Anthology of Socialism*. Edinburgh: Mainstream Publishing, 1995.

Brown, W. 'Genealogical Politics'. In *The Later Foucault: Politics and Philosophy*, (ed.) J. Moss. London: Sage, 1998.

Bryant, C. *Possible Dreams: A Personal History of British Christian Socialists*. London: Hodder and Stoughton, 1996.

Bryce, J. *Modern Democracies*, 2 vols. London: Macmillan, 1921.

Budge, I. 'Party Policy and Ideology: Reversing the 1950s?' In *Critical Elections: Voters and Parties in Long-Term Perspective*, (eds) G. Evans and P. Norris. London: Sage, 1999.

Burch, M. and Holliday, I. 'New Labour and the Machinery of Government'. In *New Labour in Power*, (eds) D. Coates and P. Lawler. Manchester: Manchester University Press, 2000.

Burchell, G., Gordon, C., and Miller, P. *The Foucault Effect: Studies in Governmentality*. London: Harvester Wheatsheaf, 1991.

Burnham, P. 'New Labour and the Politics of Depoliticisation', *British Journal of Politics and International Relations* 3 (2001), 127–49.

Burnham, W. *Critical Elections and the Mainsprings of American Politics*. New York: W. W. Norton, 1970.

Burrow, J. *Evolution and Society: A Study in Victorian Social Theory*. Cambridge: Cambridge University Press, 1966.

—— *Whigs and Liberals: Continuity and Change in English Political Thought*. Oxford: Oxford University Press, 1988.

Campbell, A., Converse, P., Miller, W., and Stokes, D. *The American Voter*. New York: Wiley, 1960.

Campbell, J. and Pedersen, O. (eds) *The Rise of Neoliberalism and Institutional Analysis*. Princeton: Princeton University Press, 2001.

Carpenter, E. 'The Value of the Value Theory', *To-day* 11 (1889), 22–30.

—— 'Transitions to Freedom'. In *Forecasts of the Coming Century*, (ed.) E. Carpenter. Manchester: Labour Press, 1897.

—— *Angel's Wings*. London: Swan Sonnenschein, 1898.

—— *The Art of Creation*. London: G. Allen, 1904.

—— *Towards Democracy*. London: Gay Men's Press, 1985.

Chong, D. 'Rational Choice Theory's Mysterious Rivals'. In *The Rational Choice Controversy*, (ed.) J. Friedman. New Haven: Yale University Press, 1996.

Clarence, E. and Painter, C. 'Public Services under New Labour: Collaborative Discourses and Local Networking', *Public Policy and Administration Review* 13 (1998), 8–22.

Clark, D. 'The Civil Service and the New Government'. Speech, London. 17 June 1997.

Clark, T., Myck, M., and Smith, Z. *Fiscal Reforms Affecting Households, 1997–2001*. London: Institute for Fiscal Studies, 2001.

Coates, D. 'New Labour's Industrial and Employment Policy'. In *New Labour in Power*, (eds) D. Coates and P. Lawler. Manchester: Manchester University Press, 2000.

—— and Lawler, P. (eds) *New Labour in Power*. Manchester: Manchester University Press, 2000.

Cockett, R. *Thinking the Unthinkable: Think-Tanks and the Economic Counter Revolution*. London: HarperCollins, 1995.

Coddington, A. and Perryman, M. (eds) *The Moderniser's Dilemma: Radical Politics in the Age of Blair*. London: Lawrence and Wishart, 1998.

Cohen, M., March, J., and Olsen, J. 'A Garbage Can Model of Organization Choice', *Administrative Science Quarterly* 17 (1972), 1–25.

Collier, R. and Collier, D. *Shaping the Political Arena: Critical Junctures, the Labor Movement, and Regime Dynamics in Latin America*. Princeton: Princeton University Press, 1991.

Collini, S. *Liberalism and Sociology: L. T. Hobhouse and Political Argument in Britain, 1880–1914*. Cambridge: Cambridge University Press, 1979.

——, Winch, D. and Burrow, J. *That Noble Science of Politics: A Study in Nineteenth-Century Intellectual History*. Cambridge: Cambridge University Press, 1983.

Commission on Social Justice. *Social Justice: Strategies for National Renewal*. London: Vintage, 1994.

Cope, S. and Goodship, J. 'Regulating Collaborative Government: Towards Joined-Up Government', *Public Policy and Administration Review* 14 (1999), 3–16.

Coughlin, R. 'Whose Morality? Which Community? What Interests? Socio-economic and Communitarian Perspectives', *Journal of Socio-Economics* 25 (1996), 135–56.

Crewe, I., Gosschalk, B., and Bartle, J. (eds) *Political Communications: Why Labour Won the General Election of 1997*. London: Frank Cass, 1998.

Crine, S. *Reforming Welfare: American Lessons*. Fabian Pamphlet no. 567. London: Fabian Society, 1994.

Critchley, S. 'Ethics, Politics, and Radical Democracy – The History of a Disagreement'. In *Laclau: A Critical Reader*, (eds) S. Critchley and O. Marchant. London: Routledge, 2004.

—— and Marchant, O. (eds) *Laclau: A Critical Reader*. London: Routledge, 2004.

Crouch, C. and Marquand, D. *Re-inventing Collective Action*. Oxford: Blackwell, 1995.

Deacon, A. 'Learning from the US?', *Policy and Politics* 28 (2000), 5–18.

Dean, M. 'Culture Governance and Individualisation'. In *Governance as Social and Political Communication*, (ed.) H. Bang. Manchester: Manchester University Press, 2003.

Den Otter, S. *British Idealism and Social Explanation*. Oxford: Clarendon Press, 1996.

Derrida, J. *Specters of Marx: The State of the Debt, the Work of Mourning, and the New International*, trans. P. Kamuf. London: Routledge, 1994.

Dews, P. 'The Return of the Subject in Late Foucault', *Radical Philosophy* 51 (1989), 37–41.

Dickens, R., Gregg, P., and Wadsworth, J. 'New Labour and the Labour Market', *Oxford Review of Economic Policy* 16 (2000), 95–113.

DiMaggio, P. and Powell, W. 'The Iron Cage Revisited: Institutional Isomorphism and Collective Rationality in Organizational Fields'. In *The New Institutionalism in Organizational Analysis*, (eds) W. Powell and P. DiMaggio. Chicago: Chicago University Press, 1991.

Dorey, P. 'The Blairite Betrayal: New Labour and the Unions'. In *The Impact of New Labour*, (ed.) G. Taylor. Basingstoke: Macmillan, 1999.

Douglas, J. 'The Overloaded Crown', *British Journal of Political Science* 6 (1976), 483–505.

Downs, A. *An Economic Theory of Democracy*. New York: Harper and Row, 1957.

Driver, S. and Martell, L. *New Labour: Politics after Thatcherism*. Cambridge: Polity, 1998.

—— and —— *Blair's Britain*. Cambridge: Polity, 2002.

Dunleavy, P., Gamble, A., and Holliday, I. (eds) *Developments in British Politics*, no. 6. Basingstoke: Macmillan, 2000.

Easton, D. *The Political System: An Inquiry into the State of Political Science*. New York: Knopf, 1953.

Elster, J. *Sour Grapes: Studies in the Subversion of Rationality*. Cambridge: Cambridge University Press, 1983.

—— *Ulysses and the Sirens*. Cambridge: Cambridge University Press, 1984.

—— *The Cement of Society*. Cambridge: Cambridge University Press, 1989.

Englander, D. and O'Day, R. (eds) *Retrieved Riches: Social Investigation in Britain 1880–1914*. Aldershot: Scholar Press, 1995.

Etzioni, A. *A Comparative Analysis of Complex Organizations: On Power, Involvement, and their Correlates*. New York: Free Press, 1961.

—— 'Toward a Theory of Societal Guidance'. In *Social Change: Sources, Patterns, and Consequences*, (eds) E. Etzioni-Halevy and A. Etzioni. New York: Basic Books, 1973.

—— *The Organizational Structure of the Kibbutz*. New York: Arno Press, 1980.

—— 'Encapsulated Competition', *Journal of Post-Keynesian Economics* 7 (1985), 287–302.

—— *The Spirit of Community: Rights, Responsibilities, and the Communitarian Agenda*. New York: Crown, 1993.

—— *The New Golden Rule: Community and Morality in a Democratic Society*. London: Profile Books, 1997.

—— *The Third Way to a Good Society*. London: Demos, 2000.

—— 'Is Bowling Together Sociologically Lite?', *Contemporary Sociology* 30 (2001), 223–4.

—— (ed.) *The Essential Communitarian Reader*. Oxford: Rowman and Butterfield, 1998.

Evans, G. and Norris, P. (eds) *Critical Elections: Voters and Parties in Long-Term Perspective*. London: Sage, 1999.

Evans, P. *Embedded Autonomy: States and Industrial Transformation*. Princeton: Princeton University Press, 1995.

—— and Stephens, J. 'Studying Development since the Sixties: The Emergence of a New Comparative Political Economy', *Theory and Society* 17 (1988), 713–45.

Everdell, W. *The First Moderns*. Chicago: University of Chicago Press, 1997.

Fay, B. *Contemporary Philosophy of Social Science*. Oxford: Blackwell Publishers, 1996.

Field, F. *An Agenda for Britain*. London: Fount, 1993.

—— *Making Welfare Work: Reconstructing Welfare for the Millennium*. London: Institute for Community Studies, 1995.

—— *How to Pay for the Future: Building a Stakeholder's Welfare*. London: Institute of Community Studies, 1996.

—— *Stakeholder Welfare*. London: Institute of Economic Affairs, 1996.

—— *Reforming Welfare*. London: Social Market Foundation, 1997.

—— *Reflections on Welfare Reform*. London: Social Markets Foundation, 1998.

Finer, H. *Foreign Governments at Work*. New York: Oxford University Press, 1921.

—— *Theory and Practice of Modern Government*. Westport, CT: Greenwood Press, 1970.

Finlayson, A. 'Third Way Theory', *Political Quarterly* 70 (1999), 271–9.

Foucault, M. *The Archaeology of Knowledge*, trans. A. Sheridan-Smith. London: Tavistock, 1972.

—— *Power/Knowledge: Selected Interviews and Other Writings, 1972–77*, (ed.) C. Gordon. Brighton: Harvester, 1980.

Francis, M. and Morrow, J. *A History of English Political Thought in the Nineteenth Century*. London: Duckworth, 1994.

Frankel, B. 'Beyond Labourism and Socialism: How the Australian Labor Party Developed the Model of New Labour', *New Left Review* 221 (1997), 3–33.

Franklin, B. 'The Hand of History: New Labour, News Management and Governance'. In *New Labour in Government*, (eds) S. Ludlam and M. Smith. Basingstoke: Macmillan, 2001.

Freeden, M. *Ideologies and Political Theory: A Conceptual Approach*. Oxford: Clarendon Press, 1996.

—— 'The Ideology of New Labour', *Political Quarterly* 70 (1999), 42–51.

Friedman, J. (ed.) *The Rational Choice Controversy*. New Haven: Yale University Press, 1996.

Friedrich, C. 'Comments on the Seminar Report', *American Political Science Review* 48 (1953), 658–61.

Galston, W. *Liberal Purposes: Goods, Virtues and Diversity in the Liberal State*. Cambridge: Cambridge University Press, 1991.

Geddes, M. and Martin, S. 'The Policy and Politics of Best Value: Currents, Crosscurrents, and Undercurrents in the New Regime', *Policy and Politics* 28 (2000), 379–95.

Gibson, A. and Asthana, S. 'Local Markets and the Polarization of Public-Sector Schools in England and Wales', *Transactions of the Institute of British Geographers* 25 (2000), 303–19.

Giddens, A. *The Third Way: The Renewal of Social Democracy*. Cambridge: Polity Press, 1998.

—— *The Third Way and Its Critics*. London: Polity Press, 2000.

Gilbert, J. 'Beyond the Hegemony of New Labour'. In *Cultural Capitalism: Politics after New Labour*, (eds) T. Bewes and J. Gilbert. London: Lawrence and Wishart, 2000.

Gillespie, R. *Manufacturing Knowledge: A History of the Hawthorne Experiments*. New York: Cambridge University Press, 1993.

Goddard, J. and Chatterton, P. 'Regional Development Agencies and the Knowledge Economy: Harnessing the Potential of Universities', *Environment and Planning C: Government and Policy* 17 (1999), 685–99.

Gordon, C. 'Governmental Rationality: An Introduction'. In *The Foucault Effect: Studies in Governmentality*, (eds) G. Burchell, C. Gordon, and P. Miller. London: Harvester Wheatsheaf, 1991.

Gore, C. *The Social Doctrine of the Sermon on the Mount*. London: Percival, 1892.

Gould, B. *Socialism and Freedom*. London: Macmillan, 1985.

Gould, P. 'Why Labour Won'. In *Political Communications: Why Labour Won the General Election of 1997*, (eds) I. Crewe, B. Gosschalk, and J. Bartle. London: Frank Cass, 1998.

—— *The Unfinished Revolution: How the Modernisers Saved the Labour Party*. London: Little Brown, 1998.

Granovetter, M. 'The Strength of Weak Ties', *American Journal of Sociology* 78 (1973), 1360–80.

—— *Getting a Job: A Study of Contracts and Careers*. Cambridge, MA: Harvard University Press, 1974.

—— 'Economic Action and Social Structure: The Problem of Embeddedness', *American Journal of Sociology* 91 (1985), 481–510.

—— 'Business Groups'. In *Handbook of Economic Sociology*, (eds) N. Smelser and R. Swedberg. Princeton: Princeton University Press, 1994.

Hall, P. *Governing the Economy: The Politics of State Intervention in Britain and France*. New York: Oxford University Press, 1986.

—— and Taylor, R. 'Political Science and the Three Institutionalisms', *Political Studies* 44 (1996), 936–57.

Harris, J. 'Political Thought and the Welfare State 1870–1914: An Intellectual Framework for British Social Policy', *Past and Present* 135 (1992), 116–41.

Hay, C. 'Labour's Thatcherite Revisionism: Playing the Politics of Catch-up', *Political Studies* 42 (1994), 700–7.

—— *The Political Economy of New Labour: Labouring under False Pretences?* Manchester: Manchester University Press, 1999.

—— 'New Labour and "Third Way" Political Economy: Paving the European Road to Washington?' In *Critiques of Capital in Modern Britain and America: Transatlantic Exchanges 1800 to the Present Day*, (eds) M. Bevir and F. Trentmann. Basingstoke: Palgrave Macmillan, 2002.

Hayward, J. 'British Approaches to Politics: The Dawn of a Self-Deprecating Discipline'. In *The British Study of Politics in the Twentieth Century*, (eds) J. Hayward, B. Barry, and A. Brown. Oxford: Oxford University Press, 1999.

——, Barry, B., and Brown, A. (eds) *The British Study of Politics in the Twentieth Century*. Oxford: Oxford University Press, 1999.

Heath, A., Jowell, R., and Curtice, J. *The Rise of New Labour: Party Policies and Voter Choices*. Oxford: Oxford University Press, 2001.

——, ——, ——, and Taylor, B. (eds) *Labour's Last Chance? The 1992 Election and Beyond*. Aldershot: Dartmouth, 1994.

Heffernan, R. 'Media Management: Labour's Political Communication Strategy'. In *The Impact of New Labour*, (ed.) G. Taylor. Basingstoke: Macmillan, 1999.

—— *New Labour and Thatcherism: Political Change in Britain*. Basingstoke: Macmillan, 2000.

Hennessey, P. 'The Blair Style of Government', *Government and Opposition* 33 (1998), 3–20.

Heywood, A. *Political Ideologies*. London: Macmillan, 1992.

Hinich, M. and Munger, M. 'Political Ideology, Communication, and Community'. In *Political Economy: Institutions, Competition, and Representation*, (eds) W. Barnett, M. Hinich, and N. Schofield. Cambridge: Cambridge University Press, 1993.

Hirst, P. (ed.) *The Pluralist Theory of the State: Selected Writings of G. D. H. Cole, J. N. Figgis, and H. J. Laski*. London: Routledge, 1989.

Hobsbawm, E. *The Forward March of Labour Halted*, (eds) J. Martin and F. Mulhern. London: New Left Books, 1981.

Hobson, J. and Mummery, A. *The Physiology of Industry*. London: John Murray, 1889.

Hood, C. 'British Public Administration: Dodo, Phoenix, or Chameleon?' In *The British Study of Politics in the Twentieth Century*, (eds) J. Hayward, B. Barry, and A. Brown. Oxford: Oxford University Press, 1999.

Hughes, H. Stuart. *Consciousness and Society: The Reorientation of European Social Thought 1890–1930*. New York: Vintage Books, 1961.

Hyndman, H. *The Text Book of Democracy: England for All*. London: E. Allen, 1881.

—— 'The Dawn of a Revolutionary Epoch', *Nineteenth Century* 9 (1881), 1–18.

Immervoll, H., Mitton, L., O'Donoghue, C., and Sutherland, H. 'Budgeting For Fairness: The Distributional Effects of Three Labour Budgets', Microsimulation Unit Research Note no. 32, March 1999.

Jänicke, D. 'New Labour and the Clinton Presidency'. In *New Labour in Power*, (eds) D. Coates and P. Lawler. Manchester: Manchester University Press, 2000.

Johnson, N. 'The Place of Institutions in the Study of Politics', *Political Studies* 23 (1975), 271–83.

Jones, N. *Sultans of Spin: The Media and the New Labour Government*. London: Weidenfeld and Nicholson, 1999.

—— *The Control Freaks: How New Labour Gets Its Own Way*. London: Politico's, 2001.

Jones, T. *Remaking the Labour Party: From Gaitskell to Blair*. London: Routledge, 1996.

Jordan, B. *The New Politics of Welfare: Social Justice in a Global Context*. London: Sage, 1998.

Kato, J. 'Institutions and Rationality in Politics: Three Varieties of Neo-Institutionalists', *British Journal of Political Science* 26 (1996), 553–82.

Kelly, G. (ed.) *The New European Left*. London: Fabian Society, 1999.

Kenny, M. *The First New Left: British Intellectuals after Stalin*. London: Lawrence and Wishart, 1995.

—— and Smith, M. 'Discourses of Modernisation: Comparing Gaitskell, Blair, and the Reform of Clause IV'. In *British Elections and Parties*, (eds) C. Pattie, D. Denver, S. Ludlam, and J. Fisher. London: Frank Cass, 1997.

—— and —— 'Interpreting New Labour: Constraints, Dilemmas and Political Agency'. In *New Labour in Government*, (eds) S. Ludlam and M. Smith. Basingstoke: Macmillan, 2001.

Kickert, W., Klijn, E.-H., and Koppenjan, J. 'Managing Networks in the Public Sector: Findings and Reflections'. In *Managing Complex Networks: Strategies for the Public Sector*, (eds) W. Kickert, E.-H. Klijn, and J. Koppenjan. London: Sage, 1998.

——, ——, and —— (eds) *Managing Complex Networks: Strategies for the Public Sector*. London: Sage, 1998.

King, A. 'Overload: Problems of Governing in the UK in the 1970s', *Political Studies* 38 (1975), 284–96.

King, D. and Wickham Jones, M. 'Training Without the State? New Labour and the Labour Markets', *Policy and Politics* 26 (1998), 439–55.

—— and —— 'Bridging the Atlantic: The Democratic (Party) Origins of Welfare to Work'. In *New Labour, New Welfare State? The 'Third Way' in British Social Policy*, (ed.) M. Powell. Bristol: Policy Press, 1999.

Kinnock, N. 'Reforming the Labour Party', *Contemporary Record* 8 (1994), 535–54.

Kitschelt, H. *The Transformation of European Social Democracy*. Cambridge: Cambridge University Press, 1994.

Labour Party. *Made in Britain: A New Economic Policy for the 1990s*. London: Labour Party, 1991.

—— *Winning for Britain: Strategy for Industrial Success*. London: Labour Party, 1993.

—— *Rebuilding the Economy*. London: Labour Party, 1994.

—— *A New Economic Policy for Britain: Economic and Employment Opportunities for All*. London: Labour Party, 1995.

—— *A New Economic Future for Britain*. London: Labour Party, 1995.

—— *New Life for Britain*. London: Labour Party, 1996.

Landau, M. 'The Myth of Hyperfactualism in the Study of American Politics', *Political Science Quarterly* 83 (1968), 378–99.

Layard, R. 'Preventing Long-term Unemployment'. In *Unemployment Policy*, (eds) D. Snowes and G. de la Dehasa. Cambridge: Cambridge University Press, 1997.

Leadbeater, C. *The Rise of the Social Entrepreneur*. London: Demos, 1997.

—— *Living on Thin Air*. Harmondsworth: Penguin, 1999.

—— and Goss, S. *Civic Entrepreneurship*. London: Demos, 1998.

—— and Mulgan, G. *Mistakeholding: Whatever Happened to Labour's Big Idea?* London: Demos, 1996.

Leonard, D. (ed.) *Crosland and New Labour*. Basingstoke: Macmillan, 1999.

Leonard, M. *Britain: Renewing Our Identity*. London: Demos, 1997.

Levitas, R. *The Inclusive Society? Social Exclusion and New Labour*. Basingstoke: Macmillan, 1998.

Lloyd, D. and Thomas, P. *Culture and the State*. London: Routledge, 1998.

Local Government Association. *Best Value: A Statement of Objectives*. London: Local Government Association, 1998.

Lowndes, V. 'Varieties of New Institutionalism: A Critical Appraisal', *Public Administration* 74 (1996), 181–97.

—— 'Rebuilding Trust in Central/Local Relations: Policy or Passion?' In *Renewing Local Democracy*, (ed.) L. Pratchett. London: Frank Cass, 2000.

Ludlam, S. 'The Making of New Labour'. In *New Labour in Government*, (eds) S. Ludlam and M. Smith. Basingstoke: Macmillan, 2001.

—— 'New Labour and the Unions: The End of the Contentious Alliance'. In *New Labour in Government*, (eds) S. Ludlam and M. Smith. Basingstoke: Macmillan, 2001.

—— and Smith, M. (eds) *New Labour in Government*. Basingstoke: Macmillan, 2001.

MacDonald, R. *The Zollverein and British Industry*. London: Grant Richards, 1903.

—— *Socialism and Society*. London: Independent Labour Party, 1905.

—— 'Socialism'. In *Ramsay MacDonald's Political Writings*, (ed.) B. Barker. London: Allen Lane, 1972.

MacIntyre, D. *Mandelson: The Biography*. London: HarperCollins, 1999.

Mackenzie, W. 'Pressure Groups in British Government', *British Journal of Sociology* 6 (1955), 284–96.

—— *Politics and Social Science*. Harmondsworth: Penguin, 1967.

Mahoney, J. 'Path Dependence in Historical Sociology', *Theory and Society* 29 (2000), 507–48.

Mandelson, P. 'Coordinating Government Policy'. Speech to Conference on Modernising the Policy Process, London. 16 September 1997.

—— and Liddle, R. *The Blair Revolution: Can New Labour Deliver?* London: Faber and Faber, 1996.

March, J. and Olsen, J. 'The New Institutionalism: Organisational Factors in Political Life', *American Political Science Review* 78 (1984), 734–9.

—— and —— *Rediscovering Institutions*. New York: Free Press, 1989.

—— and —— *Democratic Governance*. New York: Free Press, 1995.

Marsh, D. (ed.) *Comparing Policy Networks*. Buckingham: Open University Press, 1998.

—— and Rhodes, R. (eds) *Policy Networks in British Government*. Oxford: Clarendon Press, 1992.

—— and Stoker, G. (eds) *Theory and Methods in Political Science*. Basingstoke: Palgrave, 2002.

Marshall, A. *Principles of Economics*, (ed.) C. Guillebaud. London: Macmillan, 1961.

Martell, L., Anker, C. van der, Brownes, M., Hooper, S., Larkin, P., Lees, C., McCowan, F., and Stammers, N. *Social Democracy: Global and National Perspectives*. Basingstoke: Palgrave, 2001.

Miliband, R. *Parliamentary Socialism: A Study in the Politics of Labour*. London: Merlin, 1961.

—— *The State in Capitalist Society*. New York: Basic Books, 1969.

Mitchell, W. 'The Shape of Public Choice to Come: Some Predictions and Advice', *Public Choice* 77 (1993), 133–44.

Morris, W. *The Collected Works of William Morris*, vol. 16: *News from Nowhere*. London: Longmans, 1910–15.

Moss, J. (ed.) *The Later Foucault: Politics and Philosophy*. London: Sage, 1998.

Mulgan, G. *Connexity*. London: Jonathan Cape, 1997.

—— and Perri 6. 'The Local is Coming Home: Decentralisation by Degrees', *Demos Quarterly* 9 (1996), 3–7.

North, D. 'Toward a Theory of Institutional Change'. In *Political Economy: Institutions, Competition, and Representation*, (eds) W. Barnett, M. Hinich, and N. Schofield. Cambridge: Cambridge University Press, 1993.

Ohmae, K. *The End of the Nation State*. New York: Free Press, 1996.

Olivier, S. *Sydney Olivier: Letters and Selected Writings*, (ed.) M. Olivier. London: G. Allen and Unwin, 1948.

Osborne, D. and Gaebler, T. *Reinventing Government: How the Entrepreneurial Spirit is Transforming the Public Sector*. Reading, MA: Addison-Wesley, 1992.

Painter, C. and Clarence, E. 'UK Local Action Zones and Changing Urban Governance', *Urban Studies* 38 (2001), 1215–32.

Panitch, L. and Leys, C. *The End of Parliamentary Socialism: From New Left to New Labour*. London: Verso, 1997.

Paton, C. 'New Labour's Health Policy: The New Healthcare State'. In *New Labour: New Welfare State? The 'Third Way' in British Social Policy*, (ed.) M. Powell. Bristol: Policy Press, 1999.

Pattie, C., Denver, D., Ludlam, S., and Fisher, J. (eds) *British Elections and Parties*. London: Frank Cass, 1997.

Peck, J. 'New Labourers? Making a New Deal for the "Workless Class"', *Environment and Planning C: Government and Policy* 17 (1999), 345–72.

—— and Theodore, N. '"Work First": Workfare and the Regulation of Contingent Labour Markets', *Cambridge Journal of Economics* 24 (2000), 119–38.

Penty, A. J. *The Restoration of the Gild System*. London: Swan Sonnenschein, 1906.

Perri 6. *Escaping Poverty: From Safety Nets to Networks of Opportunity*. London: Demos, 1997.

—— *Holistic Government*. London: Demos, 1997.

—— 'Neo-Durkheimian Institutional Theory'. Paper to Conference on Institutional Theory in Political Science, Loch Lomond. 1999.

—— Leat, D., Seltzer, K., and Stoker, G. *Governing in the Round: Strategies for Holistic Government*. London: Demos, 1999.

Piachaud, D. and Sutherland, H. 'Changing Poverty Post-1997'. CASE paper no. 63. London: Centre for the Analysis of Social Exclusion, 2002.

Pierre, J. and Stoker, G. 'Towards Multi-Level Governance'. In *Developments in British Politics*, no. 6, (eds) P. Dunleavy, A. Gamble, and I. Holliday. Basingstoke: Macmillan, 2000.

Pierson, C. and Castles, F. 'Australian Antecedents of the Third Way', *Political Studies* 50 (2002), 683–702.

Pierson, P. 'Increasing Returns, Path Dependence, and the Study of Politics', *American Political Science Review* 92 (2000), 251–67.

Pierson, S. *Marxism and the Origins of British Socialism*. Ithaca: Cornell University Press, 1973.

—— *British Socialism: The Journey from Fantasy to Politics*. Cambridge, MA: Harvard University Press, 1979.

Powell, M. *New Labour, New Welfare State? The 'Third Way' in British Social Policy*. Bristol: Policy Press, 1999.

Powell, W. 'Neither Market nor Hierarchy: Network Forms of Organization', *Research in Organizational Behaviour* 12 (1990), 295–336.

—— and DiMaggio, P. (eds) *The New Institutionalism in Organizational Analysis*. Chicago: Chicago University Press, 1991.

——, Koput, K., and Smith-Doerr, L. 'Interorganizational Collaboration and the Locus of Innovation: Networks of Learning in Biotechnology', *Administrative Science Quarterly* 41 (1996), 116–45.

Pratchett, L. (ed.) *Renewing Local Democracy*. London: Frank Cass, 2000.

Putnam, R. *The Beliefs of Politicians: Ideology, Conflict, and Democracy in Britain and Italy*. New Haven: Yale University Press, 1973.

—— *Making Democracy Work: Civic Traditions in Modern Italy*. Princeton: Princeton University Press, 1993.

—— *Bowling Alone: The Collapse and Revival of American Community*. New York: Simon and Schuster, 2000.

Radcliffe-Brown, A. 'The Mother's Brother in South Africa', *South African Journal of Science* 21 (1924), 542–55.

Radice, G. *Southern Discomfort*. Fabian Pamphlet no. 555. London: Fabian Society, 1992.

—— and Pollard, S. *More Southern Discomfort: Year On – Taxing and Spending.* Fabian Pamphlet no. 560. London: Fabian Society, 1993.

Reich, R. 'We Are All Third Wayers Now', *American Prospect* 43 (1999), 46–51.

Reinecke, W. *Global Public Policy: Governing without Government?* Washington, DC: Brookings Institution Press, 1994.

Rentoul, J. *Tony Blair.* London: Little Brown, 1995.

Rhodes, R. *Beyond Westminster and Whitehall.* London: Unwin Hyman, 1988.

—— *Understanding Governance: Policy Networks, Governance, Reflexivity, and Accountability.* Buckingham: Open University Press, 1997.

—— (ed.) *Transforming British Government*, 2 vols. London: Macmillan, 2000.

Richards, D. and Smith, M. 'How Departments Change: Windows of Opportunity and Critical Junctures in Three Departments', *Public Policy and Administration* 12 (1997), 62–79.

Richardson, J. and Jordan, G. *Governing under Pressure: The Policy Process in a Post-Parliamentary Democracy.* Oxford: Martin Robertson, 1979.

Richmond, W. *Christian Economics.* London: Rivingtons, 1888.

Richter, M. (ed.) *Essays in Theory and History.* Cambridge, MA: Harvard University Press, 1970.

Rose, R. *Do Parties Make a Difference?* London: Macmillan, 1980.

Rouse, J. and Smith, G. 'Accountability'. In *New Labour, New Welfare State? The 'Third Way' in British Social Policy*, (ed.) M. Powell. Bristol: Policy Press, 1999.

Routledge, P. *Gordon Brown: The Biography.* London: Simon and Schuster, 1998.

—— *Mandy.* London: Simon and Schuster, 1999.

Rowe, M. 'Joined-Up Accountability: Bringing the Citizen Back In', *Public Policy and Administration Review* 14 (1999), 91–102.

Russell, C. 'New Labour: Old Tory Writ Large?', *New Left Review* 219 (1996), 78–88.

Saunders, D. 'Behavioural Analysis'. In *Theory and Methods in Political Science*, (eds) D. Marsh and G. Stoker. Basingstoke: Palgrave, 2002.

Schabas, M. *A World Ruled by Number: William Stanley Jevons and the Rise of Mathematical Economics.* Princeton: Princeton University Press, 1990.

Schoemaker, P. 'The Expected Utility Model: Its Variants, Purposes, Evidence and Limitations', *Journal of Economic Literature* 20 (1982), 529–63.

Scott, A. *Running on Empty: 'Modernizing' the British and Australian Labour Parties.* Sydney: Pluto Press, 2000.

Scott, W. *Chester I. Barnard and the Guardians of the Managerial State.* Lawrence: University of Kansas Press, 1992.

Self, P. *Government by the Market: The Politics of Public Choice.* London: Macmillan, 1993.

Seliger, M. *Ideology and Politics.* London: Allen and Unwin, 1976.

Selznick, P. 'Foundations of the Theory of Organization', *American Sociology Review* 13 (1948), 25–35.

—— *TVA and the Grass Roots.* Berkeley: University of California Press, 1953.

—— *Leadership in Administration: A Sociological Interpretation.* Berkeley: University of California Press, 1957.

—— *The Moral Commonwealth: Social Theory and the Promise of Community.* Berkeley: University of California Press, 1994.

Shaw, E. *The Labour Party since 1979: Crisis and Transformation*. London: Routledge, 1994.

—— *The Labour Party since 1945*. Oxford: Blackwell, 1996.

Shaw, G. 'The Economic'. In *Fabian Essays in Socialism*, (ed.) G. Shaw. London: Walter Scott, 1890.

—— 'The Transition to Social Democracy'. In *Fabian Essays in Socialism*, (ed.) G. Shaw. London: Walter Scott, 1890.

Skinner, Q. 'Motives, Intentions, and the Interpretation of Texts'. In *Meaning and Context: Quentin Skinner and his Critics*, (ed.) J. Tully. Cambridge: Polity Press, 1988.

Skocpol, T. *States and Social Revolutions*. Cambridge: Cambridge University Press, 1979.

—— 'Uses of Comparative History in Macrosocial Inquiry', *Comparative Studies in Society and History* 22 (1980), 174–96.

—— 'Emerging Agendas and Recurrent Strategies in Historical Sociology'. In *Vision and Method in Historical Sociology*, (ed.) T. Skocpol. Cambridge: Cambridge University Press, 1984.

—— *Protecting Soldiers and Mothers: The Political Origins of Social Policy in the United States*. Cambridge, MA: Harvard University Press, 1992.

—— 'Theory Tackles History', *Social Science History* 24, (2000), 675–6.

Smith, M. and Spear, J. (eds) *The Changing Labour Party*. London: Routledge, 1992.

Snowden, P. *Socialism and Syndicalism*. London: Collins, 1913.

—— 'The Socialist Budget 1907'. In *From Socialism to Serfdom*, (ed.) J. Hardie. Hassocks, Sussex: Harvester, 1974.

Snowes, D. and Dehasa, G. de la (eds) *Unemployment Policy*. Cambridge: Cambridge University Press, 1997.

Sopel, J. *Tony Blair: The Moderniser*. London: Bantam Books, 1995.

Stapleton, J. *Englishness and the Study of Politics: The Social and Political Thought of Ernest Barker*. Cambridge: Cambridge University Press, 1994.

Stead, W. 'The Labour Party and the Books that Helped Make it', *Review of Reviews* 33 (1906), 568–82.

Stocking, G. *Victorian Anthropology*. New York: Free Press, 1987.

—— *After Taylor: British Social Anthropology, 1888–1951*. Madison: University of Wisconsin Press, 1995.

Stoker, G. 'Introduction: The Unintended Costs and Benefits of New Management Reform for British Local Governance'. In *The New Management of British Local Governance*, (ed.) G. Stoker. London: Macmillan, 1999.

—— (ed.) *The New Management of British Local Government*. London: Macmillan, 1999.

—— 'Urban Political Science and the Challenge of Urban Governance'. In *Debating Governance*, (ed.) J. Pierre. Oxford: Oxford University Press, 2000.

—— 'The Three Projects of New Labour', *Renewal* 8 (2000), 7–15.

—— (ed.) *The New Politics of British Local Governance*. London: Macmillan, 2000.

Straw, J. *Policy and Ideology*. Blackburn: Blackburn Labour Party, 1993.

Sutherland, H. 'Five Labour Budgets: Impacts on the Distribution of Household Incomes and on Child Poverty'. Microsimulation Unit Research Note no. 41. May 2001.

—— and Taylor, R. 'The 2000 Budget: The Impact on the Distribution of Household Incomes'. Microsimulation Unit Research Note no. 35. March 2000.

Tam, H. *Communitarianism: A New Agenda for Politics and Citizenship*. New York: New York University Press, 1998.

Taylor, C. 'Interpretation and the Sciences of Man', *Review of Metaphysics* 25 (1971–2), 3–51.

Taylor, G. *Labour's Renewal? The Policy Review and Beyond*. Basingstoke: Macmillan, 1997.

—— (ed.) *The Impact of New Labour*. Basingstoke: Macmillan, 1999.

Taylor, M. 'Structure, Culture and Action in the Explanation of Social Change', *Politics and Society* 17 (1989), 115–62.

Temple, M. 'New Labour's Third Way: Pragmatism and Governance', *British Journal of Politics and International Relations* 2 (2000), 302–25.

Temple, W. *Christianity and Social Order*. London: Shepherd-Walwyn, 1976.

Thelen, K. 'Historical Institutionalism in Comparative Politics', *Annual Review of Political Science* 2 (1999), 369–404.

Thompson, N. *Political Economy and the Labour Party*. London: UCL Press, 1996.

Toynbee, P. and Walker, D. *Did Things Get Better? An Audit of Labour's Successes and Failures*. Harmondsworth: Penguin, 2001.

Tully, J. (ed.) *Meaning and Context: Quentin Skinner and his Critics*. Cambridge: Polity Press, 1988.

—— 'Wittgenstein and Political Philosophy: Understanding Practices of Critical Reflection', *Political Theory* 17 (1989), 172–204.

—— 'Political Philosophy as a Critical Activity', *Political Theory*, 30 (2002), 533–55.

Vicchaeri, C. *Rationality and Co-ordination*. Cambridge: Cambridge University Press, 1993.

Vincent, A. *Modern Political Ideologies*. Oxford: Blackwell, 1992.

—— 'New Ideologies for Old?', *Political Quarterly* 69 (1998), 48–58.

Vincent-Jones, P. 'Competition and Contracting in the Transition from CCT to Best Value: Towards a More Reflexive Regulation', *Public Administration* 77 (1999), 273–91.

Vulliamy, G. and Webb, R. 'Stemming the Tide of Rising School Exclusion: Problems and Possibilities', *British Journal of Educational Studies* 48 (2000), 119–33.

Walker, R. 'The Americanization of British Welfare', *International Journal of Health Services* 29 (1999), 679–97.

Webb, S. 'The Economics of a Positivist Community', *Practical Socialist* 1 (1886), 37–9.

—— 'Rome: A Sermon in Sociology', *Our Corner* 12 (1888), 53–60 and 79–89.

—— *English Progress towards Social Democracy*. Fabian Tract no. 15. London: Fabian Society, 1892.

—— and Webb, B. *Industrial Democracy*. London: Longmans, 1902.

—— and —— *A Constitution for the Socialist Commonwealth of Great Britain*. London: Longmans, 1920.

White, S. 'The Ambiguities of the Third Way'. In *New Labour: The Progressive Future?*, (ed.) S. White. Basingstoke: Palgrave, 2001.

—— (ed.) *New Labour: The Progressive Future?* Basingstoke: Palgrave, 2001.

Wickham-Jones, M. 'Recasting Social Democracy: A Comment on Hay and Smith', *Political Studies* 43 (1995), 698–702.

Wilkinson, A. 'New Labour and Christian Socialism'. In *The Impact of New Labour*, (ed.) G. Taylor. Basingstoke: Macmillan, 1999.

Wilks, S. and Wright, M. 'Conclusion: Comparing Government–Industry Relations: States, Sectors, and Networks'. In *Comparative Government Industry Relations*, (eds) S. Wilks and M. Wright. Oxford: Clarendon Press, 1987.

—— and —— (eds) *Comparative Government Industry Relations*. Oxford: Clarendon Press, 1987.

Williamson, O. 'Transaction-Cost Economics: The Governance of Contractual Relations', *Journal of Law and Economics* 22 (1979), 223–61.

Wilson, J. 'From CCT to Best Value: Some Evidence and Observations', *Local Government Studies* 25 (1999), 38–52.

Wood, B. 'New Labour and Welfare Reform'. In *New Labour in Power*, (eds) D. Coates and P. Lawler. Manchester: Manchester University Press, 2000.

Wright, T. *Tawney*. Manchester: Manchester University Press, 1987.

—— *Who Wins Dares: New Labour – New Politics*. Fabian Pamphlet no. 579. London: Fabian Society, 1997.

Young, R. 'New Labour and International Development'. In *New Labour in Power*, (eds) D. Coates and P. Lawler. Manchester: Manchester University Press, 2000.

Index

actions 18–20, 21–2, 29, 56
Action Teams 50
Action Zones 49, 51, 101, 152
Active Community Unit 72
Adam Smith Institute 30
agency, situated *see* situated agency
altruism 19
Amsterdam Summit, 1997 116–17
anthropology 76–9
Anti-Drugs Coordination Unit 98
Asian Tigers 47
associations 146
authoritarianism 72
autonomy 22–3, 25–7

Baby Tax Credit 93
Bagehot, Walter 6
Balls, Ed 42, 113, 116
Bank of England 113–14
Bank of England Act, 1998 113
Barnard, Chester 77, 78
Beckett, Margaret 120
Beer, Max 55
Beer, Sam 33, 34
behaviour, human 10–11, 12–14
behaviouralism 5, 8–9, 12, 15, 16–18,
    27, 32–4, 52, 76, 77–80, 87–9
beliefs 12–14, 16–21, 23–8, 52,
    83–4
Bellah, Robert 73
Bendix, Reinhard 33, 34
Benn, Tony 55
Bentham, Jeremy 5, 9, 131
Bentley, Tom 30
Best Value 96–7, 104
Better Regulation Taskforce 101, 117
Bevan, Nye 54
Bevin, Ernest 58
Bible, The 54

Blair, Tony 1, 30; and Amitai Etzioni
    73; on community 70, 71, 72, 136;
    on 'cool Britannia' 47; on duty 68;
    on economy 108, 111, 121; on
    ethical socialism 54, 72; on family
    75, 93; on globalisation 105, 109,
    116; on inflation 109–10; on joined-
    up governance 48; on labour
    markets 117–18; on pensions 94; on
    poverty 115, 121; on rights 75; and
    social democracy 61, 63; on social
    order 142; on the state 112; on
    technology 110; on Third Way 41,
    108–9; *The Third Way: New Politics
    for a New Century* 41; on trust 100;
    on values 140–1; on the welfare
    state 46, 67, 90, 91; 'Why
    Modernisation Matters' 42; *see also*
    New Labour
Blondel, Jean 8
Blunkett, David 30, 65
Booth, Charles 10
Bosanquet, Bernard 6
Brandt, Willy 58
British Institute of Public Opinion
    (BIPO) 7
Brown, Gordon 30, 31; and Bank of
    England 113–14; and Child Benefit
    93; on economic stability 64, 117;
    and equality 65, 136; on ethical
    socialism 54, 61, 63; and inflation
    107, 109–10; influence of Amitai
    Etzioni on 73; influence of Bill
    Clinton on 42; and the New Deal
    91; on the state 112; and supply-side
    economics 108, 111
Bryce, James 7
business 119–20
Butler, David 79

California 47
Calman-Hine Cancer Service
   Framework 102
capitalism 86, 129–34
Carlyle, Thomas 54
Carpenter, Edward 62, 132, 134
causation 14
Centre for Policy Studies 30
Charter Mark 97
Chartists 136
Child Benefit 93, 115
Childcare Tax Credit 93
children and poverty 115, 121
Christian Social Union 132
Citizen's Charter 100
citizenship 62, 66–9, 75–6, 81
civil service 151
civil society 74–5, 80, 88, 96, 130,
   132–3, 146
Clark, David 45
Clause IV 1, 68
Clinton, Bill 1, 42, 73
Code for Fiscal Stability 114
Cole, G.D.H. 54, 56, 135
Coleridge, Samuel 5
Collingwood, R.G. 9
Commission for Health Improvement
   101, 102
Commission on Social Justice 42,
   68
Commissions for Care Standards
   (CCSs) 102
communitarianism: and community
   140–2, 143; influence on New
   Labour 72–82, 84–5, 87–90, 103,
   124, 129, 140, 143, 153; *v.*
   pluralist democracy 148; and the
   welfare state 121; and work 91,
   96, 103; *see also* community;
   Etzioni, Amitai
community 62–3, 69–72, 81, 88, 135;
   and individualism 138–43; open
   137–43, 148; *see also*
   communitarianism
Comprehensive Spending Review
   114
Compulsory Competitive Tendering
   (CCT) 96, 104
Comte, Auguste 5, 76
Connolly, James 134
consumers 65, 66
Crick, Bernard 9
critique 136–8
Crosland, A. 81

deliberation 143–4, 148–50
democracy: liberal 144–5, 149–53;
   participatory 143–4, 146; pluralist
   146–8, 154; *see also* social
   democracy
Democrats, New *see* New Democrats
Demos 30–1, 51, 73
Department of Trade and Industry
   (DTI) 112, 119, 120
Dialog Corporation 119
dialogue 3–4, 148–53
Dickens, Charles 54
DiMaggio, Paul 30, 39
Driver, Stephen 124, 125
Durkheim, Emile 76, 77
duties and rights *see* rights and
   duties

Economic Commission 42
economy: globalisation 85–6, 107–12,
   116, 128, 136; inflation 63–4, 66,
   81, 107, 108, 109–10, 113; interest
   rates 108, 113–14; Keynesianism
   43–5, 61, 62, 63, 107, 109, 135;
   macro-economics 113–17; and
   networks 85, 108, 112; and new
   institutionalism 111–12; and New
   Labour 28, 42–8, 62, 64, 84–6,
   106–27, 153; and New Right 63–4,
   107–11, 117; public expenditure
   114–15; rules for 109, 114; supply
   side 108, 111–12, 117–21; taxation
   63–4, 70, 92–3, 110, 117–18, 122
education 50, 101, 118–19, 123
Education Action Zones 118
Egan, Beth 30
Election, General, 1997 1
embeddedness 39, 44, 45–9, 53; *see
   also* networks
empiricism, modernist 7–9, 12, 15,
   31–7, 52, 76–82, 123–4, 141
employment *see* unemployment
Employment Relations Act 93
Employment Zones 94, 96
Enlightenment 5–6, 9
equality 65–6, 136
ethical socialism *see* socialism, ethical
Etzioni, Amitai 73–4, 78–9, 88, 140,
   141–2
European Union (EU) 116–17
European Working Time Directive 116
Evans, Peter 37, 38
experience, pure 13, 14, 21, 86
expertise 3–4, 124–6

Fabianism 62, 129, 130–3, 134, 135
Fairness to Work 120
family 74–5, 75, 93
fellowship 138–40; *see also* community
Field, Frank 70, 71, 94, 95, 96
Finance Act, 1998 114
Financial Services and Markets Bill, 1999 121
Financial Services Authority 121
Finer, Herman 8; *Foreign Governments at Work* 7; *Theory and Practice of Modern Government* 7
Finer, S.E. 8, 9
Firth, Sir Raymond 79
Foreign and Commonwealth Office Panel 31
Foreign Policy Centre 30, 31
France 107
Freeden, Michael 56–7, 59–60, 61
Friedman, Milton 116
Friedrich, Carl 33
functionalism 76–9, 88

Gaitskell, Hugh 58
Galston, William 74
General Election, 1997 1
General Electric 77
General Social Care Council 102
George, Henry 54
Giddens, Anthony 42, 87; *The Third Way: The Renewal of Social Democracy* 41
globalisation 105, 107–12, 116, 128, 136
Gore, Charles 64
Gould, Brian 66
governance, joined-up 2–3, 29–30, 48–51, 89, 98–9; *see also* networks
Granovetter, Mark 30, 39
Green, T.H. 6
guild socialism 134

Hall, Peter 15, 34, 88
Hall, Stuart 136, 137
Hardie, Keir 133
Hay, Colin 125
healthcare 50, 95, 97, 99, 100, 101, 102–3
Health Improvement Programmes 99
Hegel, Georg Wilhelm Friedrich 6
hegemony 137
Heywood, Andrew 55
Hobhouse, L.T. 6
Hobsbawm, Eric 69

Hobson, S.G. 134, 135
humanism, social 9, 20, 27
Hutton, Will 47
Hyndman, H.M., *The Text Book of Democracy* 130

ideologies 55–60, 80–2
individualism 71, 88; and community 138–43
Individual Learning Accounts 94, 118
individual responsibility *see* responsibility, individual
Industry Forums 120
inflation 63–4, 66, 81, 107, 108, 109–10, 113
Institute for Fiscal Studies 122
Institute for Public Policy Research 30, 31
institutionalism 29–53; and behaviouralism 33–4; in Britain 36–7; and communitarianism 76–80; and the economy 91, 111–12, 121; and explanation 15–16; influence on New Labour 3–5, 27–8, 41–57, 84–5, 87–90, 103, 121, 124, 127, 129, 153; and modernist empiricism 31–7; and neoliberalism 85; and networks 96, 103, 153; old 87; and positivism 3–5, 12; and rational choice theory 34–6; and the state 37–41; in the United States 32–6
intentions 22–3
interest rates 108, 113–14
International Computers Limited 119
International Monetary Fund 63
interpretivism 4–5, 20–8, 51–3, 128–9, 137–40, 143–4, 148, 153–4
Invest to Save Budget (ISB) 98
Italy 47

Jevons, W.S. 6, 9, 130
Johnson, Neville 16
joined-up governance *see* governance, joined-up
justice, social 62–6, 67, 76, 81, 103, 145

Kamark, Elaine 73
Kay, John 47
Keynesianism 43–5, 61, 62, 63, 107, 109, 135

Labour, New *see* New Labour
labour market 117–18; *see also* unemployment

language 23
Laski, Harold 56, 135
Layard, Richard 116
Leadbeater, Charles 31, 45, 47–8, 51
legislation 150
Leonard, Mark 31, 47
liberalism 55–6, 135; *see also*
  democracy, liberal; neoliberalism
Liddle, Roger 61, 64, 65, 67, 70, 89,
  94, 108, 111, 117
Lipset, Seymour 34
Local Government Act, 2000 50
Local Government Programme 39
Lowndes, Vivien 30

Macaulay, T.B. 5
MacDonald, Ramsey 133, 134
MacIntyre, Alasdair 73
Mackenzie, Bill 8, 11
Macmurray, John 9, 61, 70
Major, John 124
Malinowski, Bronislaw 76, 77, 79
Mandelson, Peter: and the economy
  64, 70, 108, 109, 110, 111, 117;
  and ethical socialism 61, 63;
  influence of New Democrats on 42;
  and institutionalism 30; and
  liberalism 136; and the welfare state
  65, 67, 89, 94
Mann, Tom 130, 134
March, James 15, 79
markets 37–41, 44–5, 96–9
Marquand, David 58
Marshall, Alfred 6, 130, 135
Martell, Luke 124, 125
Marx, Karl 34, 54
Marxism 34, 129–31, 134, 135, 136,
  137, 156
Maurice, F.D. 61
Mayhew, Henry 10
Mead, G.H. 77
meaning 25
Merton, Robert 77, 78, 88
Microsimulation Unit, University of
  Cambridge 121
Miliband, David 42
Mill, John Stuart 5–6, 131
minimum wage 93
Mitterand, François 107
Modernising Government 2, 3
modernism 6–9, 12, 13
modernist empiricism *see* empiricism,
  modernist
monetarism 63, 107

Monetary Policy Committee, Bank of
  England 113
Moore, Barrington 34, 79
Moore, G.E. 6
Morris, William 130, 136; *News from
  Nowhere* 69
Mrs T (case study) 2–3
Mulgan, Geoff 30, 45, 47–8, 50

NAIRU 116
National Childcare Strategy 94
National Framework for Assessing
  Performance 50, 102
National Health Service (NHS) *see*
  healthcare
National Institute for Clinical
  Excellence (NICE) 101, 102
National Service Frameworks 102
National Survey of Patient and User
  Experience 102–3
National Taskforce on Staff
  Involvement 99
neofunctionalism 142
neoliberalism 29–30, 37–41, 63, 85,
  86, 88; *see also* New Right
networks: and the economy 85, 108,
  112; and institutionalism 39–40, 96;
  and interpretivism 53, 153; and
  joined-up governance 2, 29–30, 89,
  98–9; New Labour's use of 2,
  29–32, 45–51, 88, 89–90, 98–102,
  135–6, 152–3; study of 11
New Deals 103–4, 116; New Deal for
  the Unemployed 46, 67, 68, 94;
  New Deal for Young People 91–2
New Democrats 1, 42–3, 73
New Labour: and business 119–20;
  and citizenship 66–9, 75–6, 81; and
  communitarianism 72–82, 84–5,
  87–90, 103, 124, 127, 129, 140,
  143, 153; and community 63, 70–2,
  81, 88, 135; and consumers 65, 66;
  and the economy 28, 42–8, 64,
  84–6, 85–6, 106–27, 153; and
  education 50, 101, 118–19, 123;
  and equality 65–6, 136; and ethical
  socialism 54, 60–3, 71–2, 75, 135,
  156; and European Union (EU)
  116–17; evaluation of 121–7; and
  healthcare 50, 95, 97, 100, 101,
  102–3; and ideologies 54; and
  individual responsibility 11–12, 69,
  89, 90–5, 103; and inflation 66, 81,
  108, 109–10, 113; and

institutionalism 3–5, 27–8, 41–57, 84–5, 87–90, 103, 121, 124, 127, 129, 153; and joined-up governance 2–3, 29–30, 48–51, 89, 98–9; and networks 2, 29–31, 45–51, 88, 89–90, 96, 98–102, 135–6, 152–3; and New Democrats 1, 42–3, 73; and new liberalism 55–6; and New Right 28, 29–31, 43–6, 48–9, 52, 71, 81, 84–90, 153; and new technology 110, 119, 136; pensions 94–5, 96; and poverty 44, 91, 94, 103, 115, 121–2; and public services 43–50; and rights and duties 67–9, 75, 90–1, 95, 101; and social democracy 1, 75, 81, 84, 86, 127, 128–56; and social justice 63–6, 67, 76, 81, 103; and socialism 54–6, 58 (*see also* New Labour, ethical socialism); and stakeholders 71, 152; and supply side economics 108, 111–12, 117–21; and taxation 63–4, 70, 92–3, 110, 117–18, 122; Third Way 1, 28, 41–53, 61, 86, 87, 108–9, 153–4; traditions of 29, 56, 61, 83, 87, 127, 135–7, 154, 155; and unemployment 44, 46, 67–9, 90–5, 103–4, 107, 109, 122; and the welfare state 28, 43–8, 66–9, 71, 81, 83–105, 153, 154; *see also* Blair, Tony
new public management (NPM) 11, 38, 46, 96
New Right: and the economy 63–4, 107–11, 117; and New Labour 28, 29–31, 43–6, 48–9, 52, 71, 80–1, 84–90, 153; and public services 96; *see also* neoliberalism
Next Steps 97
NHS *see* healthcare
non-accelerating inflation rate of unemployment (NAIRU) 116

objectification 3–5, 143–8
Office for Standards in Education 101
Office of Fair Trading 121
Olsen, Johan 15, 79
open community 137–43, 148
Orage, A.R. 134
organicism 5–6
organisations 138–40, 142–3
Orwell, George 54, 136
Our Competitive Future 31

Parsons, Talcott 77, 78
pensioners and poverty 115
pensions 94–5, 96
Penty, A.J.: *The Restoration of the Gild System* 134
People's Panel 100
Performance and Innovation Unit 98
Perri 6 31, 39, 44, 46, 48–9, 50, 51
Pigou, A.G. 6
pluralism 143–8
Policy Unit 31
political science: history of 5–12; philosophy of 12–20
poor *see* poverty
positivism 3–5, 8, 12–20, 52
post-structuralism 137
poverty 10, 44, 74–5, 91, 94, 103, 115, 121–2
Powell, Walter 30, 39
practices 3–4, 18, 21–2, 29, 56, 83–4
Private Finance Initiatives (PFIs) 99; *see also* Public–Private Partnerships (PPPs)
property 145
Public Administration Committee 30
public expenditure 114–15
Public–Private Partnerships (PPPs) 98, 99
Public Sector Benchmarking Project (PSBP) 97
Public Service Agreements (PSAs) 100
public services *see* welfare state
pure experience 13, 14, 21, 86
Putman, Robert 73, 79–80

Quality Networks 100

Radcliffe Brown, A.R. 76, 77
rational choice theory 5, 9, 11, 12, 15, 18–20, 27, 29, 34–6, 85, 87, 88–9, 106
rationality 3–4
Rawls, John 72–3
recentring 24–7
Regional Development Agencies 120
Regulatory Impact Unit 101
Reich, Robert 1
rent 131, 133
Research Careers Initiative 119
responsibility, individual 11–12, 69, 89, 90–5, 103; *see also* rights and duties
Rhodes, Rod 30, 38–9, 49
Richmond, Wilfred 132

rights and duties 67–9, 75, 90–1, 95, 101; *see also* responsibility, individual
Ritchie, D.G. 6
Roethlisberger, Fritz 77
Rose, Richard 8
Rowntree, Seebhom 10
Ruskin, John 54, 61, 134
Russell, Bertrand 6

Sandel, Michael 73
Schmidt, Helmut 58
Schools Standards and Framework Bill 118
self-interest 18–19, 71
Seliger, Martin 58–60, 61
Selznick, Philip 78, 79
service delivery 96–103, 136
Service First 46, 100, 101
Shaw, George Bernard 54, 131
Silicon Valley 47
Simon, Herbert 79
Singapore 31
Single Gateway 92, 93, 94
Single Regeneration Budgets 51, 98
situated agency 22–3, 25–6, 137, 138, 142–4, 148, 154
Skinner, Quentin 9
Skocpol, Theda 34, 79
Small Firms Loan Guarantee Scheme 119
Smith, John 42
Snowden, Philip 70, 133
social categories 3–4
social democracy: and community 62, 69; history of 129–37; and New Labour 1, 41–4, 54–5, 58, 75, 81, 84, 86, 90, 127, 128–56; and New Right 52, 127; and social justice 62–6
Social Democratic Federation (SDF) 129, 131, 134, 136
social exclusion 65–6, 91, 116
Social Exclusion Unit (SEU) 49–50, 94, 96, 98
social humanism 9, 20, 27
socialism 54–6, 58, 86; ethical 54, 60–3, 71–2, 75, 129, 132, 133, 135, 156; guild 134; history of 129–37; supply side 111–12, 118, 120
Socialist League 129
social justice *see* justice, social
social security *see* welfare state

Society of Motor Manufacturers and Traders 120
sociology 76
Spencer, Herbert 6, 76
stakeholder pensions 94–5, 96
stakeholders 71, 151, 152
state, the 10–11, 37–41, 63, 131, 132–6, 145–6
State Earnings-Related Pensions (SERPS) 94
Stedman Jones, Daniel 31
Steinbeck, John 54
Stephens, John 37, 38
Stoker, Gerry 30, 31, 38–9, 48, 49, 50
Stokes, Donald 79
Straw, Jack 81
supply side economics 108, 111–12, 117–21
Sure Start 98
Sure Start Maternity Grant 115
survey research 32
Survey Research Centre, Michigan University 32
surveys, social 10–11

Tawney, R.H. 54, 56, 61, 62
taxation 63–4, 70, 92–3, 110, 117–18, 122
Taylor, Charles 73
technology, new 110, 119, 136
Teeside Chemical Initiative 120
Temple, William 61, 62
Thatcher, Margaret 66
Thatcherism 36–7, 70
Third Way 1, 28, 41–53, 61, 86, 87, 108–9, 153–4
Thompson, E.P. 136, 137
TradeUK 119
Trade Unions 117
traditions: nature of 23, 25–6, 128; and New Labour 56, 61, 83–4, 87, 127, 135–7, 138, 154, 155
Tressell, Robert, *The Ragged-Trousered Philanthropist* 54
trust 12, 45, 46, 50, 85, 89–90, 96, 100, 103
typologies 7

underclass 66–7, 73, 86, 90, 93
unemployment 44, 46, 67–9, 90–5, 103–4, 107, 109, 116, 122; *see also* labour market
United States 32–6, 42–3, 47, 72–4

Vienna Circle 77
Vincent, Andrew *55–6*, *59–60*, 61
violence 143–4
volunteering 44, 72

Wallas, Graham 7, 8
Warner, Lloyd 77
Webb, Beatrice 131, 133
Webb, Sidney 68, 131, 133
Weber, Max 34
Welfare Reform and Pensions Bill,
    1999 94, 95
welfare state 28, 43–8, 61, 62, 66–9,
    71, 81, 83–90, 153, 154; and
    markets 37–41; pensions 94–5, 96;
    service delivery 96–103, 136; welfare

to work 90–5, 104; *see also* health;
    unemployment
welfare to work 90–5, 104
Wellcome Trust 119
Wells, H,G, 54
Westminster Model 11
Whitehall Programme 39
Williams, Raymond 136, 137
women 73, 74, 98
Women's Unit 98
Working Families Tax Credit 93
World War I 6
Wright, Tony 54, 71
Wundt, Wilhelm 77

Young Enterprise Scheme 118